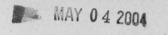

ALSO BY VINCE STATEN

Simon & Schuster
New York London Toronto Sydney

WHY
is the
FOUL POLE
FAIR?

Answers to
101 of the
Most Perplexing
Baseball Questions

VINCE STATEN

SIMON & SCHUSTER
Rockefeller Center
1230 Avenue of the Americas, New York, NY 10020

First Simon & Schuster trade paperback edition 2004

SIMON & SCHUSTER and colophon are registered
trademarks of Simon & Schuster, Inc.

Art permissions: Pages iv–v: Robert Gwathmey, "World Series,"
1958, oil on canvas, Collection of Leslie Pollack.
Pages xiii, 4, 32, 48, and 65: drawings by E. W. Kemble.
Pages 56, 132, 166, 174, 185, and 262: Copyright © *Look* 1971,
drawing by Boris Drucker (details).
Page 212: Copyright © the New Yorker collection 2003
Peter Arno from CartoonBank.com. All rights reserved.

For information regarding special discounts for bulk purchases,
please contact Simon & Schuster Special Sales:
1-800-456-6798 or business@simonandschuster.com

Designed by Bonni Leon
Manufactured in the United States of America

1   3   5   7   9   10   8   6   4   2

The Library of Congress has cataloged the hardcover edition as follows:
Staten, Vince, 1947–
Why is the foul pole fair? or, Answers to the baseball questions your father
hoped you would never ask / Vince Staten.
        p.   cm.
1. Baseball—Anecdotes. 2. Baseball fields—United States—Anecdotes.
I. Title: Why is the foul pole fair?. II. Title: Answers to the baseball questions
your father hoped you would never ask. III. Title.
GV873.S83 2003
796.357—dc21   2003041565
ISBN 0-7432-3384-0
ISBN 0-7432-5791-X (Pbk)

To the Ridgeway Hurricanes of 1959

Our team motto was: *All our games are a breeze.*

> P Lance Harris
> C Tony Wampler
> 1B Mike Wampler
> 2B Mike Cox
> 3B Mark Cox
> LF Chip Grills
> CF Butch Cunningham
> RF Michael Jarvis
> (I was the SS.)
> Sub: Donnie Jarvis
> Batboys: Eddie Isley, Phil Ketron
> Manager: Darnell Shankel

(Note that if a batter hit a ball to the right side, and the pitcher called, "Get it, Mike!" three kids would run into each other.)

ACKNOWLEDGMENTS

I'll try to make this quick, since studies show that only twelve people read the acknowledgments anyway.

The reason this book exists is editor Jon Malki and his boss Jeff Neuman. They had read my other books and thought baseball was ripe for an inside look: that's inside as in inside the concession stand, inside the ticket office, inside the stadium architect's office, not inside the pitcher's and the batter's heads. They knew the kind of inside stuff I have examined in books about supermarkets, hardware stores, drugstores, and barbershops: the histories and evolutions and psychologies of everyday objects. They wanted to read that sort of stuff about the ball park.

My ace research assistant on this book was Shirl Ryan, who did a lot of heavy lifting. Also aiding in the research were Liz Baldi and Brian Kehl. Ray Bearfield supplied a great title for this book, which unfortunately had nothing to do with the manuscript, so I'm saving it for a later volume.

Thanks to Hal McCoy of the *Dayton Daily News,* who allowed me inside his world on the baseball beat, and to Rob Butcher of the Cincinnati Reds.

First aid was supplied by Chris Wohlwend, whose last name always sets off the spell check, and Tom Jester.

The book is structured around the May 23, 2002 game between the Cincinnati Reds and the Florida Marlins, but I must acknowledge that the narrative is actually a composite of two games I attended with my son. We also went to the May 11, 2002 Reds–Cardinals game but, because the late Daryl Kile was the pitcher for the Cardinals, I elected to focus on the Reds–Marlins game, rather than distract the reader with mentions of Kile, whose death is a sad reminder of the mortality of even the finest.

And, finally, thanks to my son Will for going with me to the games, even though baseball ceased being his favorite sport about five years ago.

CONTENTS

WHY
is the
FOUL
POLE
FAIR?

Introduction:
FIELD OF SEAMS

One day it was a jumble of yards: a garden, a dog pen, a hedgerow, a garage, a line of shrubs. It was where backyards met.

The next, it was a ball field.

It hadn't been there until we needed it but, once the boys in my neighborhood came of ballplaying age, a ball field magically appeared, scotched together from six different backyards.

One day, that foot-square piece of concrete sunk in Lance Harris's backyard was a septic tank cover. The next, it was home plate.

The hedgerow between my house and Eddie Isley's backyard became the left-field wall; Papa Hawkins' garage was the center-field fence; the corner of the Harris's dog pen was third base. A scraggly pear tree became first; the rise in the middle of the vacant lot became the pitcher's mound. The swale where Papa's yard met the vacant lot became second base; and the shade tree next to Harris's garden became a dugout.

I'd never noticed a ball field there before. Lance and I

visited back and forth all the time, him strolling through two vacant lots and ducking under a mimosa tree to bring his comic books to my house, me trudging up the same path in reverse to his house, with a handful of cowboy figures. In the spring of 1957, a ball field magically appeared in the hodgepodge area between our houses.

Ball fields are like that: They don't appear until you need them, and we hadn't needed a ball field before.

That was the year our baby boom really boomed. Suddenly, the neighborhood toddler crop turned into a mess of little boys, little boys who wanted to play together.

The Wamplers tore down their back fence; my father cut a path through our hedge; Gank Price dug up his fence posts. What had been a chopped-up intersection of property lines opened up into a vast expanse of grass and dirt.

And a ball field was born.

None of my friends can recall us ever walking off the base paths, staking out base locations. They just remember that every afternoon we played baseball on that field. They remember stripping down to our short pants to beat the summer sun, begging Lance's mother for a pitcher of Kool-Aid, daring to climb into Penny's dog pen to retrieve an errant throw, watching Donnie Jarvis eat four green apples, then score from third and head on to his other home with a case of the green-apple quickstep.

We didn't have any ground rules. "Run it out," was our motto: If a long fly to left bounded into Isley's garden, run it out. If the ball became entangled in Hawkins' fly bushes, run it out. Lose the ball in the weeds behind the Shankels' tool shed, run it out.

It may be, as Hollywood insists, "If you build it, they will come," but, in my neighborhood, it was, "If you need it, it will appear."

That was our ballpark.

I still love the ballpark, the open-air emporium of hot dogs and fun. I catch a couple of big-league games every year, twice that many minor-league contests. And, every baseball game I attend today, every game I watch on television or listen to on radio, I'm really revisiting my old ball field. Every game, deep down, is a replay of my childhood, the carefree days before mortgages and tuition and adulthood, when life was just a game and Lance Harris was the pitcher and I was the shortstop.

That's why I love a ball field.

This book is an outgrowth of a conversation with my editor, Jon Malki. He knew of my love of the minutiae of life, the *whys* of everyday things, and he knew of his love of baseball. He thought we might be able to marry the two. What he didn't know was about my love of baseball, so it's a perfect marriage of editor and writer, of subject and approach.

When people have asked what I'm working on, I've said, "a book about baseball," and, for half the public, that's enough. They don't want to know more, they don't care about knowing more. For the other half, there's a curiosity: What about baseball? Hasn't everything about baseball been written?

To those people I've said, "It's about everything *but* the

players." Then, I would ask them if they knew how wide a seat at the ballpark was; none knew, although a few guessed right: 18 inches. Then I asked if they knew why it was that wide. No one knew, giving me a golden opportunity to regale them with the story of Eugene Hooton, famous for measuring criminals' heads, who was commissioned by the railroad in the forties to measure American backsides and come up with the perfect seat size.

There are statistics at the ballpark besides batting averages, and that's the subject of this book. In those carefree moments between pitches and between innings, I like to ponder if the rubber really is rubber, how they know how many restrooms to build, and why the foul pole is fair.

Curiosity did not kill this cat. This book is testament to that.

Chapter One

Take Me Out to the Ball Game

I grew up in a neighborhood of boys. Tony and Mike were on one side of my house, Darnell on the other, Lance in back, next to him Michael and Donnie and Bob, then Ronald and Billy, Phil and Eddie, across the street to Tommy, up the hill to Chip and Butch.

All you needed to do on a Saturday morning was take a bat and ball to the field, then start tossing up a few and hitting them; the crack of the bat was siren call enough. Soon, there were six, eight kids, gloves in hand, ready for a pickup game.

There was always a game going in my neighborhood: football in fall, basketball in winter, and baseball the rest of the time. We didn't have a real ball field; we cobbled one together from a couple of backyards, a vacant lot, a garden, and a dog pen. My backyard was the end zone in fall, the backcourt in winter, and the infield in spring. I remember a man whom my father worked with coming by and being greatly distressed at how we neighborhood boys had worn base paths into the grass. "Those boys are killing your yard," the man said. And I remember my father's answer. "Those boys will be gone someday. That grass will grow back."

. . .

I grew up loving baseball. When I wasn't playing it, I was watching it on TV or reading about it in the *Sporting News,* or talking about it with my best friend Lance Harris. He and I oiled our gloves together, we taped our bats together, and, on the days we couldn't get up a game, we played catch and pepper together.

The only thing we didn't do was go to games together. There was no team in our town, big-league or otherwise. There was a Class D Rookie League franchise twenty miles away, but the big leagues were as far away as my dream of someday playing there.

At the beginning of my eleventh summer, my father announced that we wouldn't be going to the beach that year. It had been a vacation tradition for as long as I could remember. "No, not this summer," he said. Instead, we were going to a big-league baseball game. Suddenly, I couldn't breathe. This might not seem like a big deal to a city kid but, to a southern boy in the fifties, this was better than finding out you'd made Little League all-stars. See, we had no big-league clubs in the South then. The Braves were still in Milwaukee, the Astros and Rangers and Marlins and Devil Rays were all off in the future.

On our way to the distant ballpark that summer we thread through the mountains into Kentucky, then up to Cincinnati for a Reds game against my favorite team, the Giants. I'll never forget that weekend. It was the longest car ride of my life.

It was the dog days of summer when we arrived at the

Queen City of the Ohio. Cincinnati is a city that's notoriously humid in the summer, but who knows from humidity when you're a kid? We unpacked in a motel on the Kentucky side of the river, then hustled over to Findlay and Western Avenue, site of the now-legendary Crosley Field.

I loved the hustle and bustle outside my first big-league park. I loved the sounds of the sidewalk barkers hawking pennants and balls and every kind of baseball trinket. I loved the crush of people scurrying to the turnstiles. And, when we finally got through the mob, a Giants pennant in my hand, and hurried up the ramp to the plaza overlooking the field, I couldn't believe my eyes. I was finally there. It was everything I had seen on television and it was in color and it was up close. Even the steel girders holding the upper deck excited me. And when we finally made our way to our seats, which were a classy green with fold-up bottoms, I was ecstatic. There, right in front of me, close enough to talk to, even touch, if I hadn't been so afraid of them, were the idols of my boyhood: Willie Mays and Willie McCovey, Jim Davenport, and Don Blasingame, and my favorite player, Orlando Cepeda.

I'll never forget my first thought: They look just like their baseball cards!

Oh, the sights and sounds that night: "Get your beer, here!" "Peeeeeeeea-nuts! Peeeeeea-nuts!" The roar when Willie Mays sent a ball over the left-field wall. The *oooooh* when Frank Robinson fanned.

It was a magic moment, one that I can never recapture, only recall.

Years later, when I married and had a son, my hope for him was that he grow up to love baseball. I named him Will . . . after my wife vetoed Orlando. Will was for two of the best players my team produced: Willie Mays and Willie Mc-Covey. My wife thought it was for her grandfather and my grandfather. She's just finding out the truth in this book.

The winter Will was born I bought season tickets to the local Triple A club, the Louisville Redbirds, and took him to every home game his first summer. (He usually slept.)

Together, we watched the Cubs on television most afternoons and the Braves most evenings. (He preferred *Thundercats* cartoons.)

I signed him up for T-ball. (He hated it and spent most of his time in the outfield picking dandelions.)

For his eighth Christmas, I bought him a baseball-card album that included an assortment of cards. (He never even took the cellophane off.)

Then, came spring of his eighth year. One day after Harry Caray began bellowing "Take Me Out to the Ball Game," he went up to his room, dug out the album kit, and tore into it. Two hours later, he had all the cards neatly tucked into the polyurethane pockets. He needed more cards, he announced.

Now, he wanted to go to the Redbirds games, he wanted to get on a Little League team, he wanted to join a fantasy league. It was all happening almost *too* fast.

I knew what would be next: A big-league game.

I called the Reds box office. My first game had been in Cincinnati, albeit at Crosley Field; his first big-league game would be in Cincinnati, at Riverfront Stadium.

Baseball had a new fan.

Over the years, we went to games together, we operated a fantasy-league team together, we played catch in the backyard, and I pitched to him at the local field.

Then, something happened. He didn't want to go anywhere with me. He was embarrassed by my wardrobe, by my haircut, by pretty much everything about me. It's called the teen years. As he got over the embarrassment of having a father, he drifted into a new phase. Now, it wasn't that he didn't want to go to a ballgame with me, it was just that, well, Steve wanted him to play golf and Drew wanted him to bowl. And there were the calls from girls.

Now, something else has happened. His friends are all heading off to college but, because his school starts later, he's willing to hang out with his dad.

So, for the first time in five years, we are going to a big-league game together. To Cincinnati, of course. Scene of my first game, and his, too.

I just *have to* get us tickets.

In the beginning, it really was a game. There were no tickets; there was no need for tickets. It was just a gang of kids gathered in a field, playing a game. In some areas of this country they called it *rounders*, after the British game of the same name. Other places called it *old cat* or *stool ball*. It was a time in America when pilgrim wasn't just a name John Wayne called his rivals, and Indians weren't just from Cleveland. It was the eighteenth century.

Whatever this early game was, it certainly wasn't baseball. The only real similarity to the modern game was the bases. Kids would take turns running the bases while other kids tried to put them out by hitting them with a ball. It's always been fun to throw stuff at other kids.

(Incidentally, getting an out by hitting a player with the ball isn't as outlandish a rule as you might think. When I played backyard baseball in the fifties, there were days when we couldn't get up enough kids for a regular game. Sometimes, we'd play with as few as four guys. In the field, you had a pitcher and a shortstop. To get a player out, you'd hit him with the ball. And, yes, it did make you want to run faster.)

Over time, these eighteenth-century ball games evolved into what was once called *base ball*.

The first reference to a baseball-like game in America comes from a Christmas Day 1621 diary entry by Governor William Bradford of the Plymouth Plantation, who notes some of his subjects "frolicking in ye street, at play openly; some at Virginia pitching ye ball, some at stoole ball and shuch-like sport."

John Newbery's *A Little Pretty Pocket-Book*, an alphabet instruction booklet published in 1784, offers the first picture of American baseball, a woodcut showing boys playing "Base-Ball."

The ball once struck off away flies the boy
To the next destin'd post and then home with joy.

The bases of the title are posts stuck in the ground. There is no bat in the scene, but one boy appears ready to pitch underhand to a second boy standing, hand on post.

It was left to a group of young New Yorkers to synthesize all the disparate elements of rounders and cricket, town ball and stool ball, and formalize the rules of this new game. These professionals had been meeting regularly since 1842 on a field at 4th Avenue and 27th Street in Manhattan to get a little exercise playing this game of base ball. In 1845, one of their number, a twenty-five-year-old stationer named Alexander Cartwright, suggested they form a club. He even had a name for it, the Knickerbocker Base Ball Club, a name derived from the Knickerbocker Engine Company, where Cartwright was a volunteer firefighter.

So, they made it official, this gentlemen's club, composed of seventeen merchants, twelve clerks, five brokers, four professional men, a bank teller, a "Segar Dealer," a hatter, a cooperage owner, and several "gentlemen." They elected Daniel L. "Doc" Adams, a physician, their president.

This was not, however, the first baseball club in New York. Baseball historians Thomas R. Heitz and John Thorn unearthed an interview Adams gave in 1896, in which he admitted to having played baseball in the city as early as 1839. "I began to play base ball just for exercise, with a number of other young medical men. Before that there had been a club called the New York Base Ball Club, but it had no very definite organization and did not last long. Some of the younger members of that club got together and formed the Knickerbocker Base Ball Club."

Adams said the players were all professional men "who were at liberty after three o'clock in the afternoon. They went into it just for exercise and enjoyment."

As president of the newly minted Knickerbocker Base Ball Club, Adams saw a need for a set of formal rules, so he put together a four-man committee that included himself and Cartwright, and sat down to write a set of by-laws. Only those four know who wrote what, but Cartwright, with his drafting skills, was called upon to draw the playing field and, as a result, his name has come to be attached to the rules, so much so that he is in the Baseball Hall of Fame.

The rules they came up with would pass for baseball even today. No more outs by lethal throw. No more twenty-five men out in the field at one time. They created the diamond-shaped field, decreed three outs per turn and invented the foul ball.

Their document was published on September 23, 1845, as the "Rules and Regulations of the Knickerbocker Base Ball Club." There were twenty rules, a sort of ten commandments times two.

Some had nothing to do with baseball, but with procedures for the club:

"1st. Members must strictly observe the time agreed upon for exercise, and be punctual in their attendance."

(Obviously, the club was having an attendance problem.)

"2nd. When assembled for exercise, the President, or in

his absence, the Vice-President, shall appoint an Umpire, who shall keep the game in a book provided for that purpose, and note all violations of the By-Laws and Rules during the time of exercise.

"3rd. The presiding officer shall designate two members as Captains, who shall retire and make the match to be played, observing at the same time that the player's opposite to each other should be as nearly equal as possible, the choice of sides to be then tossed for, and the first in hand to be decided in like manner."

On the sandlot we tossed for sides, too: We tossed a bat. One captain caught it, each putting his fist above the other 'til one or the other could cover the knob with his thumb, thereby giving him first choose. That was how we made the sides "nearly equal," by picking back and forth.

By rule four, the Knickerbocker Club was onto something: "4th. The bases shall be from 'home' to second base, forty-two paces; from first to third base, forty-two paces, equidistant."

Figuring three feet to a pace, that's 126 feet from home to second. The current rule book for Major League Baseball, in section 1.04 "The Playing Field," specifies, "When location of home base is determined, with a steel tape measure 127 feet, 3 3/8 inches in desired direction to establish second base." But, no one figured three feet to a pace in 1845: Heitz and Thorn found a contemporaneous dictionary that tabbed a pace at 2.5 feet, meaning the first fields were smaller, with base paths more in the range of 75 feet, closer to a Little League field. Those dimensions stand to reason, as the bats and balls were different too, making a smaller field necessary.

Rule 8 set a game at 21 *aces*, or runs—first team to 21

wins. (We used to play that on the sandlot.) Some of the other rules hint at a move in the modern direction.

"10th. A ball knocked out of the field, or outside the range of the first and third base, is foul.

"11th. Three balls being struck at and missed and the last one caught, is a hand-out; if not caught is considered fair, and the striker bound to run.

"12th. If a ball be struck, or tipped, and caught, either flying or on the first bound, it is a hand-out.

"13th. A player running the bases shall be out, if the ball is in the hands of an adversary on the base, or the runner is touched with it before he makes his base; it being understood, however, that in no instance is a ball to be thrown at him.

"14th. A player running who shall prevent an adversary from catching or getting the ball before making his base, is a hand-out.

"15th. Three hands-out, all out.

"16th. Players must take their strike in regular turn."

Adams, Cartwright, and company took a children's game and gave it a design that enabled adults to play it.

You don't charge admission to a game until you need to and, at first, there was no need: Baseball was a social event. And, as noted in the first rules, a way to get a little exercise.

·   ·

For better or for worse, the very setting down of a set of rules changed the game. Baseball was now—and here's the ugly word—*organized*. It was no longer strictly a playground game.

Two weeks after publishing their rules, the Knickerbocker boys played the first recorded game under these guidelines, at their club ground, Elysian Fields in Hoboken, New Jersey, a short ferry ride across the Hudson from Manhattan.

It must have been a hit because, soon, baseball clubs were forming all around the city; within a decade there was enough interest for a convention! Adams presided at the formation of the National Association of Base Ball Players (NABBP) in 1858, with twenty-two clubs from the New York area participating. Heitz and Thorn note, "It was no longer merely an amusement for exclusive, socially oriented clubs of young professional men. Workingmen were discovering the sport, and they didn't necessarily subscribe to the 'it's only a game' attitude that had been adopted from the British sporting class."

It was more than a game; it was a competition.

And, with a competition, comes rooting and fans. And following along shortly is the admission fee.

Early baseball has numerous watershed events: When the bases were established at ninety feet, when the pitcher began throwing overhand, when someone had the good sense to provide the catcher with a cup.

But no moment in the history of organized baseball is bigger than the one of July 20, 1858. It was on that day that members of the American public first paid to see a baseball game.

According to baseball historians, it was at Fashion Race Course on Long Island—at National Avenue and 102nd Street in present-day Corona—where opportunistic entrepreneurs charged fifty cents per head for a game between the New York All-Stars and the Brooklyn All-Stars. If an 1866 Currier & Ives print is to be believed, spectators stood on the sidelines and in the outfield to watch this all-star event. Fifteen hundred folks paid what would be the equivalent of $9.13 in 2001 dollars to watch the event. Among the spectators—history doesn't record if he paid or if he got the very first press pass—was Henry Chadwick of the *New York Mercury*, who would chronicle this embryonic sport for the next half century.

History also fails to record if William H. Cammeyer, a shoe merchant, was at the game but, if he wasn't, he certainly read about it and learned from it. Three years later, he leased a hollow of land in Brooklyn bounded by Harrison Avenue, Marcy Avenue, Rutledge Street, and Lynch Street. He surrounded the site with a six-foot-high board fence, named it Union Grounds, and opened it for baseball games in the spring of 1862. He allowed teams to use the field free of charge, but collected a dime admission fee at the gate from each spectator. That's about two bucks in modern money.

Enter another ugly word: greed. "Why should Cammeyer profit from our sweat?" the clubs asked. By 1864, he was splitting gate receipts with teams and the players, who felt they, too, should share the riches.

With everyone demanding their share, baseball was heading toward becoming a business; bills to pay, therefore admissions to be charged. And that, friends, is why I am preparing to call the Reds box office and buy a pair of tickets for my son and me.

It is only appropriate that I should be shelling my cash out to a Cincinnati professional club, because it was in the Queen City that professional baseball really began.

Players had been taking payments—in the form of cash under the table (or behind the dugout) or a job on the side—for a half-dozen years, when a group of Cincinnati businessmen headed by Aaron B. Champion (what a wonderful name for a baseball-team owner) decided to bring professionalism out in the open. In 1869, he created the Cincinnati Red Stockings, selling stock in the Stockings to his friends. He hired ten players—from teams in Philadelphia, New York, New Jersey, and Brooklyn, with only one player, first baseman Charlie Gould, from Cincinnati—and a manager, and put them on the road for six months. Manager Harry Wright was sure the team would score big, telling a local newspaper that people pay "seventy-five cents to a dollar-fifty to go to the theatre, and numbers prefer base ball to theatricals."

The Red Stockings were a smash hit on the field, winning all sixty games they played, but were less of a hit on the ledger books. Team payroll was $11,000, with star shortstop George Wright—Harry's brother, natch—drawing the top salary, $1,400 ($17,895.15 in today's dollars). After travel expenses, which were enormous, because the team traveled all the way to San Francisco for one series, the team netted $1.39 in profit. That's right, for their capital and labor, the owners of the Red Stockings made all of a buck and change. Even converting to today's dollars, it's not much. Would you work all year for seventeen dollars?

We don't know if Arthur Andersen was responsible for that accounting but, whatever the profit, it wasn't much, because stockholders voted the next year to return the team to amateur status, which meant that all the players left.

This is sounding more and more familiar every day.

So, that's how I have come to be on the telephone today, calling for Cincinnati Reds tickets. Except that I don't have a Cincinnati phonebook, or a Reds schedule, or any of the things I need to buy tickets.

I *do* have a computer.

When my dad took the family on our first baseball vacation in 1959, I was in charge of tickets. I sat down at the dining-room table and, in my best cursive, wrote a letter to the Ticket Manager, Cincinnati Reds, Cincinnati, Ohio. I asked when the Giants would be in town, how much tickets cost and what seats were available for the games. I licked a four-cent stamp and my father mailed it from work the next day. Two weeks later, I got a neatly typed reply. I answered it that day and, in another two weeks, we had our tickets.

From start to finish, it took a month to get tickets.

It won't take a month this time. Try five minutes.

· · ·

Buying tickets to a Reds game is a snap these days; I bought ours on the Internet. I went to the Reds website, found Tickets, clicked on it, and was guided through. I could pick either the $32 blue seats, the $24 light blue seats, the $16 green seats, the $15 yellow seats or the $14 red (upper-deck) seats. I started with the $24 light blue seats. The computer told me I could have seats 8 and 9 in row 19 of section 145. "We have reserved these tickets for ten minutes. If you do not wish to purchase them, they will be released." I called up a stadium map that showed me the exact location of the seats, in left field, just a few rows past the end of the visitor's dugout. Good enough. I clicked on "Purchase."

I had our *ducats* (that's an old word for tickets) in less than five minutes. Well, I had purchased them, that is.

Buying tickets to any major-league game is a breeze today compared to even ten years ago. When I took Will to Cleveland for a game at the new Jacobs Field in 1994, I called the box office only to discover that the game was a sellout, but they would have standing-room-only seats in left field, the lady told me.

I had no intention of standing for an entire game, not at my age.

I boasted to my family that I had never been to a game where I couldn't score tickets outside; I haven't made that boast since. You cannot buy tickets outside Jacobs Field. There are signs everywhere informing you that scalping tickets is a corporal, if not a capital, offense. And there are more cops than there are signs. I didn't even get a furtive glance from a potential scalper.

So, I went to Plan B: standing-room-only tickets. I approached the box-office window with that hangdog face. "I need two for today's game," I said to the pleasant woman inside, a woman who was about to get even more pleasant.

"You just got lucky," she said. "They just turned in the scouts' tickets."

I didn't know exactly what that meant but she explained that each club holds a number of tickets in reserve at each game for scouts from other teams. They always hold extra tickets, then sell them to the public at the last minute.

That day *we* were the lucky public. Field-level seats right behind home plate, surrounded by older men with radar guns and World Series rings.

I'm not willing to take that chance for our Reds game. You just can't count on luck. So, I buy blue seats, section 145, row 19, seats 8 and 9.

Our tickets are $24, plus a $3.58 City of Cincinnati admissions tax each, plus a $2.50 service charge for shipping and handling, even though our tickets will only be handled (we are picking them up at the Will Call window), bringing the total to $57.66.

The Team Marketing Report, a trade magazine that surveys ticket prices annually, says the average ticket to a Major League Baseball game cost $18.31 in 2002 (before local hotel, motel, and entertainment taxes, not to mention mailing, handling, and shipping surcharges).

We must be getting pretty good seats.

· · ·

According to *Crosley Field: The Illustrated History of a Classic Ballpark* by Greg Rhodes and John Erardi, my father would have paid $2.50 for our box seats in 1959. (Grandstand general admission was $1.50, and sundeck seats were 75 cents.) He got a great deal; in 2002 dollars that's about $15 a ticket. I'm paying $24 for comparable seats today. But, deal or not, we've got our seats, so, Riverfront Stadium, here we come.

Except they don't call it Riverfront Stadium anymore: It's now Cinergy Field, joining a growing list of major-league parks with for-pay corporate names, like 3Comm Park, Tropicana Field, Bank One Ballpark, even, for a brief time, Enron Field.

Cinergy is a relic of Cincinnati Gas & Electric. Its corporate report says Cinergy was created October 24, 1994 from a merger of Cincinnati Gas & Electric and PSI Energy, the largest electric utility in Indiana. Cinergy is, it brags, "one of the leading diversified energy companies in the U.S. [with] . . . a balanced, integrated portfolio consisting of two core businesses: energy merchant and regulated operations." (I have no idea what that means, either.) The report goes on to laud the company's "profitable balance of stable existing customer portfolios, new customer origination, marketing and trading, and industrial-site cogeneration."

Still, for most people, Cinergy is a ballpark in Cincinnati.

It's exactly 100 miles from my house to Riverfr . . . er . . . Cinergy Field. I live on the outer edge of Reds country; farther west belongs to the Cardinals. For years, western

Kentucky baseball fans listened to Cardinals games on KMOX radio. Head south and you start getting into Braves territory, turn north and you get into Cubs country.

It's all interstate to Cincinnati, a drive through the country that doesn't end until you hit the suburbs. Now, it's time to start worrying about parking.

That apparently is something the average major-league club doesn't worry much about.

Rod Sheard, senior vice president of HOK + LOBB, the architectural firm that has designed many new baseball stadiums, including Oriole Park at Camden Yards, Jacobs Field, and Coors Field, recommends a minimum of one parking space for every ten to fifteen spectators.

Cinergy Field holds 40,008. (It had a capacity of 52,952 until they tore out the left-field stands to make way for construction of the new Reds field, slated to open in 2003.) A quick computation with the calculator, giving Cinergy the benefit of the doubt by using the larger number of spectators per car, it looks like Cinergy should have 2,667 spaces. Before construction, it had 2,500 parking spaces on three levels, but that has been reduced considerably. There are a couple of open-air lots next door with 1,800 spots. Because of Cinergy's proximity to downtown and downtown lots it really isn't a problem finding a parking space. A close space, yes; a space, no.

Sheard also recommends the distance from the car to the stadium should be no more than five hundred yards and an absolute maximum of a mile. Will and I arrive early enough to get in an open-air lot next door, a walk of maybe a hundred yards.

It's six bucks to park, which is below the league average of \$8.79. We'll spend our savings on popcorn.

As we make our way from the parking garage to the stadium, we are accosted by a parade of strangers offering to sell us tickets. And, when we shake our heads in the negative, they offer to buy our extra tickets. Some even have professionally printed signs: I NEED TICKETS.

These are not poor souls who drove down from Dayton hoping to score good seats behind the Reds dugout. These are professional scalpers: guys—I saw one girl today—who try to turn a profit buying and selling tickets. In Cincinnati, it is perfectly legal to resell tickets—*resell* being the nice term for scalping. There are only two provisions: It's illegal to resell tickets on the plaza outside the ballpark, so scalpers must stay on the sidewalks at street level. And if you're a dealer in tickets you must have a vendor's license. All the scalpers I saw were away from the plaza level, although a couple were on the steps. One had parked atop an empty newspaper box on the road to the stadium. None displayed a vendor's license.

It's that way at ballparks everywhere. The I NEED TICKETS guys aggressively pursue customers. And these guys generally aren't, despite appearances, poor working stiffs just trying to make an extra buck: A 2002 *Boston Herald* investigation found that all the ticket resellers outside Fenway Park were professionals, many with ties to the mob. In Massachusetts, resellers can mark up a ticket two bucks over permissible costs of acquiring the ticket, meaning they can charge whatever the market will bear, and amateur ticket resellers need not apply. The *Herald* observed four members of the scalping ring beat up a nonaffiliated scalper.

The sign I NEED TICKETS has as much meaning as a Don't Walk sign on a Manhattan street corner.

There should be a translation in small letters below: I SCALP TICKETS.

We make it to the plaza without being physically forced to buy tickets. After a quick stop at the will-call window, it will be on to the game.

Except that it's not a quick stop at will call: There are four will-call windows open today, three divided alphabetically by last name, and a fourth for passes. The S-to-Z line, my line, is, of course, longer than the others.

I am twelve people from the front, although I think there are at least three sets of couples, which means I am only nine slots from picking up my tickets.

Because it is a reasonably short line, I can see the transactions ahead. They are not going smoothly. There is no ticket agent at my window; she seems to be in the back looking for something. This happens to me all the time in the grocery store: "Price check in Vince Staten's lane! Let's hold him up as long as possible!" I am used to it.

These are boring lines and, even though we are in the shade, you can feel the frustration building. People are looking backwards with that disgusted face that says, Why is that idiot at the front delaying me?

It is obvious the Reds are not familiar with queuing theory. Queuing theory explains why folks will stand in line for thirty minutes at Disney World and arrive at their ride with a smile and stand in line only five minutes at Burger World and arrive with a frown. *Queuing* is the British term for waiting in line. The average American spends 134.5 hours a year, or about twenty minutes a day, waiting in line.

Waiting in line is one of life's inevitabilities: Rod Sheard, author of *Sports Architecture,* says, "No public assembly building, least of all a large stadium, can ever hope to serve all its customers simultaneously. A spectator attending an event must inevitably stand in a series of queues, for entry at the stadium entrance, to be served at the bars, eating places or at the shop counter, to use the toilets and finally to make their exit."

So, obviously, I expected a line. Still, I am a little frustrated. After all, I'm just picking up tickets I've already purchased. If I were in line to buy tickets that would be a different matter. I would expect to wait longer if I didn't have the good sense to buy my tickets ahead of time.

Obviously, your mental state plays a big factor in how you survive waiting in line.

One reason for my frustration is the system the Reds use. Danish engineer A. K. Erlang, who published the first paper on queuing theory back in 1909, called it the *multiple parallel queue* system. Most fast-food joints gave up on it years ago, because studies showed that people didn't like it—it's the old fairness factor. With a *combined queue,* as Erlang called it, there is one line and several ticket sellers; once you reach the head of the line, you go to the first available window. With the multiple parallel system there are several lines and several sellers. Your trip to the front depends on the speed of your seller, the complexity of the orders in front of you, and pure dumb luck. Studies show that people prefer the single line system even when it means a longer wait.

Instead, the Reds use parallel lines. That way, you watch someone who arrived later than you get to the front of their line ahead of you. And you simmer. Queue theoreticians have a name for it: *queue rage*.

Another of my frustrations is what sociologists call *empty time*. I'm just standing here, doing nothing, waiting impatiently.

People at Disneyland often wait half an hour for a two-minute ride. How does Disney do it—get spectators to wait this long, then turn around and wait in another equally long line for the next ride? Sheard says, "They transform the queuing experience into a pre-event, first by ensuring that people are as physically comfortable as possible and second by enlivening the experience with interesting and attention catching diversions."

That can involve having TV sets to watch: most baseball teams have figured that one out, positioning sets where people in the beer lines and the peanuts lines can watch game action while waiting to get a brewski.

It can involve diversions: Disney sends clowns and jugglers to the queuing areas to keep visitors entertained. The Federal Republic National Bank of New York provides live music in its branches on Friday between 10 A.M. and 2 P.M., the heaviest banking hours. Customer feedback told the bank that people didn't consider the time waiting as lost time, but as time during which they were entertained.

It can even be something as simple as routing people through ropes that twist and turn, giving visitors the impression they are closer to the front of the line than they really are. "Hey, it's only a few feet away." Of course, there may be fifty people ahead, but those in line can at least see the attraction. They can look at each other, joke with each other.

That's why everyone from Disney World to Wendy's uses queuing ropes or chains to snake the crowd around. If a Disney World line were allowed to extend naturally away from the gate, it might be a hundred yards long. Those in the back would give up because the wait would seem interminable. By snaking the crowd, the park makes guests think they are closer to the entrance than they really are.

This can all be important for business. If the fan gets bored, stressed out, or aggravated from waiting in line, he's not going to enjoy the game wholeheartedly. He won't stay as long, won't spend as much money, and may not come back.

Of course, it depends on what you are standing in line for. A study by Thierry Meyer, published in a 1992 edition of the *Journal of Social Psychology,* found that people who were excited about the event estimated there were fewer people in line ahead of them than people who were only lukewarm about attending. He also found that the excited people were in a better mood.

If I were waiting in line to pick up tickets for the Rolling

Stones, I might estimate the line to be much shorter. Conversely, if I were waiting for tickets to a *Saved by the Bell* reunion, I might be really irritated.

Waiting in line does play with your head. Several years ago, the Houston airport found it was receiving an inordinate number of complaints about the baggage wait, even though it never took more than eight minutes to go from getting off the plane to grabbing the suitcase. The problem was that it was a one-minute walk to baggage and a seven-minute wait for luggage to come rolling into the baggage carousel. The airport had a simple solution: Baggage was moved farther from the terminal. It was now a six-minute walk and a two-minute wait. The complaints stopped.

Cinergy Field has ten gates. Our tickets say, ENTER GATE FOUR.

Gates open ninety minutes before game time weekdays and two hours before the game on weekends. At 12:15, exactly one hour before game time, we hand our tickets to the ticket taker at Gate 4 and, as he tears off the stub, Will and I push through the turnstiles.

Turnstiles are God's way of letting you know you are getting fat. I can still ease through, but the man in front of me must turn sideways.

The primary purpose of the turnstile is crowd control. This way, the team ensures that no one without a ticket gets in. The turnstile also keeps a spectator count

Stadium architect Rod Sheard says a stadium needs one turnstile for every 500 to 750 spectators. If the Reds are expecting a crowd of 25,000, which is about average for a

Saturday afternoon game, they need at least 33 turnstiles, three at every gate. Our gate has four.

The downside to turnstiles is they are expensive and slow down entry to the stadium. Your basic turnstile, featuring registering, guide rail, and floor tread, will run you $2,615, plus shipping. The average turnstile allows about 750 fans to pass through per hour.

The turnstile has its origins on English farms of the first millennium.

A farmer had his crop field and his livestock field, and never the twain should meet, otherwise the livestock would eat the crops. So, he separated the two with a stone fence. After tiring of climbing over the fence to go from vegetables to meat, he built a stile in the wall. There might be a couple of steps up, a short platform, and a couple of steps down on the other side, but climbing steps would get tiring.

The next step was to tear down the stile, put a post in the ground and mount a cross of wood on top, sort of like the propeller on a plane. The farmer could go from crop to livestock without climbing or bending, but merely by walking through this propeller, which was wide enough for his torso but much too narrow to allow a cow through (that is, if a cow was smart enough to figure out this new kind of gate).

The farmer's old stile had been replaced by a *turn*stile.

It would be a thousand years before anyone made an improvement on this simple turnstile. In 1928, a pair of New Englanders named John Perey and Conrad Trubenbach designed a mechanical turnstile that looked like a three-legged stool on its side. Push against the top leg and it releases while the second leg shoves you on through from behind. It's a concept that's still working three quarters of a century later, and the company founded by John Perey to manufacture turnstiles is still one of the industry leaders.

In the twenties, Perey and Trubenbach patented the two most popular styles of turnstiles: the three-wing full-height turnstile, which the company calls the Roto-Gate, and the three-arm waist-high turnstile, the Passimeter.

Today, there are all sorts of variations on these original designs, including the optical turnstile, which has no arms at all, but the basic turnstile is still the entry gate of choice for almost every ballpark, theme park, and racetrack.

Why? The Perey Company says, "There is still only one absolutely reliable way to ensure ONE entry per ticket and ONE count per person; that is the venerable turnstile."

The initial investment may be steep: forty turnstiles can run a ball club over a hundred grand, but turnstiles are durable: The average service life is thirty-five years. (Churchill Downs only recently replaced the turnstiles it purchased in 1938.) Turnstiles are virtually maintenance free, requiring only a squirt of oil every eighteen months or so. Modern turnstiles are manufactured so that you don't have to replace the entire machine; you can upgrade.

The Reds use basic Perey turnstiles. The turnstile industry is on the cutting edge today with such products as Tomsed Turnstiles, "Mantrap Turnstile," a full-height, high-security turnstile with a two-stage entry process that includes a biometric identity verification device, all for only $13,036.

We don't need this at the ballpark, at least not at any ballpark I want to go to.

As the usher hands me back my stub, I look down at it. Once tickets were a thing of beauty, gorgeously printed, something you could frame and hang on the wall. My little two-inch by three-inch remnant features cheap computer printing with only the basics on it: date, game, seat number and price. No lithograph of the field, not even the Reds logo. It resembles the cash register tape you get at the grocery store. There's even a buy-one-get-one-free Subway coupon on the back.

Somewhere in my mother's house are the tickets to that long-ago Reds game. They had the little Redlegs man with a bat, printing in multicolored ink so you could differentiate seating information from all the notices and warnings and information. Simply put, they were pretty.

My ticket today is a muddle of gray and black.

This ticket would make William Gillenwater's heart sink. Gillenwater was the president of Arcus-Simplex-Brown, Inc., which was, in 1959, the world's largest ticket printer. When Gay Talese of the *New York Times* interviewed him in his office that year, the writer remarked on all the framed tickets on the wall, for everything from World Series to prizefights to Broadway shows.

Gillenwater was proud of the craftsmanship of his tickets, proud of the look, and of the printing technology that meant none of his tickets had ever been counterfeited.

"When you tear apart one of our tickets you'll notice various colors sandwiched between the layers of the cardboard," he told Talese. "Well, we change those colors each time. Sometimes we'll have three colored layers of paper inside the ticket. Ticket takers look for this when they rip your ticket."

All that beauty, all that security and yet, he said, each ticket costs less than one cent to make.

Disappointingly drab tickets in hand and the turnstiles behind us, it's time to find our seats!

Chapter Two

Cinerfront, er, Rivergy, er, Cinergy Field

Every time I visit Cinergy Field, I think about Richie Hebner.

Hebner was the best third baseman ever to come out of the grave-digging profession. (Honest. That's what he did in the off-season!) He was a slugger back when twenty-five homers a season were enough to get *slugger* in front of your name. (Today, that makes you a second baseman.) Hebner arrived in the majors in 1968, at the beginning of what is known in the stadium-design field as the *late modern ballpark era.* St. Louis had torn down Sportsman's Park and erected multipurpose Busch Stadium; Pittsburgh was preparing to level Forbes Field and replace it with multipurpose Three Rivers Stadium; new multipurpose parks were on the planning boards in Philadelphia and Cincinnati.

So Hebner played in the old parks: Crosley and Shibe and Forbes and Sportsman's. His career also extended into the new stadium era: Veterans and Three Rivers and Busch and Riverfront. One night in the early seventies, he was standing behind the batting cage in Philadelphia's Veterans Stadium when a sportswriter asked him about the slew of multipurpose stadiums that were being thrown up all around the National League. Hebner's response was prescient: "I stand at the plate in the Vet and I don't honestly know whether I'm in Pittsburgh, Cincinnati, St. Louis, or Philly. They all look alike."

They can change the name to Cinergy Field, but the park on the Ohio in downtown Cincinnati is still Riverfront Stadium. It has been home to some great games and great names—from Bench to Griffey, from Rose to Griffey, Jr.—over the past three decades. It has *not* been home to a great field. For most of its life, Riverfront had a rock-hard carpet infield, great for rain delays and slap hitters, but not much when it came to character. It was bowl-shaped, with no distinguishing features. To Richie Hebner, it looked just like all the other bowl-shaped, carpeted, multipurpose stadiums that defined baseball in the seventies and eighties.

Fifty years from now, old-timers may recall nostalgic games at Riverfront, but no one will speak with fondness about the old stadium. Not the way they do about Crosley Field.

Yankee Stadium was grand; Wrigley and Fenway, historic.

But Crosley Field, that was a ballpark.

When local governments prepare to erect a modern ballpark, it is the neighborhood that yields. Need more parking? Sorry, that block has to go. Crosley came from the era when the ballpark made the compromises. Got a hill where you want left field? Well, we'll just incorporate the hill into our plans. A house in the way? Build around it. Crosley was like a ballpark designed by a committee: It really did have a hill—they called it the *terrace*—in left field. And no one considered closing Western Avenue to accommodate a ballpark. Heck no, just angle the right-field wall.

Crosley was a field. Riverfront is just a stadium.

The Greeks had a word for it, but they used a different alphabet, so you wouldn't be able to read their word anyway.

Their word transliterates *stade,* and we get our word *stadium* from it.

Stade was a Greek measure of length, about 600 feet, the distance of the Greek's most popular foot race, the *stade* race. Today, we would call it the 200 meters.

At first, Greek racing fans would line the race path to cheer their favorite runners; the finish line was the most popular spot, then as now. When people in the back, began complaining about not being able to see, the stadium came into existence. This would have been about the eighth century B.C., predating even Casey Stengel. These first stadiums were U-shaped and the U surrounded the finish line. The *stade* at Delphi was almost exactly 600 feet long, while the Olympia *stade* measured in at almost 630 feet.

Jumping ahead four centuries, the Romans started getting in on the stadium-building game, but, since they preferred chariot races, their stadiums needed circular tracks. In Latin, still alive and kicking at the time, that translates to *circus.* The largest Roman stadium was Circus Maximus, built in Rome in the fourth century B.C.: It was 2,100 feet, almost one-half mile in length, 700 feet wide, with three tiers of seats, enough for a quarter-million fans, and is thought to be the largest stadium ever built. It was so big that we now name casinos after it.

The last great stadium of the Roman Empire was the Colosseum—capacity 50,000—which opened in 80 A.D. with a spectacle: one hundred days of games, during which 9,000 animals were sacrificed to please a bloodthirsty crowd.

Rod Sheard of HOK is a great admirer of the Colosseum. "A sports stadium is essentially a huge theatre for the presentation of heroic feats. . . . The first great prototype, the Colosseum of Rome, did indeed achieve this ideal, but very few stadia since then have succeeded as well. The worst are sordid, uncomfortable places, casting a spell of depression on their surroundings for the long periods when they stand empty and unused, in sharp contrast with the short period of extreme congestion on match days."

I think he may be talking about Riverfront Stadium.

After the Colosseum, the days of the colossal stadium were over, at least for a long time.

As Christianity swept the world, societies turned from the building of stadiums to the building of churches. Recreation was out; religion was in. It would be fifteen centuries before humans got back to building sports arenas. Baseball would be at the forefront of this movement.

The first baseball stadium was William Cammeyer's Union Grounds, a board fence around a ball field, which opened in Brooklyn in 1862. By 1871, Cammeyer had added wooden bleachers and grandstands, so that it could seat 40,500 fans. In the next decade, wooden ballparks started popping up all over the country: South End Grounds in Boston, National Association Grounds in Cleveland, Hamilton Field in Fort Wayne, Haymaker's Grounds in Troy, New York.

Shortly thereafter, they started burning down. Union Grounds in Chicago didn't even last an entire year, burning to the ground in October 1871, during the Great Chicago Fire, only a few months after opening.

The year 1884 was the year of the ballpark fire; four parks burned down that season. Boston's South End Grounds caught fire during a game that May. Chicago Cubs players averted a disaster by knocking down the fence in front of their West Side Grounds grandstands, allowing fans to escape a blaze. The original Baker Bowl, in Philadelphia, and the original Oriole Park in Baltimore also succumbed to fire that season.

The era of the wooden ballpark ended soon, victim of its own combustibility.

The early modern ballpark era was at hand. Stadium historians trace the beginning of this era to the erection of Shibe Park in Philadelphia in 1907. It was the first park made of steel and concrete. It was literally a bandbox, a square stadium with a center field that seemed to stretch to infinity. It was 515 feet to dead center, and it was lonely; Patty Hearst could have hidden there without fear of notice in her fugitive days.

Soon, there were new parks in Pittsburgh, Chicago, Washington, and Boston, culminating in the construction of Yankee Stadium in New York. These were real ballparks with real names—Forbes, Comiskey, Fenway, Navin—not generic designations like Metropolitan Stadium and Exhibition Stadium and, of course, Riverfront Stadium.

The fans loved them, particularly for their idiosyncrasies, and still do. Old time fans still talk about those parks. And make pilgrimages to the handful that are still in operation: Wrigley, Fenway, Yankee Stadium. I feel privileged that I made it to old Crosley, old Griffith Park in Washington, and old Shibe Field in Philadelphia before the wrecking ball did.

After Yankee Stadium, the flurry of ballpark construction was over. Cleveland built a new stadium, appropriately known as Cleveland Stadium, in 1932; but, for the next forty years, the only new parks were for relocated teams.

The late modern ballpark era began in 1965, with the first indoor baseball stadium, Houston's Astrodome, and continued with Busch Stadium (1966), Three Rivers (1970), Riverfront (1970), Veterans (1971), on through Toronto's Skydome in 1989. These were, according to Sheard, "models of rationalization and economies of scale." In other words, *boring.*

What a switch from what ballparks had once been. In the ballparks of the 1870s fans found music, fireworks, fountains, pennants, flags. Sportsman's Park in St. Louis even had a roller coaster. When Riverfront Stadium opened in 1970, its fans didn't even have a view of the river.

Something happened in the early 1990s. A new generation of stadiums, conceived by forward-thinking baseball executives and architects, who had grown up with Bill Veeck's exploding scoreboard and postgame fireworks, reminded us that the ballpark should be fun again.

First came Baltimore's Camden Yards in 1992, followed, by Cleveland's Jacobs Field in '94. Texas, Denver, Atlanta, Arizona, Pittsburgh, Seattle, Detroit, Houston and San Francisco all have new, ambitious, evocative parks. Most are downtown, use the city as a backdrop, feature odd dimensions, grass fields, smaller seating capacities, and great sightlines. "The vast majority have simulated some of the surface charm of the classic parks and have added a range of amenities," write George Ritzer and Todd Stillman in a 2001 article in *Study in Leisure Sciences*. Their article, titled "The Postmodern Ballpark as a Leisure Setting: Enchantment and Simulated DeMcDonaldization," argues that the late modern ballparks, the ones built in the sixties and seventies, were *McDonaldized*, that is, too much "efficiency, predictability, calculability and replacement of human with nonhuman technology." They say the new parks are trying to bring back fun, to make the stadium more spectacular and enchanting with shopping, food courts, beer gardens, amusement rides, video games, and "many, many ATMs." At the new PacBell Park in San Francisco, ATM machines double as will-call windows!

If Richie Hebner were playing today, he could glance up at the B&O Warehouse in right field of Camden Yards. He could squint at the giant glove in left-center field at PacBell Stadium. He could envy the field-level beer garden at new Comiskey Park.

He would once again know where he was.

. . .

Will and I know where we are. We are just inside the turnstiles of Cinergy Field, but we don't know where we are going. Where are our seats? Stadium architects know that a ballpark can be a confusing place. Which way do I go? Do I take the ramp or stay on this level? Where's the concession stand? Where's my section, my row?

Rod Sheard of HOK says there are four ways to make the fan's journey easier:

- "Keeping choices simple so that people are never faced with complex or difficult decisions.
- "Ensuring clear visibility of the whole stadium so that people always know where they are in relation to exits.
- "Clear signs.
- "Good stewarding."

The Reds got it right on the third count: A clear sign directs us down the ramp to section 145.

The goal of stadium design is to make every choice a simple one. It's difficult enough when you are being jostled along in a crowd, so the stadium is designed as a series of Y or T junctions. Sheard says the fan "must be confronted with one and only one decision at a time in such a way that when he has taken the final decision he has arrived at his seat."

No complex choices: left, right, straight, up, or down. Just left-right or up-down. We're going down.

At the end of the ramp, we read another clear sign and head left.

Here's the sign for section 145. We turn right, and interact with "good stewarding." A grumpy old fellow leads us down to row 19, then over to seats 8 and 9, right in the middle of the row. He wipes off our seats, even though they seemed to be cleaner than his dirty rag, hands us back our stubs and takes his time leaving. It's called the tip pause. I give him two dollars, a buck for each seat. He doesn't even say thank you.

Should I have tipped him? You know what people who make their living in the service industry say: Tipping isn't a city in China. I'm from the old school; I grew up hearing that TIPS stood for "to insure prompt service."

I've never been a server, but I've had many friends who were, so I am pretty well trained on the subject. I tip, I tip early, I tip often, and I tip big. Not that big, not for this grouchy old guy. He would do well to read a study on tipping out of Cornell University. If he had introduced himself by name, he could expect a 53 percent greater tip than those who don't. (That might have meant $3.06 from me.) A little eye contact would see his tip increase 15 percent ($2.30), and a simple smile could have caused his tip to jump by 140 percent ($4.80 just to wipe off our seats)!

As we turned toward the ramp, we were greeted—*accosted* might be a better word—by a trio of women in red T-shirts. "Don't forget your flag," one said. Today is flag day or, more specifically, Chevrolet Cincinnati Reds Car Flag day. The first 10,000 fans ("Sixteen and over") get a free Reds flag to display proudly on the back window of their cars.

This is the first of sixteen giveaways the Reds have scheduled for this season. Among the upcoming promotions are Provident Bank Magnetic Schedule Night, Johnny Bench Bobblehead Day, Cap Day, Floppy Cap Day, Fashion Cap Day, Kahn's Baseball Card Day, and Butterball Fresh Chicken Dry-Erase Board and Recipe Night.

I almost miss getting my free flag. I hurry back to snatch one. I might be able to sell this baby on eBay.

Why are the Reds doing this? Does this really make a difference, are people really going to load up the car so they can snag a couple of cheesy car flags? According to researchers Mark McDonald and Daniel Rascher, writing in a 2000 edition of the *Journal of Sports Management* the answer is *Yes,* a resounding *Yes.*

First, a little background: The number of promotions has been steadily increasing in Major League Baseball since the early eighties. McDonald and Rascher's data from 1996 indicates the average team schedules twenty-six promotional dates per season, with an average cost of $2.19 per giveaway item. The low is 40 cents for magnetic schedules, to a high of $4.95 for youth replica jerseys.

Using complex mathematical formulae and factoring in any number of variables, including the weather, they conclude that promotions do work. The average promotion increases attendance by 3,893 fans per game. Imagine, the Reds give away a two-dollar gewgaw and four thousand more people will fight the traffic and the parking and the heat and the humidity.

The value of the giveaway also influences that attendance increase. The better the freebie, the more fans come to the game. McDonald and Rascher conclude that each one-dollar increase in the value of the giveaway draws an extra 2,688 fans.

Will wonders what the Reds would have to give away to get a sellout (Today they are about 17,000 or so fans short of capacity). The left side of my brain tells me that all they need is another seven bucks in value and it's a full house.

The field is bleached in sun, and so are our seats. We're in the sun field, something I didn't know when I bought our tickets. It's the noonday sun, though, and as the afternoon progresses the sun will move around behind us.

Stadium designers have to take care how they position the field, because you don't want the sun in the batter's eyes. The official baseball rules even have a suggestion on how to orient the field: Section 1.04 states, "It is desirable that the line from home base through the pitcher's plate to second base shall run East Northeast."

Cinergy faces due east; so do PacBell Park and Yankee Stadium. Also the Metrodome but that doesn't really matter, because, well, it's a dome. Facing east, the sun would only be a problem for the batter in a morning game. How many of those do they schedule?

The worst orientation would be facing southwest. No big-league parks face that direction. In fact, only one has any westward orientation; Houston's Minute Maid Field is rotated about 15 degrees west of north. Of the current thirty major-league stadiums, fifteen are pretty much in line with the rule book recommendation. Five face due north; another five face southeast.

· · ·

Next to me, in seats 1 through 7, is a gang of college boys. They are what the marketing folk call a *sports-priority spectator group.* They are here for the game, and the game only. They know the players; they know the strategy; and they are not afraid to voice their opinions to those around them, even those like me who don't care to hear; to those in front of them, even to the players on the field. They talk baseball before, during, and after the game, and are most likely to end up in a bar afterwards.

In short, these are the kinds of guys who usually sit around me.

The other kind of fan is called the *social-priority group.* These fans are here on business or on a social outing. For them, the game is mildly entertaining but they are more interested in doing business or sharing gossip. They are Will's neighbors, a family of six (lucky Will has an empty seat next to him), who are more interested in the hot dogs and the beer than the stats on the scoreboard. The more upscale members of the social-priority fan group are in the luxury boxes entertaining and being entertained and cutting deals.

Will and I are sitting in what the Reds call the *blue-box seats.* Yes, the Reds sell blue seats. Also green seats and yellow seats and, of course, red seats. You might think that for a team named the Reds, the red seats would be the best; oddly, they're the worst. Blue are best, followed by green and yellow. All the seats are called *box seats* except for the absolute worst of them, in the upper regions of the upper deck. They are called *red reserved* seats. If you get the red reserved seats, you would be advised to take along an oxygen tank.

Why are they called *box seats*? They're just seats, twenty-two to a row. They have a back and the bottom folds up. Nothing about them would suggest *box*. The name derives from a time when the best seats were boxed off by railing. Each boxed area would have a certain number of seats; you rubbed elbows with your fellow boxmates and didn't have to run up against the riffraff. (The *Oxford English Dictionary* doesn't speak to the word's origin, noting only that, at one time, a box seat was the seat on the roof of a railroad car.) Box seats were usually in the *grandstand*, a grand name for the wooden stand built to hold customers. Often, the grandstand was the covered area of the ballpark. Over time, park owners came to calling the best seats *box seats*, whether they were boxed off by railing or not. Churchill Downs, the racetrack in Louisville, Kentucky, still has boxed off seats, but those days are pretty much over in baseball.

There are no bleachers in Cinergy Field. When the stadium was being built, the designers chose comfort over character. Let's face it, seats with backs are much more comfortable than hard bleachers, no backs. The Great American Ballpark, the Reds' new park, won't have bleachers either—not the traditional sore-back variety—but there will be a bleacher section, at least that's what they're calling the two decks of seats in left field.

Bleachers seldom refer to uncovered benches anymore; *bleachers* just mean the worst seats in the place, the cheap seats beyond the outfield wall. It's where the rowdiest fans sit; see Wrigley Field, left-field bleacher bums. The name *bleachers* comes from *bleaching boards,* a reference to fans who sat in the hot sun, bleaching themselves on the board seats. Paul Dickson in *The Dickson Baseball Dictionary* found a mention of the term in an 1877 story in the *Cincinnati Inquirer,* which noted, "The bleaching boards just north of the north pavilion now holds the cheap crowd which comes in at the end of the first inning at a discount."

Will and I are in our seats, the sun is shining, the players are in the dugout, in preparation for their introductions. It's a great day for a game. So, why am I thinking back to a conversation I had with my hometown friend Hancel Woods? After years of living away, Hancel moved back a couple of years ago. One of the first things he did was get a haircut from his childhood barber. "I told him the seat seemed a little tighter than I remembered it. He told me, 'Seat hasn't changed in forty years.'"

That's how I'm feeling. Aren't these seats a little snugger?

They are. And it's not the seats.

It's not just me: Americans are on average a couple of inches taller and ten pounds wider than they were when the first stadiums were built a hundred years ago.

When Wrigley and Fenway were built, shortly after the turn of the century, the average seat width was 16 inches. That standard lasted until the forties, when Harvard anthropologist Earnest Hooton (no relation to Burt) conducted an extensive physical measurement program. Hooton had made his name measuring the heads of criminals. His 1939 study, *The American Criminal: An Anthropological Study,* for which he measured the heads of 13,873 criminals and compared them to the heads of 3,203 noncriminals, postulated all sorts of strange things about the criminal class: They seemed to have a greater frequency of low sloping foreheads, high nasal bridges, thin lips, and thin eyebrows. He also noted criminals seemed to have more tattoos than noncriminals. Hooton didn't address the buttocks, criminal or otherwise. He would move up in class by moving down with his measurements, charting the American fanny.

In 1944, he was hired by the Heywood Wakefield Company of Gardner, Massachussets, to measure the human buttocks. Heywood Wakefield manufactured wicker chairs for railroad cars and waiting rooms, and wanted to develop a more comfortable seat. Hooton measured commuters at Boston's North Point station—and what a line he must have had, to get people to let him measure their butts—and published his findings in 1945 in the booklet *A Survey in Seating.*

In essence, he said that chairs should be 18 inches in width to accommodate comfortably the backsides of railroad passengers. This has come to be known in the seating industry as the 18-inch rule. The standard was soon adopted for public seating of just about every kind: buses and ballparks, airplanes and movie theaters, even churches.

The 18-inch rule has, well, ruled, in seating for half a century. In the 1990s ferry officials in Seattle started noticing that more people were standing or sitting on the floor. The ferry hadn't taken out any seats and they hadn't started accepting more passengers than its 250-person limit, but the 250 seemed to be packed in more tightly.

People in other industries and venues had noticed the same thing. Eighteen inches were no longer enough to contain one heinie.

The 18-inch rule was about to fall.

Today, the average general admission seat is twenty inches wide. In the luxury boxes they go up to twenty-four inches wide. The seats at San Francisco's PacBell Stadium are two inches wider than the seats were at Candlestick Park, built just forty years ago. Same for Comerica Park, where seats are two inches wider than they were at old Tiger Stadium.

The entire seating industry has been affected by the broadening of Americans. The clerk manning the Information Booth at today's game is sitting in a 20-inch chair, now the average for office chairs. Ten years ago, it was 18 inches. In the office-furniture industry, chairs are designed to fit 90 percent of the male population (Sorry, Shaq, you'll have to get a custom model), in every dimension except seat width. Chairs are designed to fit 90 percent of the *female* population, because women are broader at the hips.

Despite the efforts to account for the expansion of the American waistline, seat width is still not a major factor in fan satisfaction. Michael Godoy, Manager of Operations Development for the stadium management company SMG, told *Amusement Business,* "It's not as big an issue as food and beverage offerings. It's not as big as access, parking and infrastructure to get to and from buildings. It's not as big as quality entertainment."

Nevertheless, it's a big issue for those of us who are now big people.

Will and I are seated, we've passed two hot dog stands and one restroom. Our next concern: Can we see the game?

It probably started back in the days of Greek foot racing. When stubby little Studius couldn't see over oafish Orifus in front of him, he knew what to do: find a rock and stand on it. In that way, he could see over the top of Orifus and have a good view of the finish line. In stadium design, they call this *sightlines*. Architect Michael Hand, vice president of HOK Sport, who is designing the Reds' new ballpark, lists sightlines as one of the four things stadium architects worry about most, along with parking, concessions, and restrooms.

If you've ever been unfortunate enough to sit behind a basketball player in the movie theater, you know what I'm talking about. It has been a problem, dating all the way back to the Greeks and Romans. Roman architect Marcus Vitruvius, who practiced his craft in the first century B.C., was already confronting the situation in his famous treatise, *De architectura*, an architectural textbook that was used through the Renaissance. In his book, Vitruvius recommended that each row should be raised twice as high as the one in front of it.

It's gotten a little more complex since then; in fact, it's gotten a lot more complex since then. Figuring out the proper *sightline*—the height a row should be raised above the one in front of it—is so complex that one of the standard texts in stadium design, *Stadia* by John and Sheard, recommends architects let a computer do the calculation.

Here, you can see why. The formula for figuring out the sightline is:

$$N = (R+C) \times (D+T)/D - R$$

Where N = riser height

R = height between eye on "point of focus" on the playing field

D = distance from eye to "point of focus" on the playing field

T = depth of seating row

C = C value

And C can be anything from six inches, if spectators are expected to see over people wearing hats, down to 2.3 inches, if people are expected to crane their necks or peer between heads rather than over them. It's the balancing act in designing a stadium: If the C value is too low, fans can't see; if it is too high, fans get dizzy when they walk down. The general rule is not to make the stands steeper than 34 degrees, which is the angle of the average stairway.

The public-address announcer asks that we rise for the singing of the national anthem. Today, the honors go to a young girl from Chillicothe, Ohio, Erica Etnale. She's a sprite, and there is a debate about her age in my section. "Is she ten?" "She has to be twelve."

As her juvenile soprano fills the stadium, I think about another juvenile rendition of "The Star-Spangled Banner." You remember, then-big star Roseanne Barr's screeching version at a 1990 San Diego Padres home game, captured on national television and preserved on videotape for the ages.

Don't blame Francis Scott Key for Roseanne's rendition; he only wrote the words. After a British shelling of Maryland's Fort McHenry during the War of 1812, Key, a lawyer and amateur hymn-writer of "Before the Lord We Bow," was so stirred by the staunch defense put up by the American boys—the flag was still there!—that he was moved to poetry, composing a four-stanza tribute he titled "Defence of Fort McHenry." That was on the morning of September 14, 1814 (the War of 1812 lasted beyond 1812). The poem was later set to the tune of an old British drinking song "To Anacreon in Heaven."

Key wasn't thinking of baseball when he composed his poem; he probably didn't know what baseball was, but credit baseball for turning "The Star-Spangled Banner" to something more than a patriotic song, into the national anthem. There are stories that "The Star-Spangled Banner" was played before the opening game at Capitolene Grounds in New York on May 15, 1862. For whatever reason, the practice didn't catch on. In fact, "Columbia, Gem of the Ocean" was the most popular band number at ballparks in the last part of the nineteenth century.

The watershed event for Key's composition came in 1918. Baseball had been unaffected by World War I during the 1917 season but, in 1918, the government classified the sport a nonessential occupation, and ordered that the regular season end by Labor Day. There had even been talk of eliminating the World Series but, when word came back that the boys overseas were anxious to get game reports, the government relented and game one between the Red Sox and the Cubs was played September 5. The *New York Times* game story mentions in passing that as the Cubs came to bat in the bottom of the seventh, there was a delay due to the band playing "The Star-Spangled Banner." It was a spontaneous move by the band and was met spontaneously by fans and players who stood, hand or hat over their hearts, and sang. Red Sox third baseman Fred Thomas, a Great Lakes sailor, was described in the *Times* as having adopted a "military pose." The performance was so moving that the song was repeated during the seventh-inning stretch for the next two games. In Boston, the band played it *before* the fourth game, prompting the *New York Times* to refer to it in its next day's editions as the *national anthem*.

Soon after, a movement began in Congress to officially adopt "The Star-Spangled Banner" as the national anthem. Only one thing would hold the movement back: The song, as Roseanne could attest, was hard to sing, with its expansive melodic range. The bill went down to defeat, as did similar measures in 1921, 1923, and 1925. In 1931 backers of the song came to Washington with a petition signed by more than six million Americans. This time, the bill sailed through and, on May 3, 1931 it was signed into law by President Herbert Hoover. The song became a regular event before World Series games and on national holidays; it wasn't until World War II, when patriotism was rampant, that the national anthem was adopted as a regular part of baseball's pregame ritual.

And no, the last two words to the national anthem are not, "Play ball!"

They are the umpire's first two words.

Chapter Three

About a Bat

Todd Walker leads off the bottom of the first with a broken bat single to right. His first at-bat of the game, first pitch, and he breaks his bat. As he trots back to first, the batboy retrieves the wooden shard from the second baseman and deposits it in the dugout, where it's relegated to a trashcan.

If Todd Walker were Ken Griffey Jr., the broken bat might end up on eBay, where it could fetch upwards of one hundred dollars but, because Walker is a twenty-nine-year-old .280 hitter, with no whisper of Hall of Fame attached to his name, the bat will arrive at the city dump, discarded. Firewood at best.

That's one of perhaps one-hundred bats Walker will go through this season. Some will break in a game, others in batting practice. A few may go to charity auctions and still others may be discarded because there are no more hits in them. That's the life expectancy of a big-league bat, a couple of games, according to Bill Williams, vice president of Hillerich & Bradsby, makers of Walker's bat, a black Louisville Slugger model C271.

In my neighborhood, bats were a precious commodity. We had two or three bats, at most, in any season, and at least one of them was a repair job, a broken bat tacked back together with finishing nails and wrapped with a half-roll of friction tape.

If your birthday was coming up and you had a choice between a new bat and a new glove, you always went with the glove. You had to have a good glove, but a bat was a shared object. "Anybody bring a bat?" was a familiar refrain. Bats were hard to negotiate on your bicycle and a pain for the walk-up players to carry, plus there just weren't that many of them around.

As a result, bats were treated with great respect. I can remember the weekend Chip Grills had some dorky kid spend the night with him, which meant the kid joined our regular Saturday baseball game. When the dork came to bat, he was waving the bat back and forth with the label aimed straight at the pitcher. That's when Tony Wampler came charging in from left field; it was his bat. "Hey, hey, don't bat with the label toward the pitcher! You'll break it!"

That was a boyhood mantra: You had to bat with the label up. When Hillerich & Bradsby branded LOUISVILLE SLUGGER into the bat, it weakened the wood. Hit it on the label and it could break.

"We all thought that," says Louisville Slugger's Williams. "That the branding of the label made the bat weak at that spot. It's not true, but that's what everybody thought. Actually, the label is branded so if you have the label up, you'll be hitting with the grain"

Batters and carpenters alike know that the *grain* (the wavy part of the wood), is the strongest part. Pick up any bat and you will see that the waves of grain—wouldn't that be a good line for a patriotic song?—are perpendicular to the label. Swing that way and you'll smack the ball against the edge of the grain, and that's the strongest part of the bat.

Williams recalls a story about the season Yogi Berra kept breaking his bats. "He complained to our rep Frank Ryan about the wood. They all complain about the wood. Frank watched him for a while and noticed he had the label facing the pitcher. Frank told him, 'Hold it so you can read the label.' Yogi looked at him and said, 'I go up to the plate to hit, not to read.' So we started burning the labels on his bats at a 90 degree angle."

The Yankees paid for Yogi's bats, so he didn't have to worry about fixing those broken bats. In the backyard, we had to keep a bat in service as long as we could. That duty fell to Darnell Shankel's dad. Walter Shankel was the perfect candidate for bat repairman. He had the patience of Job . . . plus a woodworking shop in his basement. He would brush a little wood glue on each piece of a broken bat, then carefully nudge the shattered piece back into place, making sure to match up the grain. He would hold it in his oversized hands until the glue dried, then gently ratchet the bat into his vise. He would choose just the right-size finishing nail— no heads to tear on your palms—and tap them into precise spots. Only he knew why he picked those particular spots. He covered the repair spot with shiny black electrical tape. He wouldn't let it out of his shop until he had tapped the bat firmly on the cement floor. Walter, a one-time townball star, would send us on our way, like-new bat in hand, with one admonition: "Now boys, don't hit it on the label."

. . .

I must have broken ten bats in my baseball career. My son has never broken a single one. By the time Will was in Little League, in the early nineties, the aluminum bat had taken over. Every kid on his team had his own gleaming white TPX model, Louisville Slugger's popular youth league bat. I think it cost me ninety dollars, but you want your kid to be a (Louisville) slugger.

For modern players, the bat is like a security blanket yanked from a child's hands. They grow up on aluminum bats, then if they progress into the upper levels of baseball they have to make the switch to wooden bats.

Todd Walker uses a C271 model Louisville Slugger. His is a black bat, 34 inches long and 31 ounces in weight. The C stands for Carew, Rod Carew, the Hall of Fame second baseman. The 271 means Carew was the 271st big leaguer whose last name began with C to develop his own bat model.

That doesn't mean Walker's bat is an exact replica of the bat Carew used; Rod's bats were actually an ounce or two heavier. Williams says the model number has nothing to do with length and weight, and has everything to do with design. Measure the knob on Carew's bat and it will be the same as Walker's. The handle, the taper, the barrel, all of them will match up with Carew's bat. Louisville Slugger takes eighteen measurements along the length of the bat, at roughly two-inch intervals, and it is these measurements of various diameters that determine a bat model. (The knob is a separate 19th measurement.)

You don't have to be a mathematician to figure out

that's a lot of possibilities. If you *are* a mathematician, there are 1,978,419,655,660,313,589,123,979 possible bat models. In actuality, Louisville Slugger produces only a couple of thousand different models.

C271 is one of the most popular bat models made by Hillerich & Bradsby. Other popular models include S2, Vern Stephens' model; K55, Chuck Klein's bat; and R43, Babe Ruth's timber. Year in, year out, the most popular bat has been the M110. Thirteen Hall of Famers used it. Current stars favoring it include San Francisco Giants second baseman Jeff Kent, Indians third baseman Travis Fryman and Dodgers first baseman Dave Hansen. Todd Walker's teammate Chris Sexton prefers it as well.

It's the Eddie Malone model.

· · ·

Eddie who?

Eddie Malone was almost thirty years old when he finally reached the big leagues. In parts of two seasons, 1949 and 1950, he didn't exactly terrorize the American League, finishing his career a .257 hitter with one home run and 26 runs batted in. But his legend lives on in his bat. Maybe because Eddie only used up 62 hits during his brief stay with the White Sox, his bat had a lot of life left. Because, half a century later, the bat he designed at Hillerich & Bradsby is the most popular model in the Louisville Slugger catalog.

Mickey Mantle, a notorious bat switcher, used the M110 more than any other bat during his career. He first tried it in spring training 1952, hitting .311 with 23 home runs before switching to Vern Stephens' S2 for the pennant drive and World Series. He used it for most of 1955, including the World Series, and the first two months of his Triple Crown season of 1956. It was his favorite bat from 1957 through 1960, as well as parts of the Ruth-chasing season of '61. He ordered the M110 off and on again for the rest of his career.

Al Kaline started using it in the middle of his rookie year, 1954, and kept reordering for the next seven years, five of them .300 seasons. He switched to a lighter, longer bat, Chuck Klein's K55, for most of the sixties, then returned to the M110 in the twilight of his career.

The M110 was the favorite bat of Billy Martin and Enos Slaughter and Earl Weaver; Larry Doby used it when he was trying to recover his batting stroke in 1952; Billy

Williams used it in '62, the first season he flirted with .300, ending up at .298. Eddie Mathews used it late in his career, as did Willie McCovey and, at various times in their careers, Tony Perez, Willie Stargell, Vic Wertz, and Robin Yount found hits in the old M110.

Why has the Eddie Malone bat been so popular? What makes it different? Charlotte Jones, of Hillerich & Bradsby's Pro Bat division, says it isn't that it's different, it's that it's familiar. "It has a medium handle, a medium barrel." It harks back to a player's childhood baseball days, when a one-size-fits-all bat was used by every kid in the neighborhood.

Eddie Malone, who is eighty-two now and retired from the car business—"I bought a Chevy store after I retired from baseball"—remembers the origin of his bat. It was 1939, and he was playing for the Pocatello Cardinals of the Class C Pioneer League. "Years ago, Louisville Slugger had fellows out in the field representing them. If they came across a guy they thought was going to get to the big leagues, they'd offer him a contract. You'd get either money or a set of golf clubs. We didn't know what golf was back then. But most of us were only making a hundred a month so I took the money."

On July 28, 1939, Edward Russell Malone signed on the dotted line: "In consideration of one dollar and other good and valuable considerations in hand paid and the receipt of which is hereby acknowledged, I the undersigned hereby give and grant unto Hillerich & Bradsby Co., a corporation of Kentucky, its successor and assigns, the sole and exclusive right for twenty years from date, the use of my name, autograph, portrait, photograph, picture, initials and/or nickname for trademark and/or advertising purposes in connection with the manufacture and/or sale of baseball bats. . . . I hereby endorse and have bona fide used or will so use the bats."

On the contract, Malone identified himself as a "Catcher, 19, 5' 10", 170 pounds."

There were two lines for his autograph, the one that would be used on the bat: on one he wrote Bud Malone, on the other Buddy Malone.

"They made a model just the way I wanted. I started with one model; they thinned the handle out, put a knob on it. I couldn't swing more than 34 ounces so I had to have a smaller barrel. Over the years I changed this a little bit and that a little bit." His bat card at Hillerich & Bradsby identifies his first bat as "Chuck Fullis barrel, Jimmy Foxx handle, Jimmy Foxx knob." It was 34½ inches long and 34 ounces in weight. Over the next five years, he kept refining his choices, switching to a Charlie English barrel, going up to a 35-inch model, dropping to 32 ounces.

The Eddie Malone M110 was born on January 22, 1944. That's when Hillerich & Bradsby determined that Malone's bat was different enough to declare it a unique model. The first M110 combined the barrel of the E3 and the handle of the S44. It was 35 inches long and weighed 32 ounces. It was the 110th model made for a player whose last name started with M. It was an inauspiciously dubbed model that would become such a legendary bat: The E3 was the Charlie English model, namesake of the light-hitting White Sox infielder of the early thirties. The S44 model belonged to Mel Simons, a White Sox outfielder who had all of 194 major-league at-bats in 1931 and 1932.

Malone used the M110 exclusively for the next four years but, with his career stalled in the high minors, he switched bats in spring training of 1948, trying the Marvin Felderman model. (Felderman had had a cup of coffee with the Cubs in 1942.) In spring training of 1948, he also tried Chuck Klein's K55. It worked: His hitting took off and so did his career, and his contract was purchased by the White Sox in July 1949.

(In one of the great ironies of baseball, Eddie Malone wasn't using the M110 when he made his major-league debut. He was using the K55.)

On July 20, 1949, he had a game-winning sacrifice fly in an 8–7 Chisox win over the Red Sox using the K55. The highlight of his big-league career came on September 23, 1949 when he went 4 for 4, including a triple and a double, in a 4–1 win over the St. Louis Browns before a Ladies Day crowd of 3,497. He was hitting with the K55.

Malone alternated between the M110 and the Felderman model in early 1950. He was hitting .225 in 31 games when the White Sox turned their catching duties over to the veteran Phil Masi, sending Malone back to the minors, never to return.

"I was never much of a big-league player," Malone says today. "I hit one home run in the big leagues. The most I ever hit in a season was fifteen."

But he left his mark with his bat in another way.

"I have one [M110] hanging up in my den that they

were good enough to send me. They've been very good to me. A few years ago they sent me a set of golf clubs with my signature on them. Sent me a nice letter. Said my bat was still number one. I play golf about once or twice a week. I'll be eighty-two next month. I've gone from a ten handicap to a fourteen handicap."

Malone says he's proud that he fashioned this famous bat, but has no delusions about his career. "I wasn't a very good player but I was good enough to get there."

And his bat is still there.

Chapter Four

The End of Bad Hops
in My Lifetime

Will and I watch the game differently. I focus on the short-stop. I contend you can tell what's going to happen by the way the shortstop plays: Is he straight up or is he leaning; is he shading the hitter or playing straightaway? Will, on the other hand, watches the pitcher, believing the game goes through the mound.

Yes, I was a shortstop and Will was a pitcher.

So, when Luis Castillo leads off the third by dribbling a grounder that shortstop Gookie Dawkins can't make a play on—it's scored a hit—Will pokes me in the ribs. "Good shortstop," he says sarcastically. "Is he as good as Kubek?"

Anytime a shortstop can't make a play, Will, having some fun at his old man's expense, asks me about Kubek. He's referring to a story I've told him, apparently more than once, since he was a kid, the story of the great short-stop and the tiny pebble.

It's the most famous pebble in history or, at least, baseball history. It was no bigger than a pencil eraser, but it altered the natural history of baseball, sending the mighty New

York Yankees, winner of seven of ten World Championships in the fifties, to defeat in the first World Series of the sixties. They would win four more pennants and two more World Series over the next four years, but then suffered an eleven-year drought, and that one ground ball seemed to change things. They were never as sure of themselves and their divine right to a championship again.

Had the baseball gods turned against them?

If you've forgotten the story—Will hasn't—it goes like this: It was game seven of the 1960 World Series between the vaunted Yankees and the unlikely Pirates, who finished no higher than seventh in the National League the first eight years of the fifties. The score was 7–4 Yankees in the Pirates half of the eighth and history seemed ready to repeat itself, smiling again on the Bombers. With Gino Cimoli on first, Bill Virdon hit a sure double-play grounder toward short. As he crouched to smother the ball, Yankees shortstop Tony Kubek, a former rookie of the year, seemed in control. That's when he was greeted by every infielder's nightmare: The ball landed squarely on a pebble, sending it skittering on an unlikely trajectory, skipping upward and striking the dazed Kubek in the throat, sending him sprawling to the ground.

What looked like a sure double play became a fluke single. Kubek was helped to the dugout and was taken by an ambulance to the hospital with a possible larynx fracture. He was replaced by journeyman Joe DeMaestri. But the damage had been done.

That one bad hop opened the gate and before the inning was over the Pirates had scored five and were up

9–7. The Yanks rallied for two in the top of the ninth, tying the game 9–9 and setting the stage for Bill Mazeroski's dramatic leadoff home run that won the game and the series for Pittsburgh. (And figured heavily in Mazeroski's eventual election to the Hall of Fame.)

If Kubek had turned the double play in the bottom of the eighth, I have no doubt Mazeroski would never have come to the plate in the bottom of the ninth. And the Yankees might have reigned, unchallenged, forever.

You don't see that sort of bad hop much anymore and I went to Tom Nielsen, head groundskeeper for the Reds' Triple A minor-league affiliate, the Louisville Bats, my hometown team, to find out why. Nielsen has been tending ball fields since he created one in his backyard as a grade schooler twenty years ago. He has a degree in horticulture, and has been a working groundskeeper for a decade. (I consulted him, rather than the Reds grounds crew because Cinergy Field has only had natural grass since 2001.)

I caught up with Tom on an off day. His team was on a road trip so he'd only be spending twelve hours or so at the park. When the team is in town, he routinely works sixteen-hour days, ten days in a row. "During the season I usually work 90 hours a week," he says.

Nielsen is too young to have seen Kubek's bad hop, but he's heard about it and he hopes you never see a carom like that on his field. Nielsen and his five-man crew work year-round to make sure another pebble never decides a game, much less a World Series. Nielsen's mantra? "I want to see the end of bad hops in my lifetime."

Groundskeeping was once a craft. The groundskeeper could take pride when the field he had so carefully manicured—grass just a little higher than it should be, dirt a little softer than it should be—would hold back ground balls, enabling his slower-than-molasses infielders to get to those balls. In another town, another groundskeeper would revel in his hard-as-rocks dirt that sent balls skidding through the infield, allowing his speedy players to churn out doubles from routine grounders.

There are plenty of stories from those days.

The late Bill Veeck, owner of several big-league franchises, including the St. Louis Browns and the Chicago White Sox, said that a good groundskeeper was worth ten to twelve wins per season. For instance, during a game at old Comiskey Park, during the Veeck reign, Red Sox slugger Ken Harrelson hit a scorcher that, by all accounts, should have bounded all the way into center field but, thanks to legendary groundskeeper Emil Bossard's work, the ball actually stuck in the dirt in front of home plate.

Cleveland's Bob Feller liked a high mound, so the grounds crew would elevate it to 18 inches—regulation was 15 inches—at two in the morning, with the lights out, on nights before his starts.

During the Go-Go Sox years of the late fifties, when the speedy White Sox regularly led the league in stolen bases but hit the fewest home runs, other teams would slow the ball down by letting the grass grow in the days before the team came to town. After one game in Cleveland, White Sox manager Al Lopez is reported to have pointed to the three-inch outfield grass waving in the wind, and quipped, "Wish I had brought my shotgun. There must be quail out there!"

Tom Nielsen knows all those stories. He even told me one I'd never heard. "Did you know you can make the mound higher in the visitor's bullpen than the regular mound, then when their reliever comes in, he feels like he's pitching out of a hole?"

I thought I had heard them all but I'd never heard that trick. Nielsen swears he doesn't do it. But he could, he says.

The era of the renegade groundskeeper is pretty much past. Groundskeeping is now a science. Witness the fact that many don't even call themselves groundskeepers anymore. They prefer *manager of field maintenance.*

The modern park is a marvel of engineering. New Comiskey Park, for instance, can absorb three inches of rain in a half-hour—192,000 gallons, enough to fill a public swimming pool—and be ready for a game in an hour.

Tom Nielsen is at the leading edge of that scientific movement. He was born to be a groundskeeper. He was always fascinated by lawns, turning his Wisconsin backyard into a little baseball field, complete with a mound and batter's box, nurturing it as lovingly as he does his current home field, Louisville's Slugger Park.

He interned with his local team, the Milwaukee Brewers, then went off to college to study horticulture. After stints with the Eugene Emeralds of the Single-A Northwest League and the Chattanooga Lookouts of the Double-A Southern League, Nielsen was hired by the Triple-A Bats. "We kind of move up like ballplayers," he says of his profession. He's on the doorstep of the big leagues and, at thirty-three, young enough to get there one day. For now, he's happy, very happy.

Slugger Park is his field. Ownership brought him on board before the park was constructed. He supervised the installation of drainage pipes underneath the dirt; he oversaw the importing of 550 tons of clay from Tennessee to form the base of the field; he returned the first shipment of clay because it wasn't right. He directed the grading of the ground and the positioning of the sod. He even dug the place for the unfired clay bricks that give the mound its slope. "I was in on the ground floor. That's what was unique, but that's what they wanted."

Slugger Park isn't just his field; it's his baby; and he's up early every day taking care of it. He arrives at his garage office in right field each morning by eight, and heads immediately to his computer. What's the weather going to be? He checks the major weather sites on the Internet, adding in his own instincts from three years of living in Louisville, to formulate a forecast. It's what he battles each day: the weather. All day long, every chance he gets, it's back to the computer, back to the weather sites.

Water is his enemy and his friend. Will it rain? Will it ever rain? Will it never stop raining? If the field is hard, he needs to water. If it's soft, he needs to leave the tarp on.

His first focus of the day is the infield. "Seventy-five percent of the game happens in the infield. The infield is where the game is won or lost."

Nielsen's infield is a mixture of sand, silt, and clay. He can tell by feel where it stands: Too much moisture and the ground is springy, too little and it's hard.

"Once a player came up to me after the game and says, 'Thanks for the loose teeth.' A ground ball had bounced higher than he expected and it hit him in the mouth. I told him, 'You expect there to be moisture in the tenth inning of a day game?' A bad hop, he gets hit in the teeth, he blames me."

I walk the infield with Nielsen and I am surprised: It's nothing like the infield I played on as a kid. My field was red clay that turned to dust during the summer heat, and bad hops were the rule, not the exception. Nielsen's field is springy; you can feel it in your legs as you walk. He has that clay-sand-and-silt base packed hard but, on top of that, there's a fine layer of what looks like crushed rock. Nielsen says it's called *Mule Mix*, but it looks like kitty litter. It's a finely ground commercial grade calcine clay and it conditions the soil, keeping the clay from cracking and helping it absorb excess moisture. "The key to a good infield is keeping moisture in," he says. He will go through twenty-four tons of Mule Mix in a season, almost six grand worth, at six dollars per fifty-pound bag.

Because the infield is the part of the field everyone notices, Nielsen takes particular interest in his, spending his first two hours each day raking the base paths, watering the soil, and checking the water content, leaving much of the outfield work to his assistant, Brad Smith. He waters but he has to be careful not to overwater. "It's easier to soften than harden." If the sun is out or if it's windy, Nielsen waters more liberally; if it's cloudy or if humidity is high, he cuts back.

He likes the base path a bit firmer than the rest of the infield, because that's the part that gets chewed up by players' spikes, so it gets a little less water than the dirt skirt.

When Nielsen walks the infield, he looks down, always down. "Groundskeepers always look down when they walk. It's part of the profession." He spots a single pebble, almost invisible to the naked eye, and he's down, prying it out of the clay. "I go around the infield each day screening rocks from the clay. They sift and screen but rocks still get through. I pick up a rock every day and take it home to my wife. We have a jar. We call it love rocks to let her know I'm thinking of her."

While Nielsen stalks every inch of the infield, Smith is in the outfield, riding his mower. Nielsen says they trim the grass to a height of 1¼" pretty much the standard throughout baseball. "Some cut it a little lower, some a little higher." So Smith mows and mows and mows, an average of three hours a day. He may mow in the morning, then mow over the same stretch again in the afternoon, then touch it up before game time.

Slugger Park's infield and outfield grass is predominately Kentucky bluegrass. Nielsen says it's his biggest challenge. "It gets so hot and humid by the river. The air gets stagnant and moisture just sits there, which is a formula for disease. Plus, it's hot in the summer and cold in the winter. Just north of here in Indianapolis they have bluegrass and rye, but rye can't handle the hot, humid weather here. If I can grow grass here, I can grow it anywhere."

As he says this, he stoops and pulls out two tiny weeds that only he could have spotted.

Nielsen compares his job to tending a big golf green. "People say, 'How hard could it be to keep up two-and-a-half acres of grass?' I tell them, 'Yeah, but I have big guys running around and they don't replace their divots.'"

Nielsen says it's always something: spraying fungicide every week; applying liquid fertilizer every two weeks; watering and raking and mowing; watering and raking and drying. Painting the base lines; prepping the bullpen; putting down the bases, cleaning them; hauling out the batting cage. And don't even mention the tarp. "The tarp is 170 feet by 170 feet. Brand new, it weighs half a ton out of the box. Then add wind and water, and it weighs a lot more. The wind can lift you four feet off the ground. And you have to be ready to take it off at the drop of a hat. If the sun comes out it can fry a field in an hour." That can mean pulling and replacing the tarp four or five times a day to take advantage of even a half hour window in the weather to allow air to get to the turf.

The tarpaulin (originally *tar palling*—a covering treated with tar) was invented to protect goods in a wagon from the elements. In 1884, Chris Von der Ahe, the George Steinbrenner of his day, got the idea that, if he covered the infield at Sportsman's Park with a tarpaulin, he might be able to avoid a few rainouts for his St. Louis Browns and put more money in his coffers. Other National League owners noticed and soon every park had a tarp rolled up in the outfield.

But Von der Ahe used the tarp only on off days. It was left to the Pittsburgh Pirates to originate the use of the tarp during a rain delay, pulling the canvas cover across the Exposition Park infield during a May 6, 1906 rain shower.

Over the years the tarp has played a part in the game. Kiki Cuyler was denied an inside-the-park grand-slam home run in game seven of the 1925 World Series against the Washington Senators when the first base umpire ruled his drive to the right-field wall was a ground-rule double because it had become tangled in the tarp. (The Pirates still won the game 9–7, clinching the Series.)

The most famous tarp incident came in the 1985 National League playoffs, when Cardinal outfielder Vince Coleman got his leg caught in the automated tarp before game four and missed the rest of the postseason. His team won that game anyway, with his replacement Tito Landrum singling twice in a nine-run second inning that sealed the win over the Dodgers.

· · · ·

Nielsen considers himself something like an extra player. "I work with the manager and do the field the way he wants it. If he wants the infield softer, we water it more. My manager wants it consistent. He wants it the same every game. I do, too."

He also works with the team. "I have a good rapport with the players. I want them to talk to me, tell me what they think. Sometimes, they'll come up to me and say it was really good yesterday." He likes it when players tell him the dirt around second is a tad too hard, or the spot in front of first is too soft. He *does not* appreciate it when they blame him for an error. "They do not want to make me mad. Don't say stuff to the groundskeeper. Say the third baseman gripes about me. I can make it dry around third and balls will be racing off the ground like concrete."

Nielsen and his crew walk nearly every inch of the field every day, checking for problems, weeds, fungus spots. "You gotta know grass, you gotta know irrigation, you gotta know equipment, you gotta know what you're doing. But I love this job. I love being outside. I love grass. I go to work not because I have to but because I love it."

A half hour before the game, Nielsen goes over the field for one final check. Today, he stops beside second base, studies the dirt, bends down and pries out a fingernail-sized stone. No one in the grandstand even notices as he pockets the pebble. That's today's love rock.

While the teams go through batting practice, Nielsen observes. Is it too hard at third? Maybe just a little more water . . .

One of the last things Nielsen and his crew do before the game is move the batting cage off the field. The reason that Tom Nielsen's crew, like grounds crews everywhere, have to drag the batting cage out and drag it back every game is because Welling Titus was lazy. Titus, a catcher for an amateur team from Hopewell, New Jersey, tired of chasing wild pitches and foul tips and, in 1907, patented a device he thought would save him time and energy. He called it the "base ball back stop," a wire cage that trapped all those balls that the catcher didn't. Like fire and the wheel, it was pretty much an instant sensation. Titus assigned rights to his invention to the sporting goods behemoth A.G. Spalding and Brothers and sat back (but not on his haunches) for the rest of his life, collecting royalties of six dollars per cage.

The game actually offers a break for Nielsen and his crew. They can eat dinner, repair equipment, and check the weather channel—again. They race out to drag the infield in the fifth, but then head back to the garage.

Once the game is over, Nielsen's work begins again: repairing the mound and home plate, replacing the tarp, patching problem spots, watering.

The last fan left an hour ago, but Tom Nielsen is just finishing up, finally ready to head home to his wife and his townhouse. He will be back in less than eight hours.

He takes off his ball cap, wipes his brow and heads to the garage, and then, finally, home.

Does he ever allow himself a little extra time at home during the season, to watch a little TV, take care of household chores, mow the lawn?

"Are you kidding? You spend all day at the park, the last thing you want to do is go home and mow."

If Nielsen had worked for the Reds a couple of years ago, he wouldn't have had to know how to turn a lawn mower on. That's because, from the day it opened in 1970 until Opening Day 2001, Riverfront had AstroTurf.

For its first century, baseball owners were content with what those of us of a certain age call simply grass (as opposed to the modern term, *natural grass*). Then came the Astrodome. The world's first indoor baseball park opened on April 12, 1965. A few days later, the outfielders noticed something: The grass was dying. The Colt 45s muddled through that first season on Tifway 419 Bermuda grass, but the only way to make it look like natural grass was with a can of green paint. When the park reopened for the 1966 season on April 8, 1966 the game was played on AstroTurf, a newly invented plastic carpet, laid directly on the concrete base of the field, that enraged purists but engaged owners, who had one thought: No rainouts!

This carpetlike surface soon took over baseball, much to the players' chagrin, even providing the surface in open-air parks where natural grass grew easily. Players believed fake grass caused more injuries, though a study at Cincinnati's carpeted Riverfront Stadium in 1970 reported only an increase in burn injuries to the palms and knees. The guys who patrolled the rock-hard outfield disagreed. They were sure it was doing something to their legs and knees. In the end, grass seems to have won the day; the only new stadiums with carpet are of the indoor variety. Even obsolete parks like Cinergy have reverted to natural grass.

Julian Tavarez, the Marlins pitcher, is a landscape architect. And, the longer he pitches, the more he keeps reshaping the mound to suit himself. He's fashioned a little landing pad for his lead foot, and now he's working on the front of the rubber, etching it with his cleat.

The rubber. It's a funny name, but is it rubber?

It is. And has been since 1890, when it was introduced in the rule book as the pitcher's plate to be made of rubber. It replaced the *pitcher's box*, a morphing shape that had restricted the pitcher's movement for a quarter century. Before 1865, pitchers were required to throw from along a 12-foot line. Then came this pitcher's box, which started as a 3×12 area denoted by chalk lines, grew to 4×12 the next year, shrunk to $4 \times 5\frac{1}{2}$ feet the following season, grew back to 4×6 in 1868, then was marked as a 6-foot square for 1869 and thereafter.

That first rubber was 12 inches long and 4 inches wide. Tavarez would have had trouble finding it. In 1895 it was almost doubled in size, to 24 inches by 6 inches, and it's held at that size ever since.

In the early part of the twentieth century, the mound was fifteen inches high but, in 1968, after Bob Gibson and his pitching brethren held big-league hitters to a combined .237, a record low, the mound was lowered to its present height of ten inches. By rule, it drops one inch per foot for the first six feet from the rubber toward the plate.

You wouldn't recognize the rubber as it comes out of the box. It looks like a plumbing fixture: It's a four-sided block, 6 inches by 24 inches, with an aluminum tube running lengthwise down the center. Groundskeepers can fill the pipe with concrete or dirt for longevity. And, when pitchers like Tavarez wear the rubber out with their constant picking and scratching, the groundskeeper can dig it up and rotate it to a new clean side.

Every good boy knows that the rubber is sixty feet six inches from the plate. But does every good boy know exactly where those measurements are taken? It's from the front edge of the rubber to the facing side of the plate.

Today's game is a rarity, an afternoon game during the week. The Reds call it a Business Special. They do it a lot at the end of a home stand; it gives business people an excuse to take the afternoon off, and it gives players a little extra breather. The team bus heads to the airport at five in the afternoon; the flight leaves shortly thereafter; and the team will arrive in Atlanta before dark. Players can check into the hotel and get some rest before tomorrow's night game at Turner Field.

Baseball is no longer the sunshine game. More than two-thirds of major-league games are played at night, under the lights. The last holdout, Chicago's Wrigley

Field, installed lights in 1988. No one believes night ball is as good as day ball, but it's a lot better than it used to be, and Cinergy Field has always been a league leader in the field of lighting.

There were a lot of negatives to Riverfront Stadium when it opened three decades ago: that bricklike infield carpet that caused ground balls to bounce over Joe Morgan's head (he eventually played second in short right field), the distant seats in the upper deck, the generic bowl shape, the hermetically sealed press box. Everyone agreed they got *one* thing right: the lights. Atlanta architects George T. Heery and Bill Finch filled the stadium rim with lights, creating what they called a "crown of light," which flooded the field with the closest thing to sunshine at night. It was entirely appropriate that the replacement field for Crosley should be home to the best lighting system in the majors, since Crosley had been the site of the very first major-league night game.

It's hard to believe that once baseball was a daytime activity—how did the sport survive? It helped that many weekday games started at 3 P.M., allowing day-shift workers just enough time to go straight from the factory to the field. As America's middle class started filling up, there came a need for lights.

The minors recognized this long before the majors. Minor-league teams were experimenting with lights a full five years before the big leagues got the bug. The Des Moines Demons knocked off the Wichita Aviators 13–6 at Des Moines's Western League Park on May 2, 1930 in what is generally considered the first official night game. It was a big hit, and newspapers reported ten thousand people showed up at the five thousand seat stadium. (There had been a game played under lights in Fort Wayne on June 2, 1883, not long after Thomas Edison perfected the incandescent light, but it was an amateur game. For the record, Fort Wayne beat Quincy M.E. College 19–11 in seven innings under gaslights.)

By 1932 seven of the seventeen minor leagues had lights in every stadium; it was only a matter of time before lights reached the bigs. The Reds were the leader, by a long ways, scheduling the first big-league night game for May 23, 1935 against the Phillies. It was rained out.

It was still dreary the next night, but the game went off anyway, with President Franklin Roosevelt flipping a switch 600 miles away in Washington that turned on the lights in Cincinnati. (Actually, he pushed a telegraph key that lit up a signal lamp alerting club general manager Larry McPhail to throw the switch that turned on the lights.) The field lit up like a sudden sunrise, courtesy of 632 incandescent lamps of 1,500 watts each mounted on eight 130-foot towers. The setup cost $50,000.

The Reds won an errorless game 2–1 before an announced crowd of just 20,422, the third largest crowd of the season, but still a bit of a disappointment for an historic event in a park with a seating capacity of 30,000. The chilly weather was blamed. (Maybe they should have given away bobbleheads, too.)

Still, it was a success with the press. *Sporting News* columnist Edgar G. Brands, who had traveled over from St.

Louis, proclaimed, "The fielders found that the Mazdas [lightbulbs] made the playing area as well lighted as a hazy afternoon with the sun peeking through the clouds. It was as close an approximation to daylight as anyone has ever seen."

The Reds played six more night games that season, one against each National League team. It would be three more years before another team took the plunge, when the Dodgers installed lights at Ebbets Field for the 1938 season.

The first lighted stadiums were illuminated with floodlights, the same kind grandma has on her garage. Floodlights do just that, they flood with light. The infield, where most of the lights were focused, had plenty of light and a high ceiling, but the expanses of the outfield had dark areas and blind spots.

The problem was that round spots of light were used to illuminate a fan-shaped area. These round dots of illumination would overlap and overlap, leaving some areas bright and others dim. And because lights were positioned at 130 feet, well below the maximum height of a fly ball, which can reach upwards of 200 feet (a handful of balls have hit the Hubert H. Humphrey Metrodome roof, which is 195 feet high; no ball ever hit the Astrodome ceiling at 208 feet), sometimes batted balls just disappeared, only to reappear milliseconds later in a different location and heading on a downward spiral. Playing the outfield now required a new skill: night vision.

In 1960, the Illumination Engineering Society first published *Current Recommended Practice for Sports Lighting*, a guide to illumination levels for various sports, with recommendations for locations and heights for poles and techniques for brightening dark spots and reducing glare and spill. The key then, as now, was to make sure lights were not in the direct line of sight for the players and the fans.

To truly bring daylight to the night sky would require more than just recommendations and techniques; it would require invention. No matter how excellent the guidelines, floodlights just weren't up to the task.

Teams tried high-pressure sodium-vapor lights (too inefficient) and mercury-vapor lights (too orange), always reverting to incandescent bulbs. And then came metal halide. Metal halide lights, which are a form of high-intensity discharge lighting, emit five times the light of an incandescent lamp without the intense heat. General Electric introduced this new lamp to the market in 1964, just in time for Riverfront Stadium. Metal halides have the added advantage of producing a warm, natural light. It was a perfect solution. Virtually every ballpark built today, from high school to the pros, uses metal halide because it offers the best of all possible lighting worlds: superior color, output, and efficiency. (It does, however, take five to fifteen minutes to start a metal halide lamp, so you don't want to be turning your stadium lights on and off.)

The key to ballpark lighting, according to stadium designers, is uniformity. They've even developed a way to quantify uniformity: divide the illumination at the darkest part of the field by the brightest part. The rule of thumb is that the ratio should be at least 0.7, meaning the darkest spot is at least 70 percent as intense as the brightest spot.

. . .

When Crosley Field was replaced by Riverfront Stadium, those old back-porch lightbulbs were replaced by almost three times as many lights: 1,728 1000-watt, metal-halide lamps mounted almost twice as high, on 250-foot standards. New stadiums now use 2000-watt metal-halide lamps the size and shape of hot dogs, sealed behind a 20-inch lens in aluminum housings that resemble family-size woks. Each light weighs almost one hundred pounds; a new stadium needs about five hundred of them. Individual lights project a beam that is about four by six feet at field level. Figuring out the light pattern for maximum uniformity is too complex for the human brain, but computers can create a criss-cross pattern that is implemented by good old-fashioned manpower. In the final step, pie tins are positioned at strategic points on the field and technicians climb the light towers and aim each lamp individually, sighting through crosshairs in the lamp. If the team is lucky, those sightings will last the season.

Night games, which make up about two-thirds of the Reds 2002 schedule, have changed the face of the game: The face now includes lipstick and ketchup smears as well as five o'clock shadow, as families attend the park. Almost everyone can catch a ballgame and, because of improvements in lighting technology, fans see a game that is a near duplicate of a day game, without the summer heat.

As Paul Hutchinson put it so nicely in the *Denver Post* a decade ago, "General Electric changed baseball forever by bringing good swings to light."

. . .

After Cliff Floyd singles Castillo in from second, then steals second himself, pitching coach Don Gullet goes out to steady his starter, Rijo. The announcer tells the crowd, "Now warming up in the Reds bullpen, Scott Williamson and Jim Brower."

The word *Reds* seems to strike a sour note with Will, and he mutters under his breath, "I think *Reds* is the worst nickname of any team."

I'm not going to disagree, not without at least talking it out. This is the kind of debate baseball fans love. Who is the ugliest player of all time? Will and I have had this debate before. I say Dumbo lookalike Don Mossi, a reliever for the Indians in the fifties. Will counters with E.T. stunt double Willie McGee.

Worst haircut? I say Pete Rose in his late spikey period; Will offers Randy Johnson and his eternal mullet.

Biggest butt: We agree on Tony Gwynn.

So, while things are slow on the field—just how many steps can a coach take when heading to the mound to allegedly confer (i.e., waste time), to allow the guys in the bullpen to get loose—we debate the worst team nickname of all time.

Which brings up the question: What should a team nickname say? I think it should do two things: connect a team to its town and have an element of intimidation. Los Angeles Lakers is a terrible nickname dating back to the basketball team's days in Minneapolis in the Land of a Thousand Lakes—in La-La Land it has no meaning. By the same token, no wuss nicknames work. The Reds; who's afraid of a color? The White Sox; why would you fear hosiery? The A's;

Sesame Street taught me not·to fear letters. Brewers; oooh, I'm afraid of a man who makes beer—and besides, I'm a fan of his work! Marlins; who's afraid of a fish?

Tigers are scary; Pirates are ferocious. But Reds, intimidating? Not anymore, not since the fall of the Berlin Wall.

So, Reds is certainly in contention for the worst nickname.

Nicknames don't trace all the way back to the very first baseball team, the New York Knickerbockers. That wasn't their team nickname, that was their club name: The Knickerbocker Base Ball Club. What is a Knickerbocker anyway? The dictionary says it's someone descended from New York's Dutch settlers.

Nicknames were informal in the early years of the game. The teams preferred to be known by their city name, thus the Bostons and the Brooklyns. Nicknames came from newspaper headline writers, who were desperate for something to use in the headline besides the city name. As you might imagine, the name of, say, Boston, already appeared quite a few times in that city's headlines. Thus, the frequency of colors in the nicknames, colors reflecting the team's stockings or uniforms: the Chicago White Stockings and the Providence Grays and the Boston Red Caps.

At the turn of the century in a city such as Boston, the newspaper needed a way to differentiate between the well-known National League team and the upstart American League team. They couldn't both be the Bostons. So, the new American League team was dubbed the Pilgrims and the National League team the Beaneaters. Neither nickname ever caught on with fans.

It wasn't until about 1910 that nicknames became official, and teams rushed to brand their club. Most teams just adopted their informal nickname. It was during the teens that teams began adding their monikers to their wardrobe. The Cincinnati club first put their nickname Reds inside an ornate capital C on the uniform in 1911. That remained the team nickname until 1953, when Reds in a newspaper headline meant the hated Communists. For five years, the team became the Redlegs. When the club introduced new uniforms in 1956 the name Reds was nowhere to be found.

Ohio's other team, Cleveland, was a little late to the official nickname game. The team had been known unofficially as the Naps, for its team leader, Napoleon Lajoie, since he joined the club in 1902. Then in 1914, Nap was traded to Philadelphia. What to call the team? The Napless Naps? How about the Indians?

For many years, the team has claimed the name Indians came from a 1914 newspaper contest and was suggested by a fan to honor former player Louis Sockalexis, a Penobscot Indian and the first Native American to play in the big leagues. Ithaca College professor Ellen Staurowsky, who considers the nickname Indians demeaning, and wants the team to drop it, demolished the "honor Sockalexis" theory with a little research. After reading through all the local papers of the time, she discovered that a committee of sportswriters came up with the name at the behest of club president Charley Somers. No mention was made of Sockalexis. The *Cleveland Plain Dealer* said, "The title of Indians was their choice, it having been one of the names applied to the old National league club of Cleveland many years ago." Staurowsky discovered that the Sockalexis link was first mentioned in the team's 1968 media guide.

Which brings Will and I back to our quest: What is the worst team nickname? I used to think a team name from the Japanese League, the Nippon Ham Fighters, was the worst. (What, they fight hams all day long?) Then I found out the name of the team sponsor was Nippon Ham, a Japanese sausage maker, and that changed everything. The name suddenly made sense.

It would be easy to pick a nickname from the nineteenth century—the Boston Beaneaters, the Chicago Orphans, the Brooklyn Bridegrooms—but those were never official nicknames, they were names used primarily by the newspapers.

I almost choose the Phillies. Shouldn't that be a team in the All-American Girls Professional Baseball League. It's a girl horse, misspelled, isn't it? Or is it simply a corruption of the town name? If every team drew its nickname from their city we would have a league of the Cincies and the New Yorkies.

But since we are in Cincinnati and since Will is going with the Reds, I pick the Porkopolitans. That was the unofficial nickname for the team back in the 1870s. Team owner Josiah Keck owned a meatpacking business and, thus, the name. It calls to mind a bunch of suave pigs, not exactly an image to strike fear in the hearts of, say, the Troy Trojans, another team of the era, but maybe it incited a bit of envy from the guys on an 1880 rival, the Worcester Ruby Legs. Now *there's* a wuss name.

Chapter Five

Glove, American Style

Luis Castillo leads off the top of the third with a grounder deep into the hole at short. Demonstrating all the fielding ability you would expect of someone named Gookie, Reds shortstop Dawkins snares the bouncer but is unable to throw out the fleet-footed Castillo. Infield single is the official ruling.

I wonder how many infield singles Reds shortstops have allowed in my lifetime. I'll bet not many. The Reds have been blessed with an almost unbroken line of great fielding shortstops, dating back to my era in the fifties.

Dawkins is only playing today to give the aging and brittle Barry Larkin a day off. Larkin has been the mainstay at the position since 1987, succeeding the fluid Davey Concepcion, a five-time Gold Glove winner, who had taken over the spot in 1970 and held it for sixteen years. Concepcion, in turn, had taken over for another Gold Glove winner, Chico Cardenas, who had started at the spot for most of the sixties.

And preceding Cardenas was the graceful Roy McMillan.

Roy McMillan wore glasses in an era when almost no one in baseball did. He barely hit his weight and he didn't weigh much. But, man, could he field.

How good was he in the field? In 1956, he finished sixth in National League MVP voting, despite hitting only .263 with a mere three home runs. The *Sporting News* didn't begin its Golden Glove awards until 1957 but, when they did, Roy won the first three years for shortstop.

My first glove was a Roy McMillan model. Wilson A2890 with ROY MCMILLAN FIELDMASTER branded into the oversized little finger. A modern kid might mistake it for a catcher's mitt, with its thick-padded heel and its over-stuffed thumb and little finger, but I played a lot of short-stop with that glove. The very first play of my Little League career I gobbled up a hard-hit grounder using that glove— and promptly threw the ball into the weeds behind first. Hey, our first baseman was the shortest kid on the team.

Ask anyone of my generation about their first bat and their first glove and I'll bet you hear more stories about the first glove. That's because gloves were personal. I think we had two bats in the whole neighborhood. Bats, we shared, but your glove, that belonged to you. Oh, you might let Mike Wampler use your glove if he left his at school, but when the gang gathered every afternoon for a ball game, every one of us arrived with gloves hanging on the handlebars of our bikes.

I loved that Roy McMillan glove. Every fall, when I put it away for the season, I'd rub the pocket with Vaseline, put a ball in there and rubber band the glove shut, so it would keep its pocket the entire winter.

Eventually, I had to get a new glove. I was moving up to Babe Ruth League and my old Roy McMillan had had it. I'd restrung the fingers about as many times as I could, but the webbing was coming apart. It had lived a useful life, but three years is about as much as a kid can expect from a glove.

My last glove was a Spalding Rocky Colavito model. I paid ten dollars for it at Dobyns-Taylor Hardware.

The Roy McMillan glove had stubby fingers and an overstuffed heel. The new Rocky Colavito model was sleek, with long fingers and a deep pocket, and, at ten bucks, it was the most expensive thing I'd ever bought—or charged (my dad had an account at the hardware store).

I was relieved later that night when my mother told me my dad was proud of me for buying a good glove, not something cheap that would fall apart in a couple of years. Whew. I thought I might get yelled at.

That glove lasted me into my adult years, but it was not a happy union. I missed Babe Ruth tryouts because of high-school basketball tryouts. I got stuck playing left field that season—I still considered myself a shortstop. I ended my team's season by striking out in the last inning of the tournament, my second strikeout of the game. I was disconsolate; I wanted to cry. I remember my coach putting his hand on my shoulder and walking me off the field. "Maybe you ought to concentrate on basketball."

Thus ended my baseball career.

If we could go back in time and watch a game of those original Cincinnati Red Stockings back in 1869, we could identify with the offensive game. The pitcher throws a ball, the batter swings at it with a bat. The ball and bat were more rudimentary in design but they were clearly a ball and bat. What would surprise would be the defensive side of the game: There were no gloves.

Like the facemask in football and the helmet in hockey, the glove was originally disdained as unmanly. Baseball, like boxing, was a bare-handed sport, and fielding was more determination than art. We don't have fielding statistics for that 1869 team, but we do know that shortstop George Wright, playing the same position for the Boston Red Stockings two years later, would make 21 errors. That's in 15 games, which averages to roughly 1 error every 6 innings or so. Over a 162-game season Wright would have made 227 errors, and he was considered a top-flight shortstop.

The *Sporting News'* smart-aleck columnist Caught on the Fly would most assuredly have nicknamed him Georg-E Wright. They may have had fancy uniforms and snappy red socks, but they would have looked like a pickup game at a family picnic with that sluggish fielding.

In his autobiography *A Ball Player's Career: Being the Personal Experiences and Reminiscences of Adrian C. Anson, Late Manager and Captain of the Chicago Base Ball Club* Cap Anson recalled the days before gloves. "We had a trick of making a spring-box of the fingers, the ball seldom hitting against the palm, and we could haul down even the hottest liners that way, though broken fingers happened now and then. The hands of the infielders and the catchers were awful sights, as a rule, but they stuck to their work even when bleeding fingers were useless at the broken joints."

And that wouldn't change for a decade, until a little-known outfielder named Charlie Waitt was pressed into service at first base. In a major-league career that spanned a mere 115 games, Waitt played only four games at first base, but those four stints would change the game.

It was 1875, Waitt's first big-league season. The twenty one-year-old was a reserve outfielder for the St. Louis Brown Stockings of the National Association. The Browns were playing the Boston Red Stockings, when Waitt was called upon to spell the Browns' regular first baseman, Hermon Dehlman. He took the field wearing a flesh-colored glove with the fingers cut off. In his 1911 book, *America's National Game: Historic Facts Concerning the Beginning Evolution, Development and Popularity of Base Ball with Personal Reminiscences of its Vicissitudes, Its Victories and Its Votaries*, Al Spalding, the Red Stockings' pitcher, would recall questioning Waitt, who "confessed that he was a bit ashamed to wear it, but had it on to save his hand. He also admitted that he had chosen a color as inconspicuous as possible, because he didn't care to attract attention."

The flesh-colored Michael Jackson–style first baseman's mitt was not an immediate baseball sensation. In fact, about the only one who noted it was Spalding. When he switched from pitching to first base two years later, he recalled Waitt's glove and adapted it for his own use. He took a black dress glove made of kid leather, cut off the fingers, and added a padded palm. With the respected Spalding's endorsement, suddenly it became okay to wear a glove, particularly if you played first or catcher, the two positions that handled the largest number of chances. Of course, it was not just a fielding innovation to Spalding. Ever the entrepreneur, Spalding envisioned a big market selling $2.50 fielder's gloves through the mail-order sporting goods company he had founded with his brother Walter in 1874. His intuition proved correct and the demand for the gloves and other sports paraphernalia his company sold was so high that soon there were A.G. Spalding and Brothers sporting goods stores in New York, Philadelphia, and Denver. Today, Spalding is a household name, not because Al won 253 games in his big-league career, but because his name is on gloves and balls, including at one time the official major-league baseball.

There's never been a Charlie Waitt model glove. Waitt is remembered, if at all, for his 1882 season, when he hit a puny .156 in 250 at-bats, still the lowest season batting average for a regular.

Players nicknamed the glove the *mitt*, because many were fashioned from a pair of winter mittens. For the next half century, the baseball mitt looked a lot like a work glove or a riding glove. Over time, it acquired more padding in the heel and palm and the fingers kept getting thicker, but you could still shake hands with a man wearing a baseball glove and not feel stupid.

Then came Bill Doak.

If Charlie Waitt invented the glove, then Bill Doak perfected it. Not to modern standards, but compare gloves before Doak and after, and the difference is astounding. First, a few words about Bill Doak. Standard baseball references make much of his nickname—Spittin' Bill—and nothing about his glove. He was one of the last of the great spitballers and while his lifetime record of 169–157 is a bit lackluster, he did win twenty games in one season, 1920. It was another achievement that season that puts Doak in the baseball pantheon.

Bill Doak invented the webbed glove. He asked the sporting goods company Rawlings to create a two-stringed web between the thumb and index finger of his glove, and the result was nothing short of revolutionary. Before Doak's innovation, the glove was just something to protect the fielder's hand but, with his webbed pocket, it was suddenly an instrument of defense. And ballplayers all around the league were asking for Bill Doak gloves. Rawlings kept the Bill Doak model in its catalog until 1953.

It was just a short trip from a rudimentary web to lacing the fingers together, inserting a panel into the web and, eventually, admiring Ozzie Smith going into the hole.

How much difference did gloves make? The last bare-handed fielder in the majors, Cincinnati Reds second baseman Bid McPhee, was considered the finest fielding second baseman of his era. In 1895, his last bare-handed year, he committed 34 errors in 115 games. The next season, when he gave in and began wearing a glove, he committed fifteen errors in 117 games.

The catcher's mitt evolved along a separate, barely parallel path to the fielder's glove. That shouldn't be surprising, since the catching position is different from any other. What other player views the game through bars with an authority figure looking over his shoulder? What other position could have given us Yogi Berra and Moe Berg? No wonder catchers are paranoid.

While fielders didn't feel the need to protect their fingers until 1875, catchers were experimenting with gloves as early as 1870. A dispatch in the June 29, 1870 edition of the *Cincinnati Commercial* noted, "Allison caught today in a pair of buckskin mittens, to protect his hands." Allison was Doug Allison, the catcher for the Red Stockings, the first openly professional team. It was a different position in 1870 than it is today: Allison didn't crouch directly behind the hitter, he stood several steps back and caught the ball on a bounce, much like the catcher in a schoolyard softball game. It was still hard on the hands, and he enlisted the aid of a saddlemaker in making a mitt. The end product looked like something a farmer might use in hoeing, save for the fingers being cut out, but it worked.

The catcher's mitt stayed that way until 1889, when a former backstop named Harry Decker patented the Decker Safety Catcher's Mitt, a pillowlike contraption that at least protected the player's palm. Decker patented the glove but another catcher, Joe Gunson, had actually dreamed up the design. However, while Gunson was touring the world with Al Spalding, Decker was visiting the patent office.

In the thirties, Rawlings glove doctor Harry Latina came up with a design for a deeper pocket that helped the ball stick in the mitt, but it was still little more than a round mattress with a hole. The mattress became a king-sized bed in 1959, when Orioles manager Paul Richards created a 15-inch wide mitt, roughly the size of the chest protector, to help his catcher Gus Triandos flag down relief ace Hoyt Wilhelm's elusive knuckleball. The league legislated it down to twelve inches in 1960, but Triandos was ready to abandon the experiment anyway. The oversized mitt helped stop the ball, but it was almost impossible to dig it back out and nail a base stealer.

In 1966, Cubs catcher Randy Hundley introduced the hinged catcher's mitt, which allowed one-handed catching. No more snapping the free hand over the pocket to make sure the ball didn't pop out. Today, because of the lower strike zone, the hinged mitt is a necessity. In a low crouch with the mitt at the batter's knees, it is almost impossible for the catcher to use two hands.

It starts with a cow.

It used to start with a horse but, in the thirties, glove manufacturers began switching from horsehide to cowhide because the automobile was rendering the horse less common, so it was easier and cheaper to buy cowhides. Today, all gloves are made from cowhide and all manner of synthetics, including plastic and nylon.

And they are a far cry from Bill Doak's glove. To begin with, they are almost twice the size, and arrive in the clubhouse already broken in. No need to sleep with them, oil them, pound them, or run them over with your bicycle.

Making a baseball glove requires only two weeks, but the process begins long before that. It begins with a cow. Not just any cow, but a healthy heifer, unmarked by scratches from barbed wire and unburnished by a ranch brand. When the cow is full-grown, it is taken to a slaughterhouse, where the hide is, shall we say, extracted. The hide then heads to a tannery where it is treated with chrome, which softens and preserves the skin.

Then the hide is squeezed, split, shaved, retanned, and placed in a spinning cask with oils, dyes, and hot paraffin wax, which further condition what can now be called genuine, top-grain leather.

The leather is stretched, polished, and shipped off to a glove manufacturer. There are only two left in this country: Rawlings in Ava, Missouri and Mizuno in Norcross, Georgia.

Now, it's time to make a glove.

At the glovemakers, the leather is cut into fifteen to twenty glove parts. The palm of a glove comes from the dense hide along the cow's backbone, the same area that provides ribs and sirloins, and the back of the glove is cut from the thinner hide of the flank, where we also get, not coincidentally, flank steak. The lining is from the soft skin of the belly, also home to round steak. All told, it takes about five square feet of leather and six to nine feet of rawhide lacing to make a glove.

Glove patents last only seventeen years, so the two American manufacturers and the fifteen or so foreign glove makers share a few basic web styles. There are no big secrets in glovemaking, no industrial espionage needed. The shell of the glove is sewn inside out and then turned right side out. Much of the work is done by machine but the final step, lacing the glove, is done by hand.

. . .

Infielders use the smallest gloves on the team and second basemen use the smallest of them all. A mitt made for a second baseman is usually only 11 inches long; shortstops' gloves are a half-inch longer; third basemen use gloves that are twelve inches long. Because middle infielders must dig a ball out quickly and fire a throw to first, they need lighter and, therefore, smaller gloves. Third basemen play closer to the plate and have more time to make a throw so they can use a heavier glove but, because they handle harder-hit balls, they need more protection. Most infielders prefer an open web, with space between the panels, so they can find the ball easily. They also prefer the thinnest glove heel, a trend started by longtime Cincinnati second baseman Joe Morgan who used to pull the heel padding out of his glove because he thought it unnecessary for fielding ground balls.

The first baseman's mitt, which was invented in 1941 by Rawlings and originally called the Trapper, is the longest glove. By rule it can be no more than twelve inches long. If any appear to be longer than that, I'm sure it's just an optical illusion.

Pitchers favor closed, or solid web gloves because they don't want the hitter getting a glimpse of their grip, thereby tipping off their pitch. Outfielders also like a solid web, and want longer fingers, so they can wear the glove farther out on the fingertips giving them more reach to snag fly balls.

Gloves arrive in the clubhouse game ready—no need to break them in. Glove manufacturers have accomplished this by using softer leathers. Players get their gloves free, usually four at the beginning of the season, more later if needed. They also receive endorsement money, which can be as much as $25,000 a year for a star. Or a pitcher. Or a star pitcher.

Pitchers are the most prized endorsees, because TV cameras zoom in on their gloves when they are winding up, giving impressionable young buyers a quick glimpse of that trademark Wilson *W* or Rawlings *R*.

There are a lot of those impressionable young buyers out there. The seventeen major glove manufacturers sold more than six million gloves in 2001, a $200 million take. Rawlings is the leader, with 36 percent of the market. Half of all major leaguers wear Rawlings gloves. Second in sales is Mizuno, with 22 percent; Wilson is third, with an 18 percent market share. Fourteen other glovemakers share the remaining quarter of the market.

It started with a cow, and ended with ten baseball gloves.

The current Monarch of the Mitt, the God of the Glove— let's see, can I come up with any more trite phrases?—the Doctor of Defense, is Bob Clevenhagen of Rawlings Sporting Goods. Clevenhagen is only the third glove designer in Rawlings' 115-year history. The first, the legendary Harry Latina, was famous for creating the deep pocket, the Trapper first baseman's mitt (developed for Stan Musial), the wrist adjustment on the back of the glove, and the six-finger glove (created for Cardinals third baseman Ken Boyer, but popularized by Ozzie Smith in the eighties). When he retired, his son Rollie replaced him as Rawlings' glove designer. Rollie invented the *fastback*, the cutaway section that lets a player keep one finger outside the glove. Fifty-seven-year-old Clevenhagen has held the post for the past quarter century, working with finicky big leaguers who want the ball to land just perfectly in their glove, stick long enough for an out, but still be easy to extract for a throw.

Clevenhagen doesn't do his glove designs on a computer, saying he doesn't know how you could do it that way. He keeps it all in his head. When a player calls, Clevenhagen asks a few questions, makes a few notes, drafts a design, cuts a couple of patterns, then works on coming up with a prototype before turning production over to the folks in the factory.

If Clevenhagen is the Glove King, then there is a Crown Prince, his son Brad, who works alongside him, learning the craft. So, in a few years, the mantle will have gone from Latina to Latina to Clevenhagen to Clevenhagen. It may not have the ring of Tinker to Evers to Chance, but they are all glove men.

After Walker leads off the bottom of the third by grounding out to shortstop, Encarnacion drills a long fly to right.

As right fielder Cliff Floyd drifts back, inconspicuously feeling with his left foot for the warning path, I remember a series of photos in an old baseball annual from the fifties: Dodgers center fielder Pete Reiser streaking after a long fly, stabbing at the ball with his glove, crashing into the outfield wall, rolling over, and holding up the ball to get credit for the out.

The caption, long lost in memory, mentioned Reiser's penchant for running into walls (seven concussions and five skull fractures in a nine-year career) and his near-fatal encounter with the outfield wall in '47, a crash that pretty much ended his meteoric career. *New York Times* sportswriter Red Smith counted eleven separate encounters between the reckless Reiser and the unforgiving outfield wall. The first, in '42, only a season after he became the youngest batting champ in National League history, left him with a concussion and a separated shoulder. The one in '47 was the worst; they carried Reiser off the field on a stretcher, a stunned Ebbetts Field crowd standing in silence. At the hospital, a priest performed last rites. If he was reckless, Reiser was also resilient. He returned the next year, but his batting stroke didn't. He was soon traded to the Braves, then went on to the Pirates and Indians.

In 1948, too late for Reiser, the Dodgers installed padding to the outfield wall, and carved out a warning track as a caution to hard-charging fielders. Other parks followed: Wrigley in Chicago the next year, then Braves Field in Boston and Shibe Park in Philadelphia. Today, there isn't a ball field that doesn't have a ten-foot dirt strip in the runup to the fence.

When Reiser went to that great ballpark in the sky in 1981, the *Washington Post*'s Byron Rosen wrote, "If such protection had been provided in his day Harold Patrick 'Pete' Reiser might be in the Hall of Fame."

Cliff Floyd makes it look so effortless, drifting back, then one-handing the ball. I must have caught a million fly balls in my lifetime, and dropped a couple of hundred. I still couldn't tell you how to judge a fly ball.

I've read Willie Mays' explanation about the crack of the bat. When my son Will was first starting to play baseball, I could only teach him through practice. Catch a pop-up, then a higher pop-up, then a fly, then a sky-high fly.

To me, judging a fly ball is like turning on the television. I don't know how it works, I'm just glad it does.

Physicists have been studying the fly ball for years. Since 1968, the leading hypothesis has been the so-called *optical-acceleration-cancellation theory* (also referred to in the literature as the *linear optical trajectory* or LOT theory). In short, a fielder judges a fly by moving to the spot where the ball appears to be climbing upward at a constant rate of speed. If the ball looks like it is accelerating, it's going to drop behind you, so take off backwards; if it looks like it is decelerating, it's going to land in front of you, so hightail it forwards.

That, of course, is not how Willie Mays explains it.

With two out in the bottom of the third, Sean Casey lofts a long fly ball to left. I long for deep fly balls because I love to hear the crowd's collective gasp. Even routine fly balls can elicit an excited *aaaah*. This one isn't quite deep enough for a home run, but it carries over the head of the left fielder who was shading the left-handed-hitting Casey towards center. The ball one-hops to the wall and Casey—a wonderful name for a power hitter, isn't it?—thunders into second standing up.

The ball bounced off a sign on the left-field wall: HIT THIS—SUPER LOTTO PLUS.

It's an homage to the most famous fence advertisement in major-league history, the old HIT SIGN, WIN SUIT that decorated the right-field wall at old Ebbets Field. The Brooklyn clothier who created the sign, Abe Stark, claimed he gave away a couple of hundred suits during the twenty-five years that his ad graced a narrow strip under the scoreboard in right center field. When *Newsday* columnist Stan Isaacs did some checking he discovered Stark *might* have given away twenty-five suits in those twenty-five years.

Stark's sign was only 344 feet away, definitely hittable, although a couple of factors worked in Stark's favor. The sign was just three feet high, and it was tucked under the scoreboard where a good right fielder, say Carl Furillo, could protect it.

Danny "Suits" Sparrow of the Negro League's San Francisco Treats claimed to have hit the sign five times in an exhibition game against the Dodgers. Stark gave him one suit and promised him a new suit anytime he needed it, if he'd just quit aiming at the sign.

When he first bought the space in the early thirties, Stark paid $275 per season. By the time the Dodgers moved after the '57 season, rent had rocketed to $2,500. It was worth more than that for the exposure. The sign made Stark a personality, boosting his visibility, and enabling him to win the race for Brooklyn borough president.

Old Crosley Field had its answer to the Abe Stark sign. In left field, just on the other side of the fence, was the Superior Laundry building. It was a famous landmark, and Reds radio broadcaster Waite Hoyt would spot home runs for his listeners by telling them the shot was "on top of the laundry," "off the laundry," or "in front of the laundry." There was a billboard on top of the laundry building promising "Hit this sign and win a Seibler suit." Reds right fielder Wally Post took Seibler's up on its offer, hitting the sign a record 11 times.

The fence where Casey bounced his double is eight feet tall and 375 feet from home plate. That's easily within the rules, which specify that all outfield fences must be at least 250 feet from home plate. The preferred distances, according to the rules, are 320 feet down the foul lines and 400 feet to center. No current park has fences anywhere near 250 feet from home. The right-field corner at Yankee Stadium was only 296 feet from home in 1961, the year Maris and Mantle assaulted Ruth's 60 home-run record, and the second deck of the Polo Grounds' left-field stand had a 21-foot overhang, meaning that you could hit a 250-foot pop fly—like a checked swing for big Adam Dunn—and trot the bases. Right field wasn't much tougher; the fence was only 258 feet.

Meanwhile, in the last few years, the hit-this-win-that signs have come back into fashion. And adjusted to the rise in the cost of living. At San Francisco's Pac Bell Park, the hitter who lands a smash in the glove in left field wins a million bucks. A similar poke off the Coke sign in left at Atlanta's Turner Field nets the same million smackeroos. Neither sign is in much danger, since both targets are more than 500 feet from home plate.

According to Robert Adair, Yale University's Sterling professor emeritus of physics and author of *The Physics of Baseball*, 450 feet is about as far as a player can hit a ball under normal conditions. Under optimum conditions, say a high-nineties fastball, a 100-degree day, a falling barometer, a breeze, a ball wound a little tighter than normal, a player wound a little tighter than normal, it *might* make it 500 feet. Might. And even then the ball has to be hit in the perfect spot. So, while it's possible for a player to collect the million bucks by launching a 500-foot bomb, the actuaries at the insurance companies would say it's improbable. That's why the eventuality is covered by an insurance policy, not the Giants or Braves.

I know what you're thinking. I left something out of those optimum conditions—muscle juice. So, let me say a few words about steroids because, as we all know, the only baseball players who use steroids are retired.

While I have no inside knowledge of what big leaguers ingest, I ask myself: Why wouldn't a major-league ballplayer take steroids? There's no penalty, but there are huge rewards and, moreover, steroids work. Scientific studies have shown that anabolic steroids mimic testosterone, and stimulate muscle tissue to grow bigger and stronger. However, these studies also stress that, to work, the steroids must be combined with a rigorous physical training program and a high-protein diet.

I could run a steroid drip 24/7 and still couldn't hit the glove 501 feet to left at Pac Bell. There are two reasons for this: I have no intention of beginning a rigorous physical training program, and I can't hit a curveball.

So, yes, the steroids all those retired players ingested could wreck the record book. Even with all those steroids, the players had to work very hard and they had to be able to hit a curveball.

And the new no-surprise-tests drug program accepted by the players' union pretty much ensures that steroids will continue to be used . . . by former players.

Chapter Six

The Trail of Beers

I've been watching a seven-year-old and his dad two rows down. The dad announced to no one in particular earlier that this is his son's first big-league game, so I'm curious how the kid will respond to this new adventure. So far, his response has been what you might expect, restlessness . . . and incontinence. The game hadn't even started, and they'd already been to the bathroom twice and to the concession stand once. Now, in the bottom of the third, they are heading to the restroom again. They're not alone; there's a trail of beer drinkers behind them, fellows who've already downed a few brews and need to get rid of one or two of them.

The average American male goes to the bathroom eight times during his waking hours. That's about once every couple of hours or so. Since the average bladder capacity is 12 to 18 ounces and the average beer is 16 ounces, I can understand the line of men heading up the aisle. At about eight ounces, you start feeling what the medical textbooks call *bladder pressure* and what you and I call *the urge*.

Fortunately for those fellas feeling it now there's a restroom close by: up eight steps, then right about thirty feet.

Cinergy Field may be three decades old, but they did a good job with the restrooms. There are plenty of them and they're spread out around the park. Rod Sheard of the stadium-design company HOK says restrooms should be spaced so that no spectator is more than 200 feet from the nearest facility. The walk from our aisle is about half that.

In the first great ballpark-building boom, in the early years of the twentieth century, parks typically had four men's rooms for every ladies' room, a logical ratio at the time. If you look at old grandstand photos, men made up more than 80 percent of the spectators. That's changed—women now make up almost half the spectators at a baseball game—and so have the restroom ratios.

When the Reds' new park opens this year, there will be 15 women's restrooms, 14 men's restrooms, and 6 family restrooms. That's the way to go, according to the International Association of Auditorium Managers, which recommends more ladies' rooms than men's. That's because women take two-and-a-half minutes per bathroom visit, while men require only one minute. And no, it's not because we don't wash our hands! Those numbers are independent of good hygiene.

Anyone who's ever been to a Rolling Stones concert knows that, sometimes, the demand for toilets is overwhelming. I use that as an example because I've never been to a Stones concert and not seen a desperate woman in the men's room. Sheard explains that, "Demand comes in extreme peaks. . . . For brief periods, toilet facilities can barely cope with the number of users, while for most of the time they are completely unused."

You couldn't build a stadium with enough restrooms to prevent those restroom rushes, unless you had one toilet for every seat. So, stadium designers have to come to a happy medium.

The International Association of Auditorium Managers suggests one urinal for every 70 men, one toilet for every 600 men, and one washbasin for every 300 men. For women, it's one toilet for every 35 women and one washbasin for every 70 women.

There are three other factors that affect how many restrooms a stadium needs:

The first is beer. That's an issue here. Any stadium where large amounts of beer are consumed needs more restrooms than an alcohol-free facility.

The second is the season. People go to the bathroom more in winter weather. That's not a major consideration at Cinergy. This is a baseball stadium, not a football stadium; at least, it's not a football stadium anymore. Not since they built the new Paul Brown Stadium for the Bengals, next door.

That explains why Paul Brown Stadium has 1,200 bathroom fixtures (toilets and urinals) for 65,535 seats—one for every 54 spectators—while the Reds' new stadium will have 455 bathroom fixtures for 42,053 seats, a ratio of one for every 92 spectators. People pee more when they're cold.

The final factor is altitude; that's no factor here. It means that, for example, Coors Field in Denver's mile-high atmosphere needs more restrooms because people go to the bathroom more at higher altitudes.

The Cinergy toilets are equipped with automatic flush-ers, called *sensor-operated flushometers*. I love the name; it sounds *so* 1950s. These snazzy devices are a godsend for the squeamish who don't like to touch the toilet handle. You know who you are, you who step back and flush the toilet with your foot. They are also a blessing for those in line behind the guys whose mothers didn't teach them to flush after each potty.

The flushometer works by emitting a beam of light. When a user comes up to the urinal, the light reflects back to a sensor that puts the flushing mechanism on hold. Once the user leaves, the loss of reflected light triggers a one-time flush. The circuit then automatically resets for the next user.

Cinergy's toilet stalls, meanwhile, have giant toilet paper dispensers that seem to take up half the stall. These are Fort James brand tissue holders with two giant rolls. The tissue holders have a lock. Those who went to college know why: College students are notorious for stealing toilet paper for their apartments from public restrooms.

I've never seen the Fort James brand name anywhere except in a public restroom, but it turns out it's produced by a well-known company. The Fort James Corporation is a division of Georgia-Pacific and, in addition to its public bathroom brand, Fort James, which the company calls *high-capacity bath tissue,* it also manufactures such well-known supermarket brands as Quilted Northern toilet tissue, Brawny paper towels, Dixie paper plates, and Vanity Fair paper napkins.

I'm sure the old Crosley Field had individual-sheet dispensers for toilet paper. Each sheet was about the size of your palm and the consistency of cardboard. The Fort James toilet paper isn't exactly baby soft, but at least there's lots of it. The switch to the giant rolls was purely economic. In a stadium with, say, 100 restroom stalls and a single-roll, 500-sheet dispenser in each stall, it would cost about $2,040 in labor a year just to refill the dispensers, assuming a labor rate of $6 per hour. Switch to 2,000 sheet rolls of toilet paper and the labor cost drops to less than $600 per year.

And I'm sure they use that savings to reduce ticket prices. Or pay Ken Griffey, Jr., a little more. Wonder if Junior knows that. Part of his salary comes from toilet-paper labor savings.

When the man and his son return, I discover I was wrong. They didn't leave for another bathroom break; they're back from souvenir-stand shopping and the boy is proudly showing his mother his newest acquisition: a stack of baseball cards.

I saw the card set on my way in. I am an inveterate souvenir-stand connoisseur: I love to see what they are hawking. The Reds stand is pretty pedestrian as ballpark souvenir shops go: T-shirts, hats, and pennants in every variation predominate. You can buy an autographed team ball—printed, not really signed—for ten dollars, or a Cincinnati Reds bobblehead for twenty dollars.

The kid made the right purchase. Of all the gimcrack the Reds are selling to their fans, the cards will be something he will hold onto as a souvenir of his first game. A set of twenty-four cards in a clear plastic box—to protect your investment!—is only five bucks. The top card, in every box, is Ken Griffey, Jr., the reluctant star, who is out today, again, with an injury. Adult fans hold this against him but the kids don't mind. It seems half the kids in the park are wearing Griffey's number 24 on something or other.

Forty years ago, when I attended my first game, you couldn't buy baseball cards at the game. The souvenirs they sold at the park were unique. Pennants, autographed balls, megaphones, picture packs. Stuff you couldn't buy at the local grocery store or department store. You had to go to a ballpark to get them; that made them special, genuine souvenirs.

Lisa Love and Peter Sheldon, in a 1998 issue of *Advances in Consumer Research,* identify souvenirs as "objects that tourists acquire when traveling on vacation." If a day at the park isn't a vacation, I don't know what is.

There's even a classification system for souvenirs, created by Beverly Gordon in a 1986 edition of the *Journal of Popular Culture.* She identified five types of souvenirs:

- Pictorial images
- Pieces of the rock
- Symbolic shorthand
- Markers
- Local products

I think baseball cards easily qualify as pictorial images, along with postcards and Polaroids.

Pieces of the rock are found souvenirs; Gordon calls

them "things from nature." A piece of infield grass, a pebble from the dirt, a foul ball, gum from under your seat.

The Reds minibats fit the category of symbolic shorthand, a miniature version of the real thing.

Least interesting of all souvenirs are markers, which Gordon identified as "things that are merely inscribed." A pillowcase with "Reds" on it—$7.95 in the shop—is a marker. I don't see any Red relaxing in the dugout on his Reds pillow.

The only local products I could find at the park are concession items: Skyline Chili dogs, Kahn's hot dogs, Montgomery Inn barbecue.

Nelson Graburn, in a 1986 issue of *Annals of Tourism Research,* a journal that I must read more often, nails the souvenir phenomenon: "Souvenirs are tangible evidence of travel that are often shared with family and friends but what one really brings back are memories of experiences."

Souvenirs are proof that you went to the game. When I was at my first game, I could take back a picture pack, a set of glossy five-by-seven photos of twelve or so players, and impress my best friend Lance Harris. That proved I had been at the game. You couldn't buy a picture pack anywhere else. But I could look through those pictures later and it would bring back memories of the game: Brooks Lawrence's strong relief appearance, Jerry Lynch's towering home run.

That's what I think is wrong with today's marketing-driven souvenirs. You can buy team merchandise everywhere, at the park, at sporting goods stores, in minimarts, even on the Internet. More money in the team coffers, but a devaluation of the souvenir itself.

Love and Sheldon say, "While souvenirs can be perceived as simply functional or decorative objects, close inspection reveals tangible expressions of meaning and expression of the experiences these meanings represent."

Ballpark souvenirs should mean one thing: I was there.

A quick glance at my little first-ballgame buddy two rows down finds him squatting in front of his seat, laying his cards out on a make-believe field. All those players are on the field in front of him but he prefers squatting on the concrete, creating his own game. He'll do that a hundred times with those cards in the next few weeks, and I applaud him. That's what baseball cards are for: playing with. Not for hermetically sealing in albums.

His cards are Upper Deck, a premium card, sort of the Mercedes to Topps' good old Chevy.

Topps may have a stodgy reputation among modern card collectors, but to me and my pals—Lance, Tony and Mike, and the Jarvis boys—Topps was tops.

Topps didn't invent the bubble gum card—Goudey and National Chicle and Gum, Inc. were using cards to sell gum in the thirties—but it has certainly lived up to its name, dominating the industry for the last half century.

Topps happened into baseball cards at just the right time. The first wave of baby boomers were entering school in 1952 when Topps issued its first set of cards. The year before, the company had put out a weird playing-card set, with Bob Feller as a Strike, Duke Snider as a Single, and Del Ennis as a Stolen Base. (Ennis averaged three stolen bases per season over his fifteen-year career!)

If timing is everything, Topps owes its success to the loins of World War II's returning servicemen. There were more little boys between the ages of seven and thirteen in America in 1952—eight-and-one-half million according to census estimates—than there had ever been. There were a full half-million more little boys than there had been twelve years earlier, and that little boy bulge would continue to grow over the next fifteen years as the baby boom boomed. I was a part of that baby boom, and 1952 was the year I got into cards.

I entered the card-collecting scene through the back door—my family's back door. I can still remember my next-door neighbor Darnell Shankel lugging his old cards into our house one spring day, and asking me if I wanted them. He was thirteen, the traditional age when boys give up cards and turn their attention to girls. The cigar box was heavy with Topps 1952 and Bowman 1951 and 1952 cards.

I still have those cards.

There were 310 cards in that first Topps series in 1952. Topps sports director Sy Berger and company artist Woody Gelman designed the cards on Berger's kitchen table. It's a simple design, a Kodak Flexichrome photo of the player with a white box inset near the bottom. Printed in the box is the player's name, a facsimile autograph, and his team's logo. Simple, but elegant, unlike previous bubble gum cards from Bowman Gum and Leaf Gum, which merely featured photos with names. Topps added the autograph and the team logo, giving designer Gelman more to work with. Berger also raised the ante on the card backs, including statistics from the "past year" (they used that phrase instead of the year number, fearing the cards wouldn't sell and they would have to push them the next year too) and brief player bios. Bowman cards were crude drawings with little narratives on the back that read like they were written by the candy salesman: "Mickey is the Yankee rookie of whom so much is expected in 1951. Everyone was talking about him in spring training in which he batted over .400. Kept on clicking when the regular season got under way."

Berger also made the cards bigger; Bowman cards were just 3 inches tall and 2 inches wide. Berger bumped that up to $3\,^3/_4 \times 2\,^5/_8$ inches. It was the statistics line that separated the two cards, Bowman learned, and added that feature to its 1953 cards.

When the first 310 Topps cards hit the stores, they were an instant hit, so successful that Topps decided to add a second series of ninety-seven cards. By then it was late in the season; Bowman's football cards were hitting the stores, and Topps got few orders from candy merchants. So, cards stacked up in the warehouse waiting to be packaged . . . and waiting and waiting. The company couldn't even give the second series of '52 cards away; carnival owners, offered the cards at a half-cent each, all said no. Finally, seven years later, Topps cleared out its warehouse, sending two dump trucks full of the '52 high numbers—as they are now called—to a garbage scow, which eventually dumped them into the Atlantic.

There were untold numbers of what are now known as Mickey Mantle rookie cards in that cleanup, turned to sludge in the bottom of the ocean. A 1952 Mickey Mantle card, number 311 in the set, can fetch upwards of one-half million dollars in today's market. Maybe it wouldn't sell for so much if all those surplus cards hadn't been sent to sea.

Here's how Topps worked back then.

Sy Berger or one of his associates went to spring training camps each year to take photos for the cards. (That's why you occasionally see palm trees in the background.) Each player was photographed with and without his cap, in case he was traded before the card was printed.

In the early fifties, Topps paid $75 for rights to the player's image, $125 if the player would agree to an exclusivity clause. Since Bowman was only paying $100, Topps got a number of exclusive deals. Bowman sued Topps, claiming contract infringement and, while the matter was being litigated, Topps steered clear of several players including Mickey Mantle. That's why there were no Topps Mantle cards in 1954 or 1955.

In 1956, Topps bought out Bowman, ensuring a bubble gum-card monopoly for the next quarter century.

In 1958, Gay Talese noted in the *New York Times*, "The bubble gum man is expected to visit the Giants soon to sign players up for the first San Francisco bubble gum cards this year. Bubble gum manufacturers give a gift to each player (such as furniture or a hi fi set) for the right to distribute his picture with bubble gum."

As Talese points out, Topps also offered gifts in lieu of money. Many players' wives liked this better, picking a television or patio furniture from Topps' premium catalog.

One hundred twenty-five dollars was the standard fee

paid through the sixties. By 1975, Topps was signing minor leaguers to binder contracts for $5. When the player reached the majors, he was given a $250 bonus. Each year, Topps paid the player another $250 plus royalties, which usually brought the total to about $400. Today, players receive about $500 per year from Topps.

The company printed 132 cards to a sheet, cut them apart (sometimes not very precisely—if you have any old cards, you know about nonexistent borders), then ran them through a collating machine. That was a miracle contraption; it mixed them up so that the same card wouldn't show up twice in a six-card pack. I don't know how that machine worked, but it worked! In all my years of collecting, I never once got two of the same card in a pack. I got untold cards that I got in the pack before it, but never two of the same card.

Another miracle machine was the one that inserted the gum in the packs. Unlike Topps bubble gum wad, Bazooka gum, baseball-card bubble gum was brittle. That's because the gum was pushed into the packs. If it had been soft, it would have buckled.

In the fifties, baseball cards were more than just pastime, they were a status symbol. I remember one nerdy boy in my fifth-grade class who brought in a huge wooden box with his card collection on Hobby Day. From then on, everyone looked at him differently.

Another schoolmate of mine, Dommie Jackson, remembers, "When word got out at school, sometimes it was late March, some years it was early April, that the first baseball cards were in, all the boys at school would start getting nervous. They couldn't wait to get out and get the first cards. 'Cause if you got out and they were all gone, you were hurting. Then we'd stay home the rest of the afternoon and play with the cards and look at them and everything. During the spring ball cards were it. You just survived the winter waiting for ball cards. From the age of six to about thirteen, ball cards were like girls were from about age fifteen to eighteen. Only ball cards were probably a little more important."

In the fifties, I would occasionally order cards from Gordon B. Taylor or Sam Rosen, a couple of New Yorkers who advertised cards for sale in the back of the *Sporting News*. They were among the handful of adults who were involved in card collecting in the fifties. They were the ones who laid the groundwork for the modern business of card collecting. In 1960, my last year of card collecting (I was about to turn thirteen), I ordered the entire set from Taylor. It cost me fourteen dollars but I didn't have to figure out what to do with 800 pieces of bricklike gum. If I still had that set it would be worth, oh, a couple of trillion dollars.

Taylor and Rosen were part of the second generation of serious card collectors but, if baseball card collecting has a father, his name is Jeff Burdick.

Burdick was an unlikely choice to found the hobby. He was a parts assembler at Crouse-Hinds, an electrical-parts manufacturer in Syracuse. According to columnist Sean Kirst of the *Syracuse Post Standard*, "To the best knowledge of his surviving friends, he never attended a professional baseball game. He spent much of his life in a small Crouse Avenue apartment, where he devoted his energy to perpetuating what he always called his 'hobby.'"

Burdick never attended a baseball game, because his interest wasn't baseball cards; it was collecting, particularly collecting what is called *paper ephemera*. He collected baseball cards, yes, but also greeting cards, postcards, playing cards, printed advertisements for everything from meat products to women's shoes. He even collected paper dolls.

In a 1955 story in the *Syracuse Post Standard*, he explained his fascination: "Card collecting is primarily an inherited love of pictures."

Burdick was a bachelor—duh—who could devote his time and disposable income to his hobby. In 1936, he published a short article about collecting cards in a national hobby magazine and was inundated by letters from collectors. He was, by all accounts, an eager correspondent and soon there was a network of adult collectors trading information and cards back and forth through the mail. Burdick, because of his interest and free time, was self-selected to collect and collate this material. In 1937, he mimeographed a thirty-six-page catalog of cards, a precursor to his omnibus reference work, *The American Card Catalog*, a 1939 book that would serve as the hobby standard until the eighties, when *Beckett Baseball Card Monthly* replaced it.

Baseball-card collecting before Burdick—he pretty much quit collecting in the late forties—was a kid's racket. Only a handful of adult collectors were around, and they all seemed to know one other.

Jefferson Burdick wasn't the *first* baseball-card collector. Companies had been turning out baseball cards long before he was born in 1899. What he did was bring organization to a hobby. In the process of trying to acquire every trading card ever printed, Burdick invented a system for categorizing all the disparate cards that tobacco companies, gum companies, and candy companies, had been turning out at least since Old Judge cigarette cards in 1887.

The fact is nobody knows who the first collector was, because no one knows who put out the first baseball card. *Trade cards*, as they were called, were a popular form of advertising after the Civil War. Salesmen passed them out or left them on store counters. To attract attention, printers used a variety of pictures, from Currier & Ives scenes to portraits of famous people, including baseball players.

The Library of Congress offers a Champions of America card as the first baseball card. It is a card and it does have a baseball team on it, the 1865 Brooklyn Atlantics, but it wasn't created for kids or for trading. (What could they have traded for? There were no other cards.) It was a commemorative, a photo of the "Champion Nine," as the team called itself. Early in the 1865 season, the Atlantics presented a framed team photo to each opponent. Some of these photos were mounted on stiff cardboard to create a card.

Goodwin & Co., a New York cigarette manufacturer, inserted baseball cards into its Old Judge and Gypsy Queen cigarette packs as early as 1887. These primitive cards, really nothing more than sepia-toned photos pasted onto cardboard, were used to stiffen the cigarette pack as much as to promote the brand.

They became popular, and soon other cigarette companies followed suit with card sets from Allen & Ginter's Cigarettes, Gold Coin Chewing Tobacco, S.F. Hess Creole Cigarettes, Mayo's Cut Plug, and Yum Yum Tobacco.

To keep all these cards straight, Burdick created a classification system. His method was so simple that even a child could figure it out. Hey, card collecting was a kid's hobby. He used prefixes and numbers to refer to each set. So, the most famous old card set, the T206 set, meant it was the 206th set he identified from a tobacco company. It was Burdick who labeled the famous T206 Honus Wagner, the fabled cigarette company card that sold at auction in 2000 for $1.27 million. Only sixty or so are known to exist, because Wagner demanded the company withdraw them from circulation. (At one time, the story went that Wagner was opposed to smoking and didn't want to be seen promoting tobacco; since then, photos of Wagner smoking and chewing have surfaced, leading most to believe Wagner wanted more money.)

In Burdick's system N prefix cards were from the nineteenth century; M cards were those printed by magazines and newspapers; E meant early gum and candy company cards, primarily from the teens and twenties. Cards from the thirties and forties received an R—for Recent—designation.

In 1947, Burdick, who was only forty-eight, but was already suffering from arthritis, decided to find a place for his collection. He had no heirs, so he wanted to donate the cards to a museum. A. Hyatt Mayor, curator of prints for the Metropolitan Museum of Art from 1946 to 1966 recalled his first meeting with Burdick in an oral-history interview with the Smithsonian Institute in 1969. "He was a very remarkable man indeed. He had no money. He earned his keep by assembling electric switches for mines and flour mills that wouldn't give out sparks. He collected, first, cigarette insert cards over the years, and then all sorts of ephemera related to that. And he corresponded with everybody all over the country and abroad to swap, buy, assemble, until finally he had a matter of, I don't know how many thousands, perhaps hundreds of thousands, of these things. And he came to me once, asked if we had that kind of thing. I showed him what we had, which was very little. He said he wanted to give his collection—I did not know then how large it was, I must say, I would maybe not have been so cavalier about it if I'd had any idea—and he didn't know where to put it. So I said he'd better go around to the other places in town where that kind of thing might be used and might be looked for, the Public Library, Cooper Union, and other places outside of town; I said he should look at the Boston Museum and various other places like that."

Burdick did just that, taking a week's vacation, but he ended up back at the Met. "He said he liked the way we took care of things and showed them, and he'd like to give us his collection. So, at the end of every year several cartons of these things would come. And we had absolutely no idea how to arrange it, you see. They were all nicely tied up and labeled, but how do you make them available to people so they won't be pocketed."

Over the next dozen years, Burdick would ship two to six cartons of cards a year to the Met. His friend and co-worker John DeFlores would help him. In 1993, DeFlores told Syracuse columnist Kirst, "Sometimes I'd ask him what one card was worth, and (he'd say) that card might be worth a fortune. But he didn't want to sell them. He said he'd rather leave them for posterity."

In 1959, Burdick retired from the assembly plant and moved to New York City to devote his time to his collection. Mayor recalled, "He really got too arthritic, came down here and, for several years, he arranged all these things in scrapbooks, making about two hundred scrapbooks."

Burdick worked feverishly according to Mayor, as if he were in a horse race. "Then one Saturday he said, 'It's finished.' He mounted the last card and he finished the last album. And I helped him on with his hat and his coat. He went home. And that Monday he went to the hospital and was dead in about six weeks. He had done it and that was the end of it."

Burdick left the Metropolitan Museum for the last time on January 10, 1963. He checked into University Hospital the next day and died on March 13, 1963 at age sixty-three. Today the J.R. Burdick Collection of Paper Americana comprises 306,503 items, and the baseball cards in it frequently tour the nation's ballparks.

Among the cards is the T206 Honus Wagner, which Burdick had valued in his 1960 *American Card Catalogue*, the last one he edited, at fifty dollars. No other card in the catalog was valued at more than ten dollars. Four decades later, the Honus Wagner card is worth more than a million bucks. And Burdick's collection and contribution to card collecting is, as they say in the commercials, priceless.

Today, every card has a value and every kid knows its worth. In my card-collecting days, that was part of the fun of trading, trying to snooker someone else.

My old schoolmate Dommie Jackson remembers. "The best trade you could make would be a swindle. What I'd do was go out and buy a whole bunch of cards and get two of everybody and then pretend like I only had one and trade with the other boys in the neighborhood. 'Course, some-times they were doing the same thing you were so it was kinda like a counterespionage and double agents. There were a lot of double agents in our neighborhood."

Which brings me to the legend of Andy Pafko.

Andrew Pafko of Boyceville, Wisconsin was what they call today a *nice* player, *nice* having nothing necessarily to do with his temperament. He was good enough to hang around the big leagues for 17 seasons, from '43 to '59. A five-time all-star, he topped .300 four times, finishing as a career .285 hitter. In his declining years, he was still good enough to platoon in the outfield on two Braves World Series teams, in '58 and '59.

Nice ballplayer. Bobby Thomson without the Shot Heard 'Round the World; Bobby Murcer without the pinstripes; Carl Furillo without the rifle arm. And the only way he'll get in the Hall of Fame is by buying a ticket. So, why in heaven's name is his 1952 Topps card worth $80,000? He wasn't even an all-star that year—those days were behind him by then. His only notable achievement that season was leading the league in getting hit by pitched balls.

I'll let *USA Today* explain why someone paid $83,870 at auction in 2000 for a mint 1952 Topps Andy Pafko:

> [Pafko] was Card No. 1 in the 1952 Topps set, which meant kids put him at the top of their stack before wrapping their cards in a rubber band and sticking them in their pockets or school bags. As a result, it's rare to find the card in excellent condition today.

It may be hard to find the card in excellent condition today, but I think that's more a function of the fact that it's hard to find any half-century old card in excellent condition. In 1952, we didn't pull cards straight out of the pack and slide them into plastic holders. We put them in cigar boxes and on bicycle spokes and in rubber-banded stacks.

We didn't put Andy Pafko on top because he was number one in the series; we didn't put Andy Pafko on top. This is a myth that has spread throughout baseball card collecting, probably originated by a baseball card dealer.

Just to make sure, I surveyed two dozen of my childhood friends, other guys who collected cards and traded cards in the fifties, to see if any of them ever, even once, put Andy Pafko on the top of a rubber-banded stack.

"Numeric order? They had a numeric order? I didn't know that," said my friend Tom Poe, who grew up in Tennessee and now lives in northern Virginia.

Bruce Haney, whom I've known since nursery school,

said, "I'm not sure I even knew they were numbered until I went to college. You learn the damndest things in college. I do remember rubber banding them but I didn't pay attention to the order. So that business about the number one card always being damaged by rubber bands didn't happen."

Tom McNeer agrees. "I didn't even remember that they were numbered. For sure, nobody ever organized them that way."

Rod Irvin, who was in my second-grade homeroom, says, "It was my opinion the numbers did nothing but take up space."

Larry Magnes remembers keeping cards in a stack organized by teams. "Like a deck of cards with all the cards from the same suits next to each other."

Joie Kerns says, "I kept mine by team with my favorite players on top with rubber bands around them."

Greg Johnson adds, "The guys in my neighborhood also had a special banded-together group of 'active' cards that were potentially ripe for trades, so that nobody had to take the whole box with them to another guy's house—you just grabbed the active stack and did some hoss trading. That also meant you could lie about what you had back home. The biggest travesty in baseball cards came when people started collecting them in photo albums. Cards are cards, not proof sets of Roosevelt dimes, and they ought to be stacked and handled like cards. Keeping precious, little mint-condition baseball cards inside plastic sheets is like trying to play poker by laminating the cards into a book and then just pointing at your winning hand. Put a band around 'em, jam 'em in your jeans and don't be such a priss. Sheesh!"

As you can see, my old gang doesn't have much truck with modern card collectors.

Except maybe for one thing. Envy.

My grade-school pal Tim Thayer told me, "I get pissed off every time I think about my old baseball-card collection because my mother—being her immaculate, organized self—threw my card collection in the trash sometime while I was in college. Damn . . . I could be retired now living off the interest from the sale of those cards! I need to get over this, 'cause Mother's Day is just around the corner."

My mother didn't throw my cards out; she knew how important they were to me. So, I can't blame *her:* I gave mine away, or most of them anyway, to my girlfriend's little brothers back in 1965. In fact, the last time I saw Kenny Patton, I asked if I could have them back. He said, "Sure."

Today, adult collectors rule the quarter-billion-dollar per year baseball-card market. Fully 70 percent of new cards are sold to adults, according to Topps. So, it's nice to see the little kid two rows down enjoying his new possessions. I hope he takes them home and puts them in his bicycle spokes.

On my way out today I may buy a box of those cards. For old time's sake. Or my bicycle spokes.

Chapter Seven

Here's the Windup,
Here's the Pitch

Jose Rijo, once the Reds' young gun, is now the team's miracle man. He joined the team in 1988 at age twenty-three, and was the staff ace for the first half of the nineties, before succumbing to shoulder surgery in 1995. Five operations and six years later, he made a dramatic return to the Reds in 2001, compiling an ERA of 2.12 in 17 relief innings. This year, at age thirty-seven, he returned to the rotation and has been as effective as any Reds starter. He mixes his pitches up, alternating his forkball with a slider and a fastball that one writer said "leaves the radar gun bored."

In Rijo's previous start, Giants slugger Barry Bonds complained to catcher Corky Miller, "He's throwing too slow." Later, Bonds doubled, and ribbed Rijo from second, yelling, "Break the speed limit! Break the speed limit!"

After Rijo was relieved by Scott Williamson in the fifth today, fans began to turn their attention to a display in right field. Rijo's fastball had been struggling to hit 82 mph on the radar gun, not much to follow, but the fireballing Williamson has registered 98 mph on a couple of pitches, much to the crowd's delight.

. . .

It used to be the only time anyone glanced at the upper deck in right was if there was a monster home run or a fight. Now, it's a regular object of attention, since the Reds installed a radar-gun readout. The gun is on full time, so you can see how fast Rijo is throwing during warm-ups (not very) or get a line on Tavarez' speed today (pretty hot). And, when a reliever comes in, no one watches his form; everyone watches his speed.

Now, speed is everything. When is the last time you heard someone called "a pitcher" as a compliment? The only thing anyone wants to know is how fast a hurler can throw.

Blame John Paulson. In 1970, the Little League dad, unhappy with the pitching machines on the market, set out to craft a better machine for his two boys to practice on. Soon after, the Oregonian created a company, JUGS, named for the old baseball expression the *jug-handle curve*, which broke with the same curvature as a jug handle, and an entire line of sports products, pitching machines, football-passing machines, tennis-serving machines, and the well-known JUGS radar gun. It is the JUGS gun that has changed our perception of the game.

Before the portable JUGS gun, radar guns were pretty much confined to highway-patrol cars on southern backroads. Paulson's handy creation—it fit in a duffel bag— was an immediate hit with baseball scouts. No more looking for the *good face*, scout terminology for some nebulous big-league quality you could spot in a kid's countenance; now, you could send a report back to the front office with hard facts. "This kid hits ninety-five on the gun. Plus he has a good face."

Almost a decade ago, when Will and I visited Cleveland's Jacobs Field, *sans* tickets, we went to the ticket window at a fortuitous time. The front office had just turned in the unused scout tickets and we were able to buy box seats, behind home plate, in the middle of the scouts. There were five different teams represented around us, and each scout had his own radar gun. It was amazing to see Jack Morris at age thirty-seven outgunning Oakland's young pitcher, twenty-four-year-old Miguel Jimenez. Morris was consistently hitting 90 on the scouts' guns, and the only other pitcher to top 90 that day was Cleveland closer Jose Mesa who blew away 90, registering an occasional 95 and 96. Watching the gun quickly became addictive. I can understand fans watching the scoreboard radar readout. You forget the game, and concentrate on the speed.

The scouts in Cleveland were using two different guns. Three used the JUGS brand, the other two had Rayguns. Scouts call the Raygun the "slow gun," because it usually gives a reading of 4 mph less than the JUGS gun. So, naturally, Will and I zeroed in on the JUGS guys. Both guns look like souped-up cordless drills with a red display on the back. If you want to be your own scout, you can buy one for eight hundred bucks.

Pitching radar guns work on the same principle as police radar guns. The gun's lens shoots a narrow beam of microwave radiation. These microwaves bounce back to the gun in a steady stream. If they don't encounter a moving object, they reflect back with the same even space between each wave. If the waves hit an object that is moving, however, each successive wave will have less space between it than the preceding one. The gun measures this decreasing distance—actually a change in wave frequency—and calculates the object's speed. The JUGS gun locks in on the strongest return—the highest rate of speed—and displays that.

Don't worry if you are sitting in front of a scout with a radar gun. The microwave output is harmless, in the 15–50 milliwatt range, a long ways from that needed to pop popcorn. A typical radar gun has a range of three-quarters of a mile.

Radar guns are *not* foolproof. For example, there is the famous speeding palm-tree story: In 1979, a Miami TV station showed a radar gun clocking a palm tree at 86 mph—interference was the culprit. That was almost a quarter century ago, and technology has advanced considerably. Still, guns can be fooled because of interference from airport radar, CB radios, cellular phones, mercury-vapor lights, and other radar guns, though it doesn't happen very often.

Still, if Jose Rijo should clock 98 on the stadium radar readout, it might be time to check the batteries.

I'd bet the second most popular topic of debate among baseball fans, after who was the greatest player of all time (Ted Williams, I say) is: Who was the fastest pitcher of all time? When the *Sporting News* asked that question for its book *Baseball's 100 Greatest Players,* former manager Gene Mauch surprised younger fans with his number five selection: Steve Dalkowski. Kids knew Nolan Ryan and Roger Clemens, and they'd heard of Bob Feller; but Steve who?

Steve Dalkowski never pitched an inning in the big leagues, barely caused a ripple in Triple A, but, man, could he throw.

I saw Dalkowski pitch when I was a ten-year-old. In 1957, he was playing for the Class D rookie league team in my hometown of Kingsport, Tennessee. I wasn't there the night he tore the ear off an opposing player with a fastball, but I read about it. All I saw him do was strike out 24, walk 18 and lose a no-hitter 8–4. When one of his wild pitches, and there were many, hit the concrete base of the stadium, the stands shook. He scared the crap out of every batter he faced because not only was he fast and wild, he was also an alcoholic. Of course, I didn't know that at the time; sports pages didn't report such things. They did odd things like cover the game. Of course, all the players on the opposing team knew, and they knew he might even be sauced while pitching.

Dalkowski was the model for Nuke LaLoosh, the fire-balling wild man of the movie *Bull Durham*. Nuke, you may recall, plunked the opponent's mascot with a wild pitch. Dalkowski once hit a fan who was standing in line to buy a hot dog. During his one season on my hometown team, he struck out 121 and walked 129 in 62 innings. He finished the year 1–8 with an 8.13 ERA, and probably would have been demoted, except that Class D rookie ball was as low as you could go.

There were no radar guns in 1957, so we will never know exactly how fast Dalkowski was. Orioles manager Earl Weaver, who managed him in the minors in 1962, told *Newsday* in 1979 that Dalkowski threw "a lot faster" than Nolan Ryan.

The Orioles, who owned his rights, tried to find out how fast in 1959, when he was pitching for Aberdeen, South Dakota of the Northern League. They took him to the local Aberdeen Army Proving Grounds, where military radar clocked his fastball at 98.6 mph. Of course, he had pitched the previous night, throwing 150 pitches, he was throwing off flat ground, not a mound, and he had to throw for an hour before he finally got a pitch in the radar's range—he was that wild. So, throwing with a fatigued arm on flat ground he managed to hit almost 99 mph. On a JUGS gun he could have probably hit 110.

Can you imagine the crowd reaction if Dalkowski were pitching for the Reds at Cinergy Field today and the gun in right field registered 110? There'd be dancing in the aisles.

Dalkowski injured his arm in spring training in 1963 in one of life's little ironies. He wasn't pitching, but fielding a

Jim Bouton bunt and throwing to first when he heard a pop in his elbow. He missed that season, returning in 1964, but his fastball didn't join him and by 1966 he was out of baseball. Today, he lives in a rest home in his native Connecticut suffering from alcohol-related dementia.

His final line: 1,396-1,354. That's 1,396 strikeouts and 1,354 walks in his nine-year minor-league career. That's a lot of pitches.

The fans watching the radar readout are treated to a look into the Reds dugout on the adjacent JumboTRON TV. They cheer for Ken Griffey Jr., who is on the disabled list, but expected to return for tomorrow's game. He acknowledges the cheers not with a tip of the cap but in his own way, by blowing a bubble, and the fans cheer louder.

When I see Junior or any modern player blowing a bubble-gum bubble, I think of Rocky Bridges. Rocky never blew bubbles. When he was playing with the Reds, in the mid-fifties, no baseball players blew bubbles—it was a different era. No, they blew up their cheeks with giant chaws of tobacco, and no one had a bigger chaw than Rocky. I have all his baseball cards from my collecting days, '57 to '60 and, in every single one, he has a wad of tobacco in his cheek. Trumpet player Dizzy Gillespie can't get his rubber cheeks to swell as much as Rocky did with his tobacco.

Tobacco is now officially *verboten* in the minor leagues, which banned the stuff in rookie leagues in 1991, A-ball in 1992, and all minor-league dugouts in 1992. Baseball's protective union hasn't seen fit to allow such a ban in the big leagues—that would be an infringement on a player's individual rights, blah blah blah—but you don't find buckets of plug tobacco or the so-called smokeless stuff, snuff, sitting around the clubhouse anymore. Clubs have banned the tobacco products, so buckets of free chewing tobacco and snuff have been replaced by tubs of free sunflower seeds and bubble gum.

Tobacco and baseball go back a long way, almost to the very beginning. It's no surprise that the first baseball cards were inserted in cigarette packs and pouches of chewing tobacco.

Chewing tobacco was a popular male habit in the middle years of the nineteenth century, when baseball was gaining a foothold. Baseball players particularly liked chewing because it kept their mouths moist while standing out in the hot, dry, dusty field, and a little squirt of tobacco juice in the glove kept it soft, too.

Then came tuberculosis. When newspapers reported that doctors believed the disease could be transmitted through spitting, around 1890, the practice of chewing went out of favor everywhere, except in the ballpark. Chewing managed to hold on in baseball because of a recent invention, the spitball, a breaking pitch with many fathers, from Frank Corridon to Bobby Matthews to George Hildebrand to Elmer Stricklett, and no DNA evidence to determine conclusively its paternity. We don't know who invented the spitball. Perhaps it was invented at the same time by many different pitchers; it's not hard to imagine that an accident of drool from too much tobacco chaw was the real father. The spitball kept tobacco chewing alive in baseball. Even though the pitch was banned in 1920, seventeen pitchers who were using it at the time were allowed to continue the practice. The last spitball pitcher was Burleigh Grimes who retired after the 1934 season. If you believe that, you never saw Lou Burdette or Gaylord Perry pitch.

By the forties, chewing tobacco was as important to a ballplayer as his glove. Former Dodger pitcher Rex Barney, who signed with the Dodgers in 1942, told Roy Blount, Jr., for a 1977 *Sports Illustrated* story, "When I first broke into the Dodgers system, I was just a kid, eighteen years old. And we had a coach, an old guy named Barney DeForge. . . . I was sitting in the bullpen one night, and DeForge said to me: 'Kid, you want to get into the Major Leagues?' I said, 'Sure, that's what it's all about.' He says, 'You don't chew tobacco, do you?' I said, 'No.' He said, 'Well, you'll never get there unless you chew tobacco.' In those days, if you had twenty-five players, twenty-four chewed tobacco. Very naive, I said 'OK.' I tried it. The only thing I remember is chomping down a couple of times and getting deathly ill. I was supposed to start the next night, and I was still so sick I couldn't even leave the hotel. I said to myself, 'If that's what it takes to make the Major Leagues, I'll never make it.'"

He did make it, as the one in twenty-five who didn't chew, but chewing was about to go out of favor again. The pendulum shifted in the fifties, when a number of baseball players signed to endorse cigarettes and began making the switch to smoking tobacco. Their teammates, except for Rocky Bridges, also made the switch. Whole teams seemed to be identified by a cigarette brand. The Giants? Chesterfields, because of spokesman Willie Mays. The Yankees? Camels, following Mickey Mantle's lead.

Then, the Surgeon General deemed cigarettes harmful to your health in a landmark 1964 report, and baseball players began switching back to chewing tobacco and snuff, thinking they were safe alternatives to smoking. The industry helped by providing free samples in the clubhouse.

That's pretty much where it stands today, despite considerable evidence that snuff and chew are just as bad, in their own way, as cigarettes.

A 1987 survey of seven big-league clubs found one-third of the players used smokeless tobacco. That gradually increased over the next few years to 40 percent. Then Joe Garagiola founded the National Spit Tobacco Education Program, which has been credited with reducing major-league players' use of smokeless tobacco to 35 percent.

Despite the 1992 ban and a potential fine of $300, use in the minor leagues is still 29 percent. Minor leaguers can't use on the field or in the clubhouse or on the bus, but they break out as soon as they get to the apartment. Dip is one tough habit to break and I know why: One tin of smokeless tobacco contains the same amount of nicotine as sixty cigarettes.

On the half full side of the glass: If 35 percent of players are dipping, then 65 percent aren't. What are they doing? Chewing bubble gum and eating sunflower seeds, which teams and manufacturers are more than happy to provide. David & Sons ships tons of sunflower seeds to major-league clubhouses every spring, and Topps, the baseball card people, supplies every clubhouse with a season's supply of Bazooka Bubble Gum, both regular and sugarless. Teams add to the freebies according to player preferences. In Miami, the equipment manager picks up packs of Wrigley's gum at the local Sam's Club to give players some variety in flavors; in St. Louis, the team adds Dubble Bubble to the mix; here in Cincinnati, the Reds provide Bubblicious, a player favorite.

What's the appeal of gum? Chewing gum keeps your mouth moist and works off nervous energy. Chewing bubble gum is also said to keep you from crying, a perfect fit for the game, since we all know—everyone in unison—"there's no crying in baseball."

Bubble gum and baseball have been a pair since at least the 1890s. There's a vintage newspaper story at the Hall of Fame about Giant catcher John "Chewing Gum" O'Neil, who thought a nickel pack of gum a game brought him good luck. It must not have brought him a lot of good luck—he played only 4 games, getting 15 at-bats in the bigs.

Hall of Fame second baseman Eddie Collins was a gum devotee, if a not particularly hygienic one. He would stick his gum on top of his cap when he came to the plate, then retrieve it when his at-bat was over.

This was all chewing gum; bubble gum didn't come along until the tail end of Collins' career, which ended in 1930. Not that Fleer hadn't been trying: The chewing gum company first offered a bubble-gumlike product in 1906, Blibber-Blubber. The fact that you've never heard of it is testament to its bubble-gum capabilities.

Real bubble gum didn't hit the market until 1928. That's when a young Fleer accountant named Walter Diemer was experimenting with gum recipes, not part of his job description. He noticed his concoction was less sticky, more stretchy, and full of bubbles. He knew what he had and after teaching the company's salesmen to blow bubbles, Dubble Bubble gum was soon everywhere. In modest fashion, he told the *Lancaster Intelligencer Journal* in 1996, "It was an accident. I was doing something else and ended up with something with bubbles." Bubble gum was pink right out of the gate: It was the only food coloring Diemer had on hand.

Diemer's gum was all natural, if chewing rubber is natural, and even today's varieties include synthetic polymers in the gum base. Typical bubble gum composition: 25 percent gum base, 20 percent corn syrup, 2 percent color and flavoring, and 53 percent sugar. Weight-watchers note: There are 20 calories in a piece of bubble gum.

Today, there are photos in the newspaper of Mark Mc Gwire blowing bubbles at first base, Ken Griffey Jr. blowing them everywhere. When the Twins held Bobblehead Night in 2002, Doug Mientkiewicz insisted his doll be blowing a bubble.

You have players trying to get in the Guinness record book by chewing bubble gum. Marlins pitcher Josh Beckett did set a major-league record in 2001; to his teammates' delight, he managed to stuff 30 pieces of bubble gum into his mouth at one time. The record didn't stand long: Ryan Dempster, now with the Reds but then a Marlin, crammed

48 pieces of Bazooka Joe in his mouth while the club was in Cincinnati—an omen perhaps, since he was traded there in 2002. Dempster bragged to sportswriters later, "I couldn't really talk or swallow, but I could chew. And my mouth was sore for about three days afterward." Unfortunately, Dempster got lockjaw for nothing. He wasn't even close to the world record, held by one Richard Walker who managed 135 pieces.

Just because baseball players love their bubble gum doesn't mean that love translates to the general population. While overall gum sales have been up for the last five years, the sales of gum with sugar—that would be bubble gum— have been in free fall. Gum sales have dropped every year since 1997, 1.7 percent that year, another 3.1 percent in 1998, 1.3 percent in 1999, and 4.9 percent in 2000. The candy industry has figured out how to stem that decline. For 2001, the industry lumped sugar and sugarless gums together. Sales were up.

Bubble gum in the big leagues is everywhere, literally. Dayton *Daily News* sportswriter Hal McCoy likes to tell the story about the time then-Reds manager Lou Piniella took out his wrath after a loss on a washtub of bubble gum in the manager's office. "Writers walked into his office and found the floor completely obscured by wrapped bubble gum, a carpet of Bazooka. Obviously, Piniella had kicked over the tub, scattering gum everywhere. As we walked in, Lou softly and calmly said, 'Watch the gum, guys.'"

Bubble gum is so ubiquitous in the big leagues that every team keeps gum remover in the clubhouse, near the medicine kit, and every ballpark has a gum squad that patrols the field, shovels and brooms in hand, immediately following the game to pick up what the players left behind.

The gum squad might also be called the shell brigade because they also sweep up sunflower seed shells, of which there are thousands on the field, in the dugout, and under the bullpen bench. Unlike those of us in the stands, who hand shell our peanuts and carefully put the empty shell back into the bag, making the cleanup crew's job easier—yeah, right—baseball players spit their seeds everywhere; and the operative word is *spit*. According to Angels pitcher Shawn Boskie in the *Wall Street Journal,* not a single player hand shucks sunflower seeds. "No player'd be caught dead opening a seed with his fingers."

The sunflower seed is as All-American as popcorn. Introduced into the culture by Native Americans, who used them for everything from curing snakebites to flavoring bread, sunflower seeds, became a snack favorite in the nineteenth century. Then, just as suddenly, the sunflower seed went out of fashion. In his book, *The Sunflower,* Charles Heiser Jr. says that for almost a century the only place you could find the mother plant, the sunflower, was camouflaging "a garbage can or a privy."

Sunflower seeds were a late call-up to the big leagues. I never heard of them when I was playing in the fifties and sixties. I don't even remember hearing about them in the seventies. My first memory of sunflower seeds and baseball comes from 1987. That was the year Texas Rangers reliever Greg Harris went on the disabled list after injuring his elbow flipping sunflower seeds into the stands.

It took the seeds a long time to make inroads in the dugout and bullpen and, when they finally did, it was mostly due to the backlash against tobacco. Players who had taken out their nervous energy on a tobacco chaw started relieving those nervous tensions by shucking sunflower seeds with their teeth and spitting the shells, in creative ways. In the Reds bullpen, they play a home-run derby contest that involves flipping sunflower seeds. In the Braves bullpen, they keep base coaches alert by flicking seeds at them.

The baseball players' favorite brand, David & Sons (because it's free), got started in Fresno, California in 1926. Grocer David DerHairbedian roasted sunflower seeds in his grocery store, packaged them in individual bags, and sold them for a nickel—and sold them and sold them and sold them. Three quarters of a century later, the company, run for many years by the sons, is owned by the conglomerate ConAgra. If a conglomerate wants you, you know you are a success.

Baseball players excepted, most sunflower seeds are sold as birdfeed or crushed to make cooking oil. Only a fourth of the annual crop is roasted and salted for the snack-food market. Sunflower seeds are very efficient. One sunflower can produce 1,000 seeds, and about 18,000 of the plants can be grown on an acre of farmland. Do the math: one acre can produce eighteen million sunflower seeds a season. Then, consider that former Cubs and Yankees slugger Glenallen Hill, who was an acknowledged sunflower seed spitter extraordinaire, eats 30 to 40 an inning and you can see why it's good that the sunflower is so prolific.

Chapter Eight

Eye in the Sky

Julian Tavarez is pitching Sean Casey carefully in the fifth. He hasn't forgotten the curveball that Casey drilled into left for a double in the third. With Encarnacion dancing at second and the count 0-1, Tavarez tries to slip a fastball past the batter, almost fooling Casey. The left-handed hitter swings behind the pitch, just getting under the rising ball. It soars over the backstop, smacking into the press box window and caroming back into the stands, a souvenir for a lucky little boy.

It is the only time all day that the crowd even looks in the direction of the press box. As far as the spectators are concerned, the entire cadre of writers and broadcasters is invisible, the news media held hostage behind Plexiglas. They *are* virtual hostages, agrees Hal McCoy, looking up from the laptop computer where he is pounding out a story for tomorrow's edition of the *Dayton Daily News*. "This is the worst press box in baseball, without a doubt."

In his 1910 book, *The National Game,* Alfred H. Spink, founder of the *Sporting News,* claimed that the first baseball beat writer was one William Cauldwell, who covered the

New York Mutuals while also editing the *New York Mercury* in 1853. Cauldwell, who had known Walt Whitman when both worked at the *New York Aurora,* soon tired of reporting on baseball and editing the paper and turned over the baseball beat to Henry Chadwick.

Neither Cauldwell nor Chadwick enjoyed the benefit of covering the game from a press box. They sat in the stands with the hoi polloi and did the best they could. But soon other New York papers—the *Express,* the *Mail,* the *Times,* the *Tribune,* and the *World*—were staffing games and the press needed room for their notebooks. At first they were seated on the top row of the grandstand, then boxed into their own area in the stands, into an area that soon came to be known as the press box. One of the first teams to build an enclosed space for sportwriters was the Washington Olympics, who were accused by shareholders in 1870 of squandering money on a press box at their new ballpark, Olympic Grounds.

By the early years of the twentieth century, the press box was home to more than the press, with assorted interlopers and hangers-on increasingly taking up space. The situation came to a head during the 1908 playoff game in New York between the Giants and the Cubs: *Chicago Examiner* writer Hugh Fullerton lost his seat in the press box to Broadway actor Louis Mann, a friend of Giants manager John McGraw. Fullerton attempted to sit in Mann's lap but ended up sitting on a box in the aisle. This disrespect continued through the World Series when the Tigers put out-of-town writers in the back row of the grandstand, and the Cubs reciprocated by putting Tiger beat writers on the roof of the first-base pavilion.

The writers had had enough and, led by Jack Ryder of the *Cincinnati Enquirer* and Joseph S. Jackson of the *Detroit Free Press*, they formed a group, the Base Ball Writers Association of America (BBWAA), to negotiate press problems with the leagues. Dues were set at two dollars per year. Not every writer was on board until 1910, when the Yankees and Giants played an exhibition series and refused to allow anyone who wasn't a BBWAA member into the press box. Predictably, those two dollar dues flooded in.

Hal McCoy knows press boxes. He's been in all of them, from PacBell to Pro Player. He's been covering the Reds for thirty seasons, 162 games a season, plus 30 spring training games, plus the playoffs and the World Series. "All total, about 200 games a year for 30 years. What's that, 6,000 games? That's a lot of balls and strikes."

And he is convinced that the press box at Cinergy Field is the worst, hands down. "It's the only press box you can't open a window. It's like working in a hermetically sealed mayonnaise jar. This press box makes it harder to write during the game; you don't have the roar of the crowd to bring you back in. Plus the roof leaks when it rains. And they can't regulate the climate control. It's either 90 degrees or 50 degrees. We're the only writers in America who bring jackets to games in August when it is 100 degrees outside."

Hal McCoy has survived the indignities of Cinergy's press box long enough to become the dean of America's baseball writers. He's been covering the Reds for three decades, "longer than anybody else has covered one team." In 2001, he missed getting into the writer's wing of the Hall of Fame by one vote. So, stories about him now say "future Hall of Famer" Hal McCoy.

His first year on the beat for the *Daily News,* 1973, the Reds won the National League West, but they were still a player away from dominance, from becoming the vaunted Big Red Machine. That player arrived midway through McCoy's second season on the beat in the form of Ken Griffey. For the rest of the decade, until a cheapskate front office drove away the heart of the team, the Reds would dominate baseball.

Three decades later, the Reds are a scrappy bunch that have clawed their way to the top of the National League Central while awaiting the return of their best player, again named Ken Griffey, but known simply as "Junior." McCoy's tenure spans the Griffeys'.

Junior is due to come off the disabled list tomorrow and McCoy wants the story, and he wants it exclusively. That's how McCoy has become the dean of baseball writers, by doggedly pursuing stories, by bringing a reporter's skills to a beat often filled by fans. Most of the Pete Rose stories you read during Rose's scandal-plagued years as the Reds manager came from McCoy's pen. He says Rose won't even return a phone call anymore; "Kill the messenger," McCoy comments.

The *Cincinnati Enquirer,* the Reds' hometown paper, has gone through sixteen Reds beat writers during McCoy's tenure. McCoy's paper is an hour away, in *Dayton,* for God's sake.

This season Hal has been all over a Griffey-back-to-Seattle rumor, just as he was all over the Griffey-coming-to-Cincinnati story two years ago.

. . .

He arrived at today's game three hours early, as is his habit. "I never go in to the newspaper. This is my office." He headed almost immediately down to the clubhouse, seeking out Griffey. If Griffey does return to the lineup tomorrow, one of the worst-kept secrets in Cincinnati, Hal wants to have a story about it. And he'd prefer an exclusive.

He hangs around the clubhouse, waiting for the moment to pounce. Today, it doesn't happen. He can't get Griffey alone and his interview looks like one of those you see on the eleven o'clock news: microphones and tape recorders thrust from everywhere toward Griffey's face.

"As soon as anybody sees you talking to him, they're right there," says McCoy. "They don't want to be scooped. I should be flattered, but they all follow me around. I have to try and slip off or say, 'Hey, this is private.'"

No private interview today. At least he has a story, a GRIFFEY RETURNS story.

He folds up his notebook and it's back into the elevator, back up to the fifth floor, to the press box, his office.

As he eases into the 1,350 square foot, three-tiered room directly behind home plate, McCoy stops by the table in the rear to pick up the press releases. McCoy and his sportswriting brethren get plenty of help from the Reds publicity office, not that Hal needs it. The Reds and the Marlins have stacked forty-three pages of press material, most of it printed back and front, about half of it legal size, on a table at the back of the press box.

There's a three-page, single-spaced (front and back, legal size) release from the Reds, titled "Game Information" mentioning virtually anything a sportswriter might need to know about today's game:

- Probable pitchers
- The Reds' record at home and on the road
- Barry Larkin's chase to catch Johnny Bench for third all-time on the Reds Doubles list
- Starting pitcher Jose Rijo's record for the season, game by game
- Tidbits on all the Reds pitchers and all the regulars

If Hal needs to know Austin Kearns' batting average with runners in scoring position, it's right there, top left, page five: .280 (7-25). Should Adam Dunn homer today, Hal can check the sheet and discover that his last homer was May 7, a three-run blow against Milwaukee.

There's this kind of information for every player, updated to today's game: Reds starts by position; the disabled list, who's on it, why, and when each is eligible to come off; the back page is devoted to "2002 Day-By-Day Results."

The Marlins press office has provided a similar sheaf, only it runs to five pages, back and front, and also provides a recap for each of the Marlins' minor-league clubs.

There's a six-page packet, single-spaced, front and back, on Homer Bush. There is more information than anyone could ever want about Homer Bush. Want to know his slugging percentage for 1992, when he played for Charleston in the Sally League? It's there (.289). It tells you that Bush hits .263 when the count is 0-1. What it doesn't say in all this info is why Reds writers are getting all this information on Homer Bush, of all people. Hal knows: "The Marlins just signed him."

There's a three-page (single-spaced, front and back) stack on the Marlins' starting pitcher Julian Tavarez. The most interesting fact is that he lives in the off-season in Broadview Heights, Ohio. He pitched for Cleveland in '96. He must like the weather.

There's a four-page packet of Reds supplementary biographies, featuring Carlos Almanzar and Reggie Taylor. The Reds purchased Almanzar's contract from Louisville yesterday; they picked up Taylor from the Phillies for one of those players to be named later.

There are eight pages of box scores from yesterday's games around the league and a thirteen-page packet of stats from the league, including standings, records, averages of all kinds, even this: National League, Hardest to Double Up. Who do you think it is? It's the Cardinals' J. D. Drew—he hasn't hit into a double play in 167 at-bats.

There's a one-page fact sheet about The Ballparks, Cinergy and The Great American Ball Park, which is "scheduled to open in 2003." There's a one-page note from Major League Baseball reminding writers that the application deadline for All-Star media credentials is May 20. There's even a scorecard with all the pertinent information: lineups, rosters, bench by left- and right-handed hitters, bullpen by left- and right-handed pitchers.

And *after* the game there'll be a four-page Post Game Notes, complete with box score and pitch counts.

Hal says the volume of press handouts is in sharp contrast to the Marge Schott era. Schott was a local car dealer who inherited the team when her husband died, and made her name primarily because of her loutish behavior and her everpresent St. Bernard, an obnoxious mutt named Schottzie.

In 1995, after her payroll had jumped by a million dollars, she decreed that the press office cut the daily press notes from four pages to one, in order to save paper. She rescinded the decision after a sportswriter noted in print that it would take 9,271 years to make up the million-dollar deficit that way. The lords of baseball, a sportswriting term for baseball's ruling council, forced Schott out in 1999, after she demonstrated her mastery of history and diplomacy by telling ESPN that Hitler was "good at the beginning, he just went too far."

They still remember her wistfully, if not fondly, in the Reds press box. She did make for good copy.

The term *press box* is so familiar everyone feels like they know what goes on there. They think they've seen glimpses of the action in movies like *Major League* and in television coverage. They haven't. They've seen the broadcast booth.

The press box is home to writers, not broadcasters. Reporters stacked up three and four high, laptop computers in front of them. (Typewriters in the old days.) The press box has been home to sportswriting luminaries like Damon Runyon, Heywood Broun, Ring Lardner, Grantland Rice, Roger Angell, and Roger Kahn. It's where legends are made, of both the on-field and sportswriting variety.

It's where Bill Furlong wrote of shortstop Ernie Banks, "He swings his bat as if it were a buggy whip, striking at the ball with the swiftness of a serpent's tongue"; where Ring Lardner wrote of pitcher Walter Johnson, "He's got a gun concealed about his person. They can't tell me he throws them balls with his arm"; where Red Smith wrote of pitcher Lefty Grove: "He could throw a lamb chop past a wolf."

There are a few irregulars in the press box today but most are what are called beat writers. Baseball is their beat; they cover it year-round.

If you look from the box seats up to the Reds press box, that's Hal McCoy in the front row, one seat left of center. He's tall and angular and, at sixty-one, still quick on his feet. It's his regular seat, staked out by a small red plaque: *Dayton Daily News.*

This is Cincinnati, his home turf, so he and the other Reds writers are in the front row. It's a baseball tradition. Visiting writers sit in the second row. Irregulars, occasionals, and interlopers occupy the top row. Hal says it's the same on the road. "It's funny, we don't have assigned seats on the road, but everybody just sits in the same place."

Spread out in front of him, sort of Hal's tools of the trade, is an assortment of items that resemble the sale table at Office Max. The center spot is taken by his iBook laptop computer; to the left of the computer—Hal is left-handed—are his miniature Sony tape recorder, Labtec headphones, a cell phone, a TI-1706 calculator, two ballpoint pens, a yellow marker, the Reds Media guide, a pocket notebook, two reporter's pads, and a tin of Altoids cinnamon. On the right, his worn scorebook, a bottle of whiteout, a *Sporting News 2002 Baseball Register* and a cup of coffee. Stuffed in the briefcase situated behind him are more pens, more reporter's pads, more reference tomes.

A calculator? This really is his office.

In a nation where people fear speaking in public and doing math more than dying, baseball is an anomaly. Baseball is all math. What other newspaper reporter carries a calculator? The movie critic? The courthouse reporter?

No sport is so number-intensive. Every pitch, ball or strike, every foul, every hit, every fielding play, every at-bat, every inning, every game—it's all recorded and sorted and analyzed, often by a guy sitting in the third row of the press box who covers the Reds for STATS, Inc. a baseball database company. His job is to log every pitch. Every pitch. (For those who need to know every pitch, it's all posted after the game on the Reds website, but really, no one needs to know *every* pitch.)

The press box has thirty-nine spaces, but only sixteen writers are here for today's Reds-Marlins game, including three beat writers from Marlins country. Regulars in the Reds press box, in addition to McCoy, are the *Cincinnati Enquirer*'s John Fay, the *Cincinnati Post*'s Jason Williams and Tony Jackson, Associated Press writer Joe Kay, *Cincinnati Post* columnist Lonnie Wheeler, the *Columbus Dispatch*'s Jim Massie, and Mark Schmetzer, a freelancer who covers the Reds for the *Sporting News.*

For many years, the *Post*'s Earl Lawson, doubled as the *Sporting News*'s man in Cincinnati. That was back in the glory days, when the St. Louis-based paper justifiably called itself the *Bible of Baseball,* and gave a national audience to baseball's local beat writers.

Any kid growing up in the fifties could reel off the names of the *Sporting News* writers: Dan Daniel covered the Yankees, Shirley Povich, the Senators. Watson Spoelstra reported on the Tigers; Bob Broeg, the Cardinals; Edgar Munzel, the White Sox; Hal Lebovitz, the Indians; Les Biederman, the Pirates. Dick Young had a column; so did Red Smith and Bob Addie.

These were giants of the game, the sportswriting game.

I used half my allowance every week—twenty-five cents—to buy my copy. I'd ride my bike to the Garden Basket every Wednesday, when the latest issue arrived. When I got older, I subscribed. My friend Dommie Jackson didn't just buy it, he studied it. He would underline the things he wanted to remember.

Economics, and the arrival of *USA Today*'s *Baseball Weekly* and *ESPN The Magazine* have pinched the *Sporting News,* forcing it to change. It went from a tabloid newspaper to a four-color magazine. I'd been a subscriber for more than thirty years but, after a while, I dropped it. It just wasn't essential baseball reading. I've since picked it back up, but it's not on the top of my magazine stack.

I called my old friend Dommie the other night, to see if he still gets it, if he still marks it up with his yellow highlighter. "I dropped it about six years ago. It had become sort of the *People* magazine of baseball. I didn't want that. I just want the facts."

Rijo's first pitch of the game had barely settled into the catcher's glove, when Reds director of media relations Rob Butcher, seated on the end seat of the second row, pulled down a stand microphone and announced over the press box loudspeaker that the game started at 12:35. It was the first in a series of announcements aimed at making the baseball beat writers' jobs easier.

Butcher had no sooner pushed his microphone back up when one writer called out to another, "Gary, what's the game-time temperature?"

The response: "Seventy beer drinking degrees!"

When Preston Wilson went down swinging, another sportswriter, imitating Butcher, proclaimed, "Wilson strikes out on a 41-mph fastball." He was referring to the incorrect reading on the center-field scoreboard radar gun.

As Cliff Floyd stepped into the batter's box, another writer inquired, "Were the ribs good?" He was asking about the food in the press-box dining room. Ribs top the menu today, along with fried chicken, corn on the cob, beans, coleslaw, two kinds of cake, and soft drinks.

The quick response to the ribs question: "Got a lot of fat on them."

When Butcher announced "Career hit number 500 for Encarnacion," Hal shakes his head. "Just a number."

It's an odd atmosphere in the press box. The writers joke around, they help each other. When Hal misses a play, Columbus's Jim Massie fills him in: "6–3." There's a camaraderie, but it's restrained. That's because these colleagues are also competitors. Every big-city newspaper beat reporter has competition, but only on the baseball beat do the writers work together and travel out of town together. It's as if the Reds and Marlins shared the same locker room after the game.

Inside newspaper city rooms, sports is referred to as the *toy department*. In the editorial and executive suites, it gets more respect. That's because publishers and high-level editors know how important sports is to readers. In a 2002 readership study by the Newspaper Association of America, 57 percent of men read the sports section. That puts sports second in male readership, behind news, which scored with 66 percent of readers. Among female readers, sports finishes eleventh, ahead of only travel and science.

The game on the field is in full swing now, but Hal can't devote his complete attention because it's Thursday, deadline day for his Sunday "Ask Hal" column. He's typing in questions from readers, forty to fifty emails gleaned from the day. "And the paper expects me to answer every one of them." He does, using a selection to fill the Sunday column.

Hal McCoy is the latest in a line of great sportswriters who have covered the Reds. Three are in the Baseball Hall of Fame: Si Burick of Hal's paper, the *Dayton Daily News*, Ritter Collett of the *Dayton Journal Herald*, and Earl Lawson of the *Cincinnati Post*.

Burick was famous for his gregarious nature. I met him in 1976, and the first thing he told me was that he hadn't had a promotion in forty-eight years. McCoy has heard the line, too. "Yeah, he was like the boy sports editor. He was nineteen when they gave him the job." Burick interviewed everyone from Lou Gehrig to Lou Piniella. Collett covered every World Series from 1946 to 1990 and was, for a time, McCoy's boss. Lawson was on the Reds beat for thirty-four seasons, beginning in 1951. Only New York, Chicago and St. Louis can rival Cincinnati when it comes to Hall of Fame writers.

McCoy says he profited from knowing all three; "But Earl Lawson was my mentor. He took me under his wing. He was the greatest. For two or three years, I just sat back and watched and listened." And learned his lessons well; he will be number four when he is inducted in August 2003.

As the game progresses, Hal puts on his headphones, but it's not music he's listening to. He's transcribing his Griffey interview. Finished with the "Ask Hal" column, he turns to a feature story for tomorrow's paper on Griffey's return. As he types away, he shakes his head again. "It's always something."

"That hit for Dawkins snaps an 0-16 streak," announces Butcher. Dawkins began the day hitting what Dizzy Dean would have called "a cool .083."

Hal turns to Massie: "And another funny thing happened . . . Gookie Dawkins got a hit."

It's an inside joke: McCoy explains to me that, years ago, Bob Herzel of the *Enquirer* wrote in his game story, "And another funny thing happened . . . Darrel Chaney got a hit." Chaney was a light-hitting shortstop for the Reds in the early seventies. Light hitting and thin-skinned.

"Chaney didn't much like it, did he, Mass? Almost caused fisticuffs, didn't it?"

Massie nods yes.

Hal is writing away on his Griffey story but he never misses marking in his scorebook. He says he won't begin the story on today's game until it's over. "Day games, I don't work on the story until after the game. Night games you have to write on it along." That's because of deadlines: The paper may not show up on your doorstep until 6 A.M., but there's a long process between McCoy's computer and your kitchen table. Once he finishes his story, he sends it over the Internet to the *Daily News* offices sixty miles away in downtown Dayton, where it will be edited, a headline written and printing plates burned. The presses roll at midnight, and Hal's story has to be there.

Next time you read the newspaper story about a night game, notice the story's structure. It usually begins with the game's highlight—the late-inning, game-winning home run, the tense showdown in the ninth between closer and slugger—then quickly shifts to an inning by inning scoring summary. Sportswriters work on the scoring summary as the game goes along. Then, if the game ends too late for a full-blown article with quotes from players, the writer can still get the game results in the morning paper.

After the last out of the game, Hal turns to his neighbor Jim Massie. "What's the story, Mass?"

The Columbus writer jokes, "There's a story?"

It has been an uneventful afternoon, no sterling pitching performances, mostly a lot of errors on the Reds' side of the ledger. Hal is thinking out loud, searching for a story amongst all the notations in his scorebook. "What'll Boone say? 'We didn't bring our A game?'"

Massie laughs. It's a frequent comment from manager Bob Boone after a loss.

McCoy grabs up a notebook and heads for the elevator. "The first requirement is talk to the manager before we go into the clubhouse."

The writers, TV and radio reporters and cameramen (they are all men) gather in a waiting room outside the clubhouse door. After a few minutes, Rob Butcher sticks his head out and says, "The Reds announce Gookie Dawkins has been optioned to Chattanooga. An announcement on his roster spot will be made later." Everyone groans. They know his spot will be filled by Griffey.

Hal stands back as the door to the clubhouse opens. "We let the TV guys get their sound bites first." After all the cameras have entered, he and the others of the pencil brigade troop in.

The manager's office is smaller than I have imagined from reading baseball stories for forty years. There's just enough room for a desk, a couch, a television, and seventeen sportswriters.

Boone stands silent, waiting for a question. The first one is a softball, but he treats it as if he has never heard it before. He doesn't spar or bait the writers; he answers questions, smiles, answers more questions. He's not happy with a loss, but he's an old hand. He knows that, even in their record-breaking season, when they won 116 games, the Seattle Mariners still lost 46 games. Losses come with the game.

While the TV types ask away, I check out Boone's bookshelf. There's the usual assortment of baseball records and guides, but there's also *How to Be Like Mike,* a motivational book based on interviews with Michael Jordan's associates; *Sermon on the Mound,* an inspirational tome whose subtitle is *Finding God at the Heart of the Game; Covering Home,* a book about fatherhood; and *The Golden Dream,* football coach Gerry Faust's cautionary tale about his failure to make the leap from high school to Notre Dame. Clearly, Boone has more on his mind than numbers—his job is to motivate and inspire twenty-five men half his age, and he's looking to a number of sources for guidance. I am reminded of Casey Stengel's secret to managing a baseball team: "Keep the five guys who hate you away from the five who aren't sure."

After five minutes of routine questions, the TV corps heads into the locker room, leaving behind seven writers. Boone marks the event by sitting down.

Hal asks the first question. "Did the team not bring its A game?"

Boone doesn't know this is a bit mocking. He responds, "You're not going to have your A game every day." Then Boone opens up his laptop. After a round of questions, the room falls silent. This interview is over; it's on to the lockers.

Hal joins three others around starting pitcher Jose Rijo's locker. They ask questions, he answers softly. When two more writers join the crowd, McCoy slips off, chatting briefly with second baseman Todd Walker, then easing in next to Adam Dunn. "We just didn't get the big hits like we've been getting," Dunn says. "That's going to happen." As soon as a TV camera comes up Hal walks away. He doesn't want to use quotes that readers saw on television the night before. He slides in next to Sean Casey for a couple of quick quotes, while the TV gang descends on Barry Larkin.

Two lockers down, Gookie Dawkins sits in a chair in front of his locker staring off into space. No one is talking to him, despite the fact that he broke out of a slump with two hits. Dawkins has suffered the ultimate indignity: He may have suspected he would be moved to make way for Griffey's return to the roster, but he broke out of his slump today with two hits, and then was sent all the way to Double A, bypassing the Reds Triple A affiliate in Louisville. It was a double slap.

As he heads out of the locker room, Hal drifts by Gookie Dawkins' locker. Dawkins is still in shock. Hal doesn't ask any questions, he quietly shakes the twenty-three-year-old's hand and wishes him well. For the first time, Dawkins allows a small smile to spread across his face. He's touched.

It's 4:30, and McCoy heads out to his car to fetch a cigar. "I can't smoke my cigars during the games, so I chew 'em. After games, when the smoke police are gone, and there are only the regular beat writers pounding away on our laptops, I light that baby up."

He waits patiently for the elevator, thumbing through his notes, before heading back upstairs to his office, where he'll stare into his computer and light up his cigar. The hard part is over. Now, all he has to do is write the story. It was one of McCoy's colleagues, the late *New York Times* sportswriter Red Smith, who said it best. "Writing is easy, you just sit down at the typewriter and open up a vein."

When Reds fans in Dayton pick up their morning paper the next day, this is what they read from Hal McCoy:

"Manager Bob Boone's mantra of recent times is that if his Cincinnati Reds put their A game on the field, they'll win most games.

"On Thursday afternoon, the Reds put their E game on the field against the Florida Marlins—as in E for errors of commission and omission.

"Some rare slippage by starting pitcher Jose Rijo and some late sloppage on defense by the Reds led to an 8–4 defeat to the Florida Marlins in Cinergy Field."

Hal McCoy found his story.

Chapter Nine

The Ball Game

Adam Dunn and pitcher Julian Tavarez have quite a little duel going here in the bottom of the fifth. After looking at two quick strikes, Dunn can't afford to let anything close get by him. He looks at ball one; fouls a grounder into the visitor's dugout; takes ball two, taps a dribbler foul that bounces into the seats along first; fouls one back to the screen; and pulls one foul down the line into the first-base seats.

I tell Will it reminds me of Richie Ashburn. My dad had cousins in Philadelphia, so he took me to a Giants–Phillies game at old Shibe Park in 1961. I have two memories of that day: Willie Mays blasting one into the upper deck in left, and Richie Ashburn fouling off what seemed like a hundred pitches until he finally got one to his liking.

Will tells me it reminds him of something he once read: The average life expectancy of a major-league baseball is six pitches.

During Dunn's at-bat, it's even fewer. Nine pitches, three balls into the stands, and another one tossed out because it was scuffed by its collision with the dugout wall.

He ends the major-league career of four balls before one survives his at-bat, as he grounds to the first baseman for the third out.

Some baseballs don't even last an at-bat; others may hang around for a half inning, maybe an entire frame. But most are gone in two batters.

It wasn't always that way. When the *New York Times* analyzed the finances of a typical big-league team in 1909 it found that each club used forty dozen balls per season. A season! That's 480 balls, or 6 per home game. Scuffed balls, dirty balls, all were kept in play, and if a foul went into the stands, the bat boy went in after it.

By 1916, teams were using 154 dozen balls a season or about 24 balls per game and today, the average is 47 balls per game. The umpires rub down six dozen baseballs before each game, just to be safe.

Compare that to the average sandlot baseball that winters on the garage floor, and endures spring puddles, summer heat, and autumn frost. In my neighborhood, we could get at least a season out of a ball before we had to cover it with electrical tape and turn it into a warm-up ball, but Major League Baseball has decreed that every pitched ball must be perfect. No scuffs, no spots, no rips, or snags. Even the stitches have to be perfect.

That perfection begins at the Muscle Shoals Rubber Company, which, oddly enough, is not in Muscle Shoals, Alabama, but in Batesville, Mississippi.

The Muscle Shoals Rubber Company is the exclusive manufacturer of the pill. I thought the pill *was* the ball—

we used that as a slang term when I was playing—so I figured this was it, beginning and end. However, in Major League Baseball vernacular, the *pill* is the hard center of the ball. In baseball's dark ages it might have been a rock or a walnut; now it's a compressed mixture of cork and rubber, jacketed by two layers of rubber. Muscle Shoals has been making major-league baseball pills using the same materials and the same methods since 1948, when the company *was* in Muscle Shoals.

The cork comes from Spain and Portugal *via* Maryland Cork, which has been supplying Muscle Shoals Rubber with cork since 1948. The rubber comes from Indonesia *via* Goodyear, which has also been supplying Muscle Shoals Rubber since 1948.

The virgin cork is ground fine, mixed with rubber and other ingredients, and compressed into a sphere. It's then covered with a molded black rubber cover, then those two layers are covered with a molded *red* rubber cover. The black layer may contain rubber from the last set of tires you traded in, but the red layer is pure Indonesian rubber. Before nesting the center in the two jackets, all three pieces are polished to remove seams from the molding process. The nesting is done by hand, then it's all molded together with heat and pressure, polished again, and inspected. Only perfect—there's that word again, *perfect*—pills pass. That's generally on the order of 95 percent.

That perfection in production continues through D&T Spinning, a yarn plant in Ludlow, Vermont. Like Muscle Shoals Rubber, D&T Spinning is the exclusive provider of the wool yarns used in official baseballs and has been since

1984. Major League Baseball prefers wool yarn to synthetics, because wool pulls back to its original shape quicker than, say, the polyester in a leisure suit. Moreover, baseball windings have always been made from wool.

Next stop on the way to perfection is Tennessee Tanning in Tullahoma, Tennessee. Tennessee Tanning is not a tanning salon; it has been the sole supplier of the leather used for the covers of official baseballs since 1961. Here, fresh cowhides—not horsehides—are tanned and shaved to a consistent thickness of 0.046875 inches to 0.048828125 inches. For comparison, a sheet of paper is about .004 inches thick, so the cowhides are the equivalent of a stack of ten pieces of paper.

So, why do they call it the old horsehide, as in "You want to toss around the old horsehide?" Well, because it used to be horsehide. In 1974, with the horsehide market in a downward spiral—just not that many excess horses anymore since the automobile took over in, oh, 1905—Commissioner Bowie Kuhn quietly issued a directive that official league balls be made from cowhide. And no one noticed.

The aim for the perfect ball then moves to the Rawlings Baseball Factory in Turrialba, Costa Rica, in that Central American country's coffee-growing region. That's where it all comes together: Hides from Tennessee, pills from Mississippi and yarn from New England converge with low-paid foreign workers to create the perfect orb.

There, the perfect yarn is wound around the perfect pill: high-tension machines wind 363 feet of blue-gray yarn around the pill, then a layer of 135 feet of white yarn, followed by 159 more feet of blue-gray yarn, topped off with 450 feet of white yarn. That's 1,107 feet, almost a quarter mile of yarn in each baseball. With four baseballs, you could knit a man's pullover sweater. An ugly, blue-gray-and-white pullover sweater.

Why the different colors? At one time, the second layer was leather instead of yarn. When it was replaced with wool early in the twentieth century, the manufacturer used white yarn to look like the white leather. After the yarn is wound tight, the balls receive a coat of glue, which must set up for twenty-four hours.

It's almost a ball now. The hides are cut into figure-eight pieces, then dampened to make the leather pliable. These hides are transported to the sewing room three at a time, so they won't dry out, and there a highly skilled and lowly paid seamstress hand sews the cover on by threading two 44-inch lengths of red waxed cotton string through 108 punched stitching holes. A good seamstress can sew six covers per hour.

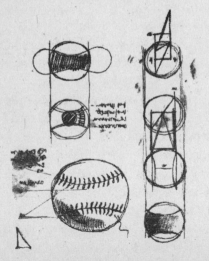

Why 108 stitches on a baseball? To hold the cover on. (You probably fell for the old "why does a fireman wear red suspenders?" joke back in grade school, too.)

If you saw *Bull Durham,* you know there are also 108 beads in a rosary. What does prayer have to do with the stitches on a ball? Maybe it's where "Spahn and Sain and pray for rain" came from. Actually, there are 108 stitches because there have always been 108 stitches. That's just how the sewing worked out a century ago.

The balls are rolled on a wooden press for seventeen seconds to tamp the stitches, then allowed to dry overnight to shrink the cover tight. After being stamped with the Rawlings label and the Official Major League Baseball brand, they are packed up and sent back home.

The final stop on the road to a perfect baseball is the Rawlings plant in Ava, Missouri, where a fellow by the name of Gary Ellison spends his days shooting randomly selected test balls out of a pitching machine at a speed of 60 miles per hour to see how far they will bounce off a wall of ash wood. This is to simulate the ball meeting the bat, although even Stu Miller on a bad day threw harder than 60. The rebound speed of the ball is divided by the speed of the pitch (60 mph) to arrive at what is called the *coefficient of restitution.* (Didn't Congress pass a law against that?) In short, the coefficient of restitution tells how far the ball bounces. The rule is the coefficient of restitution can't be more than 0.578 or less than 0.514. In layman's terms, if you were to drop the ball onto a piece of ash, the ball has to bounce back just a hair more than half the distance from where you dropped it. Balls that bounce back more than the upper-end number will be rabbit balls, suitable only for years when attendance is down. Check any balls that don't bounce at least halfway back. They probably have Ty Cobb's autograph on the cover.

Rawlings has been the official supplier of baseballs since 1976. For a hundred years before that, the contract belonged to A.G. Spalding, which manufactured the Spalding brand ball for the National League and the A. J. Reach brand for the American League. Spalding gave up the contract in the bicentennial year, claiming it was losing money on the operation.

Rawlings goes through this elaborate process to produce three-quarters of a million baseballs a year for Major League Baseball, ensuring that each one of those balls is perfect. Or just about perfect, anyway.

The ball makes one more stop before arriving in the pitcher's hand: the umpires' room. In 1921, when spitballs and emery balls and all manner of scuffed-ball pitches were banned in the aftermath of Indians batter Ray Chapman's death after being beaned by a doctored ball, pitchers complained that the balls were too slick, and they couldn't get a good grip on them. So, umpires began the practice of rubbing the balls with dirt and shoe polish and tobacco juice and spit—anything that would knock off the shine— before each game. That practice continues today, only they no longer use dirt or spit. And the umpires don't do the rubbing. They've handed the dirty work over to clubhouse attendants.

The official rub of Major League Baseball is Lena Blackburne's Rubbing Mud, a creamy concoction with just a hint of grit, perfected in the thirties by Russell Aubrey "Lena" "Slats" Blackburne (he had two nicknames), a journeyman White Sox infielder in the teens, later an Athletics coach. Slats became the official rub supplier for the American League in 1938 and the National League in 1939. The source of the mud is a closely guarded secret; Blackburne would only say it was a river he played in as a child. Speculation is that it's the Pennsauken Creek, a Delaware River tributary in Burlington County, Pennsylvania.

Nobody gets rich on this deal. One 16-ounce can of the stuff costs a hundred bucks but it will last a season for a team. You can multiply that by all the teams in organized baseball, major, and minor league—and they all use it—and you're only selling a couple of hundred cases, 360 pounds, a year.

There was a surge of interest in the mud in the early eighties, and a Princeton professor conducted a spectrometer test—using his university's expensive equipment—to discover that the mud contained finely ground quartz from the Ice Age.

After all the effort Rawlings goes through to make that perfect virgin-white baseball, it takes a clubhouse attendant only about five minutes to turn it a homely brown.

The baseball didn't begin as a perfect ball, though. It began as a rag ball. Literally. In the early days of the game players made their own balls, which meant some days they'd be hitting a rock and, other days, a marshmallow.

Doc Adams, one of the founders of the Knickerbockers team of the 1840s, recalled in a late nineteenth-century interview, "We had a great deal of trouble in getting balls made and for six or seven years I made all the balls myself, not only for our club but also for other clubs when they were organized. I went all over New York to find someone who would undertake this work, but no one could be induced to try it for love or money. Finally I found a Scotch saddler who was able to show me a good way to cover the balls with horsehide, such as was used for whip lashes. I used to make the stuffing out of 3 or 4 ounces of rubber cuttings, wound with yarn and then covered with the leather. Those balls were, of course, a great deal softer than the balls now in use."

Softer, smaller, lighter. It was because these balls had the flight characteristics of a badminton birdie that the position of shortstop came into being. Originally, there were four outfielders but, because the light ball could only travel a couple of hundred feet, there was the need for a short fielder to relay throws back into the pitcher. Short fielder became shortstop.

The first rules didn't speak to the bat's size or shape, but the ball was required to weigh 3 ounces, about what two golf balls weigh today. In 1854, sensing that the game needed more offense, the rules committee increased the weight of the ball from $5\frac{1}{2}$ to $6\frac{1}{2}$ ounces, and 11 inches in circumference, almost softball size.

Eighteen years later, reacting to complaints about this blubber ball, the rules committee settled on a ball weight of between 5 and $5\frac{1}{4}$ ounces and a circumference of 9 to $9\frac{1}{4}$ inches, and that's what it's been ever since, for over a century and a quarter. End of story.

Not so fast. If you follow baseball, then you know that's not the end of the debate—it's only the beginning. The discussion now turns to rabbit ball, nitro ball, juiced ball, lively ball, dead ball.

"The rabbit ball will not be caged," writes the *New York Times*. "The so-called lively sphere which has been responsible for the home run epidemic, according to many followers of the game, will remain the official horsehide in the National League."

The *Times* wrote that in 1926. The year *before* Babe Ruth hit sixty home runs. Variations on that story have been appearing ever since. In 1926, professor Harold A. Fales, of the chemistry division of Columbia University, conducted experiments on the 1914 ball, the 1923 ball, and the 1925 ball and concluded that rules changes, in particular ones restricting the pitcher and replacing scuffed balls sooner, and not a rabbit ball, were responsible for the increase in home runs.

The chemistry department?

In 1954, the civil-engineering department of Cooper Union concluded that the 1953 ball was 8 percent more lively than the 1952 ball but, since nobody assaulted Ruth's record, no one much cared.

In 1962, the *New York Times* hired the firm of Foster D. Snell, consulting chemists and engineers, with, the *Times* pointed out, no rooting interest, to do another ball test. Snell subjected seven balls, one each from '27 and '36, and five from '61, to scientific analysis, including surgical dissection and battering from an arm's ram, and concluded: "The technologists do not find anything in any of the balls to show clearly that a home run has been any easier to hit in any one period of baseball than another."

And, in 2000, two years after Mark McGwire and Sammy Sosa smacked around Roger Maris's home-run mark, Major League Baseball was so concerned about a loss of faith in the game that it hired the University of Massachusetts at Lowell's Baseball Research Center to test the ball. The conclusion: "The performance differences between the 1999 and 2000 baseballs are minimal."

So, as we can see, there have always been rabbit balls and rumors of rabbit balls.

In a related matter, what kind of degree would you get from a university Baseball Research Center?

In the Cincinnati half of the sixth, Wilton Guerrero, pinch-hitting for reliever Scott Williamson, bunts his way to first, then steals second, setting the stage for Todd Walker. With two outs, Guerrero is off with the crack of the bat, streaking around third on Walker's line single to left and beating the throw to the plate easily.

Guerrero doesn't run like Willie Mays, but the way he made the big wide turn at third, never hesitating, reminded me of the way Mays could score from second on a line single to left. There is one difference, though: by the time Mays was past the third base bag, his hat would be flying in the air. Guerrero's helmet is planted firmly on his head.

Willie Mays was the most stylish ballplayer of my era. Imitations of his basket catches probably caused more Little League errors than mud clods in the infield. His loosey-goosey batting stance, leaning back on his right leg, then almost diving with the bat, was widely imitated in my backyard. But the one thing we all tried to copy was the cap. I could never get my hat to fly off naturally; I learned to wear it back a tad and tip my head and shake and, occasionally, it would come off. Usually, I had to brush it off, hoping none of my teammates was watching.

Why couldn't Willie keep his cap on? And why couldn't I get mine to come off? Mays intentionally wore his cap a size too small so it would fly off. Who would have thought of that in the fifties?

Imagine if Willie Mays had been born a century sooner: Instead of breaking in with the New York Giants in 1951, he had broken in with the New York Knickerbockers in 1851. His headgear wouldn't have been a billed cap but a straw hat. That's what the Knicks wore in the early days. They looked more like a bunch of dandies on a picnic than an athletic squad.

Would it have been the same, Mays racing around third, his straw hat flying in the wind? I imagine many straw hats flew off in those early days, which may have been the reason the Knicks switched to mohair caps during the 1851 season.

There was no standard hat in the early days. "Early teams were often associated with military units or fire department units and they wore their service caps as part of the game," according to a spokesman for the library of the Baseball Hall of Fame. So, some teams looked like they were on a picnic, others looked like they were searching for a fire to put out, still others were waiting for war to break out. It literally was a free-for-all when it came to headwear.

Boating caps, bicycling hats, even jockey caps were popular.

Then, the Chicago White Sox, one of the most popular teams of the era because of their star Cap Anson, introduced a pillbox hat in the 1870s. This Chicago-style cap, with a flat top, horizontal stripes around the cap, and a short visor, became the baseball hat of choice. Of course, it made all the teams look like part of the Prussian Guard.

About the turn of the century Chicago-style was sup-

planted by Boston-style, a round-top, large-billed cap with a button on top, first worn in 1860 by the Brooklyn Excelsiors, but popularized by the Boston Red Stockings of 1900.

The ball cap as we know it, the ubiquitous fashion statement that you see everywhere from the golf course to the mall, arrived in the forties. The great leap forward for ball caps came when latex rubber was developed to replace buckram (coarse cotton) in the visor. Now, bills could be longer, providing more shading for players' eyes.

All the caps the Reds and Marlins are wearing in today's game were manufactured by New Era Cap of Derby, New York, the official manufacturer of Major League Baseball caps. In fact, the cap that flew off Willie Mays' head was also a New Era. The company has been providing caps to the big leagues since the twenties, and claims among its cap alums Ty Cobb, Rogers Hornsby, and Babe Ruth.

Styles have changed since those stars donned New Era

models, but the cap is still a fitted wool hat—not adjustable, but cut to size—with logos embroidered on the brow and the back. The stylized overlapping NY of Ruth's cap was hand embroidered by a seamstress working from memory. Today, a computerized embroidery machine, working from hard-drive memory, does the work, about 5,000 stitches for the Major League Baseball logo on the back of the hat, up to 35,000 stitches for some of the more complicated team logos.

New Era Cap Co. Inc. was founded in Derby, a city fifteen miles south of Buffalo, in 1920 by Erhardt Koch to manufacture caps for school and Little League teams. New Era is the only company still manufacturing baseball caps in this country. They have four plants: One in Derby, another in Buffalo, and two in Alabama. Major League Baseball caps, in fact, all the company's high-end caps, are manufactured in Derby and cost about $2.80 to make. By the time they reach the retail store that price is around $23. The company's economy line, caps with the adjustable strap (only attractive on someone with a ponytail), are made in Alabama, cost about $1.10 per hat in manufacturing costs and sell for around ten bucks.

The Reds are wearing vest shirts today, one of three official uniforms they wear. The Reds weren't the first team to don vests—the Chicago Cubs wore vest tops in 1942—but the Reds popularized the vest when they brought the style back in 1956. Then-manager Birdie Tebbetts raved to the press about how the design freed the ballplayers' shoulders and arms, but everyone knew the real reason for the change; it was Ted Kluszewski. The Reds first baseman had Paul Bunyanesque biceps—Mark McGwire is the proverbial ninety-eight-pound weakling in contrast—that he liked to flaunt, to give the pitcher something to think about. He did his own shirt surgery, snipping off his uniform sleeves at the top of the shoulder. This was a violation of league rules so, rather than cover up Ted's triceps, the Reds adopted his style, to make all their uniforms uniform.

Like the name says, uniforms are supposed to be uniform, to make everyone on your team stand out from the players on the other team. That's important in football, where a quarterback has to pick his receiver out of a tightly bunched pack, and in basketball, where the player with the ball has a millisecond to decide whether to pass to the player breaking for the goal. In baseball, it's much less important, but it's still the rule.

The first baseball team to adopt uniforms was, not coincidentally, the first team, the New York Knickerbockers. In 1849, they impressed their fans with snappy blue and white cricket-style outfits: blue woolen pantaloons, white flannel shirts and dapper straw hats. They were not true to their name; their uniform pants were not knickers. No team would wear knickerbocker-style pants until 1876, when the Cincinnati Red Stockings took the field in high waters.

Uniform styles weren't at all uniform at first. Different teams, different seams. For example, the Cleveland Blues of 1879 wore shirts and ties!

What set teams apart in the 1870s weren't their uniforms or their hats (on A.G. Spalding's White Sox, every player had a different colored cap), it was the socks—the stockings. After all, many of the teams took their names from their socks: the Boston Red Stockings, the Chicago White Stockings, the Cincinnati Red Stockings. Most teams wore plain wool socks. The White Sox, who considered themselves the league's elite, wore silk stockings. Ooo la la.

Baseball's first color line referred to uniforms. In 1882, the league assigned sock colors by geography: the Boston clubs were designated red; Buffalo received gray as its sock color; Chicago got white; Detroit was assigned old gold; Troy, New York got green; and Worcester, Massachusetts was given blue.

Uniform colors were also assigned in 1882, but not by team. They were determined by position. That's right, by *position*. If you played first base, you wore scarlet and white; if you were a second baseman, your uniform was orange and black. Position colors were supposed to aid neophyte fans in appreciating the game, but the players didn't appreciate the rainbow-hued uniforms, calling them "clown suits," and the experiment was scrapped after that one season.

Uniforms would return to the basics for a couple of decades, until 1901, when the Baltimore owners got the bright idea to outfit their players to match the team nickname. The Orioles road uniform was black with orange highlights. Yes, other teams "crowed" over that birdlike ensemble. No team would look that silly for another fifteen years, when the New York Giants introduced a purple plaid uniform. See, the Houston Astros of the seventies weren't ahead of their time, they were behind it.

It was at about this time, the early years of the twentieth

century, that wool uniforms were supplanted by heavy flannel ones. The suits weren't as hot as they sound; after all, if it keeps out the cold, it keeps out the heat, too. However, the baggy look favored by players at the turn of the century made it appear as if they were playing in their pajamas.

In the century and a half since the Knickerbockers adapted the cricket uniform to baseball, the sport has seen more than 3,000 uniform designs. The most famous, considered the epitome of style and taste, is the Yankees' classic white pinstripes. They weren't the first team to don that style: The Cubs were wearing pinstripes in 1907, and the Yankees' cross-town rival, the Giants, had pinstriped uniforms in 1911, four years before the Yankees adopted them.

For many years, all uniform shirts buttoned up the front (or zipped up the front in the thirties and forties) and pants were hitched up with a belt. Then came the seventies, and the introduction of synthetic fabrics. The Pittsburgh Pirates gave us double-knit, and we don't thank them for it. The Pirates were the first team to use polyester fabric in their uniforms. When the Pirates overhauled their uniforms, they went all the way, scuttling not just flannel fabric but also traditional designs. Their polyester outfits were form-fitted with pullover shirts and elastic waistbands. (No buttons. No belts.) No more baggy uniforms. Of course, they did look like a softball team sponsored by French's mustard.

One thing that did endure over the years was the tradition of teams wearing white at home and gray on the road. Maverick owner Charles O. Finley—the only owner ever to name a mule after himself—changed that in 1962 when his Kansas City Athletics modeled uniforms of "wedding white, kelly green, and Fort Knox gold." That's a fancy description of uniforms that were a hideous green and yellow. (As if playing for the A's in those years weren't insult enough.) The colorful uniforms debuted against the A's frequent trading partners, the New York Yankees (who, at the time, regularly stole hot young players from the A's for washed-up veterans). History records that anytime a decked-out A got within earshot of a Yankee in that game, he was taunted with a blown kiss.

Finley was just ahead of his time, and you know how problematic it is to be too far ahead of the curve. In the seventies, it seemed that all of baseball adopted the "softball look." The Cleveland Indians tried an all-red suit in 1977 that Boog Powell compared to a giant blood clot. The '81 Mariners used that upside-down pitchfork logo that they preferred to call a trident. The uniform everyone remembers, and abhors, belonged to the Houston Astros. For a decade, beginning in 1975, the Astros looked like a brown and gold sunset. When *Sport* magazine picked the worst baseball uniforms of all time in a 2000 issue, the winner—or loser—as everyone expected, was the Astros of '80. I think "Hawaiian pajamas" was the nicest phrase used. The '81 Mariners were a distant second, followed by the '80 Orioles, the '77 Twins, and the '77 Indians.

To put it all in perspective, those brash uniforms were just a part of seventies culture. Remember what regular people were wearing in those years. On second thought, don't remember what regular people were wearing in those years.

The magazine omitted the White Sox's notorious Bermuda shorts uniform of 1976, designed by none other than Mary Frances Veeck, wife of iconoclastic owner Bill Veeck, because they belong in a class of their own.

Veeck is also credited with being the first owner to put names on the backs of uniforms. That's only technically correct: He was the first *baseball* team owner. The NHL's New York Americans briefly tried the experiment in the '30s. Veeck, claiming he did it for the TV cameras, put names on the shoulders of his 1960 White Sox. Later that year, several teams in the fledgling American Football League followed suit.

Fears of lower scorecard sales held other baseball teams back for a time but, as other sports picked up on the idea, baseball teams fell in line. Today, names are required on jerseys in the NBA, the NFL, and the NHL. Only baseball has no rule about the practice. Still, twenty-eight of thirty big-league clubs have names on jerseys. Only the Giants, and, of course, the tradition-bound Yankees are holdouts.

The Reds and the Marlins are a study in contrasts, the Reds in their traditional white vests, the Marlins, an upstart team that only joined the league in 1993, wearing trendy teal and black.

If you could somehow put those '56 Reds on the field today, next to their modern counterparts, the contrast would be even greater. The old Reds in baggy pants and billowing jerseys, the modern Reds in sleek, form-fitting outfits; the old Reds looking strictly off the rack, the modern Reds tailored.

That's because today's Reds *are* tailored. In the fifties, teams used tailors to repair torn seats and ripped sleeves. Today, tailors arrive in spring training to custom fit jerseys and pants. Almost 80 percent of big leaguers require tailoring on their uniform pants (20 percent require alterations on their uniform shirts) and the companies that supply the majors—Russell Athletic and Rawlings among them—send tailors around during spring training to poke and prod and measure and mend.

There's almost a formula to the tailoring. Center fielders want tight pants, to cut down on wind resistance when they chase down flies. Third basemen need a roomier crotch because of the protective cup they wear (in case a hard-hit grounder takes an inopportune hop). First basemen want their uniforms baggier than average because of all the moving they do around the bag, stretching for throws. And catchers, they're vain. They wanted squared-off shirt tails in case theirs pull out; that way they won't look unkempt. (Catchers also need a roomy crotch, for obvious and potentially painful reasons. Pitchers need more room in the shoulder of their throwing arm. They don't want the uniform binding when they start their delivery or when they finish.)

Speed merchants, the guys who steal a lot of bases, want a tighter fit to cut through the wind and pick up those milliseconds that could be the difference between being called out and being called safe.

Today's uniform fabrics are a great improvement over

the wools and flannels of the past. They are more comfortable, more carefree and more durable. That last part is especially important, since the equipment manager washes uniforms after every game.

What happens when a player is traded? The uniform companies hustle. All three promise a forty-eight-hour turnaround for a traded player. If the player makes it to his new team faster than that, he crosses his fingers and hopes the equipment manager has an extra uniform in his size.

Why all the fuss about uniforms? I mean, they're just uniforms. Everybody else on the team wears the same outfit. It's spelled out in baseball's rules: Uniforms must have the same "color, trim, and style," including the same length sleeves and the same size numerals on the back (six inches tall). Why the press conferences to announce a new uniform design or a new team logo?

Here's baseball's official explanation for changing uniform and logo design: It generates fan interest and keeps the team fresh in the fans' eyes.

Here's the real reason: $$$.

When the Seattle Mariners changed in 1993 from their drab blue-and-gold jerseys with the unimaginative M logo to the stylish "Northwest green and ocean blue compass," sales of caps and jerseys at the stadium tripled, from $372,000 in '92 to $1.1 million in '93. Between 1996 and 1999 the New York Mets phased in two new black game jerseys and fans responded by purchasing twice as much Mets apparel. As the *Washington Post* put it in 1999: "Planned obsolescence of uniforms has become a tool for goosing profits, turning the tradition of having just home and away uniforms into a relic."

And buying the latest apparel of your favorite team is as much a part of baseball as labor strife.

There are two types of licensed caps and shirts out there for your consideration: authentic and replica. What's the difference? About ten dollars when it comes to caps; more than one hundred dollars for jerseys.

Authentic apparel is exactly like what the big leaguers wear. Replica apparel offers the same logos and designs but is made from less-expensive fabrics and features lower-grade craftsmanship. Die-hard fans buy the high-end authentic stuff; more casual fans purchase replica stuff. Authentic merchandise accounts for about 10 percent of big-league apparel sales.

This new uniform, new cap, new logo stuff was getting out of hand for a while; even the least cynical saw it as a ploy to sell stuff. So, the leagues stepped in to stem the tide. NHL teams can change uniforms only every three years. For NBA teams it's every four years. In the NFL teams have to ask for league permission eighteen months in advance, assuring uniforms will last a couple of seasons. Only baseball allows teams to change uniform design at will.

The uniforms the Reds are wearing today have a classic look: the vest, the stirrup pants. To me, they look like the outfits they were wearing the first time I saw the team, back in 1959. But there are differences, albeit subtle ones. Even a tradition-bound team like the Reds make occasional uniform-design changes.

How do baseball teams change their uniform design? It's not just a couple of guys, sitting in a room, saying, "Looks good to me." Most teams call in baseball's in-house expert, Anne Occi, the vice president of design services for Major League Baseball. Occi, an art-school graduate, makes suggestions on everything from colors to materials.

She was responsible for the Mariners' understated compass logo that made its debut in 1993. Earlier, the team's hats boasted a less-than-compelling M, which could have worked generically for Milwaukee, Montreal, or any other M town, even Moscow. She settled on the compass, she says, because a mariner works on the water and people in the Seattle area are outdoor oriented.

She also helped the Marlins, today's opponent, when they joined the league in 1993, recommending teal as the predominant uniform color, not because it was trendy, but because it fit: Florida's waters are teal and the team's namesake, the marlin, has teal shadings.

She helped Baltimore change its insignia from a cartoon oriole to a bird to be taken seriously.

The Reds sought her advice when they updated their uniforms in 1999, although she admits the Reds don't make big changes. "They stay pretty close to what they have. I've assisted them with updates where we've gone in and fine-honed the original work."

Her advice was simple. "We added a black-drop shadow to the letters that pops them out when you look at them."

After Occi's input comes the litmus test: Volunteers, usually front-office employees, don the mock-up uniforms and stand on the field to see how the new designs look in natural light, how they look in artificial light, how they look on television, and how they look on the stadium's big-screen television. How about in photographs? Do they look good from the box seats and from the bleacher seats? Do the new logos show up or do they blend in?

This uniform design stuff is important, at least for bragging rights, if not for extra money. When the White Sox changed from red, white, and blue uniforms to black, white, and silver in 1991 (shortly before Occi joined Major League Baseball), their licensed merchandise jumped from eighteenth most popular among big-league apparel to second (behind the Colorado Rockies). They didn't get any extra dough—Major League Baseball Properties divvies up the royalties equally among all thirty major-league teams—but they walked a little taller knowing they were second in something.

Occi's design input is valuable for another reason: She knows about fabric durability and the tensile strength of various threads. She advised one team against using metallic thread because it is brittle and could break. And, as she said, "When a player slides, you don't want his uniform falling apart."

Chapter Ten

Get Your Beer Here!

It wasn't that long ago, maybe twenty years, that I would be at the ballpark and notice that people around me were standing up. "What's going on?" I'd think. Then I'd look at the scoreboard. Oh, yeah, it's the seventh-inning stretch.

It was possible then to stay seated and catch up on your scorecard during the seventh-inning stretch, uninterrupted and undistracted. Today, it's impossible. You might as well give in, stand up and sing.

It's the middle of the seventh now, so, prompted by the scoreboard and the drunks around us, Will and I stand up and join in the singalong.

This singing of "Take Me Out to the Ball Game" is a recent development, and I blame cable television.

In particular I blame WGN, the superstation. The Chicago TV station brought Cubs baseball and, with it, the singing voice of Harry Caray, to millions of American homes. Instead of breaking away for commercials, WGN would uncharacteristically stay at the park after the visitor's half of the seventh, the camera would zoom in on the announcer's booth, and a bigheaded man of dubious sobriety would stick his face, his thick glasses and his microphone out: "All right . . . let me hear ya! A one, a two . . ."

Then, in a hoarse, alcohol-fortified voice that could sink a ship, Caray would lead the assembled throng, many of them equally bombed, in an off-key and out-of-sync version of baseball's national anthem, "Take Me Out to the Ball Game."

Harry Caray and his signature tune weren't always synonymous, though. He never led fans in the song during his twenty-five years as announcer for the St. Louis Cardinals. He got the boot from team owner August A. Busch III in 1969, supposedly because he was having an affair with Busch's wife. Though Caray eventually denied the affair, he later explained why he didn't comment on the rumors at the time: "Half of St. Louis and nearly the entire National League thought that no young, beautiful woman could resist my charms. If you were me, would you have denied rumors like that? Hell, no."

After a year in purgatory, er, working for Charlie Finley's Oakland A's, the White Sox hired Caray to do radio work in 1970. He was about to be fired in Chicago when a fortunate thing happened; the Sox were sold by straitlaced John Allyn, who didn't like Caray criticizing players, to maverick owner Bill Veeck, who did, and he retained Caray. From his years in St. Louis as Browns owner, Veeck knew that Caray often sang the ditty in the broadcast booth. Early in 1971, he secretly fed the radio signal over the public address system for all of Comiskey Park to hear.

It was a hit with the fans, who sang along, and soon it was a regular seventh-inning feature. Veeck told Caray, "The fans like singing with you, because they know they can sing better than you."

Caray moved from the Southside to the Northside for the 1982 season, joining the Cubs, where the Bleacher Bums adopted him as their own. He already was their kind of guy, regularly meeting his fans in Rush Street pubs. With the arrival of cable television came the appearance in America's living rooms of Caray's singing, and an institution was born.

Harry Caray practically lived at the ballpark, broadcasting 180 games a year for fifty-three years; Jack Norworth never saw a baseball game until he was sixty-one. And yet, the two are linked forever by the game. It was Norworth who wrote Caray's favorite song, "Take Me Out to the Ball Game."

The year was 1908 and the then-twenty-nine-year-old vaudevillian was riding the elevated train into Manhattan when he was intrigued by a placard on a station wall: "Base Ball Today—Polo Grounds." The New York Giants, led by Christy Mathewson, were in the thick of a pennant race with Pittsburgh and Chicago, and all of New York had baseball fever.

The year before, Norworth and his wife, the songbird Nora Bayes, had had much success with a song they co-authored, "Shine on Harvest Moon," and Gentleman Jack, as he was known, was anxious for another hit. The sign gave him an idea, and he began scribbling away a story song he would call "Katie Casey Was Baseball Mad."

> *Katie Casey was baseball mad,*
> *Had the fever and had it bad:*
> *Just to root for the hometown crew,*
> *Every song Katie blew.*
> *On a Saturday, her young beau*
> *Called to see if she'd like to go*
> *To see a show but Miss Kate said,*
> *"No, I'll tell you what you can do."*

That's the part of the song no one sings. Then comes that famous chorus:

> *Take me out to the ball game,*
> *Take me out with the crowd,*
> *Buy me some peanuts and Cracker Jack,*
> *I don't care if I never get back.*
> *Let me root, root, root for the home team,*
> *If they don't win it's a shame,*
> *For it's one, two, three strikes you're out*
> *At the old ball game.*

Norworth still had a few stops to go, so he kept composing.

> *Katie Casey saw all the games,*
> *Knew the players by their first names;*
> *Told the umpire he was wrong,*
> *All along, good and strong.*
> *When the score was just two to two,*
> *Katie Casey knew what to do.*
> *Just to cheer up the boys she knew,*
> *She made the gang sing this song:*

You know what comes next—the chorus again.

It took Norworth all of half an hour to scrawl the lyrics on a piece of scrap paper (now enshrined at baseball's Hall of Fame in Cooperstown). Even though he had never been to a major-league game, he obviously had some familiarity with the sport, enough to know it was three strikes to an out.

Husky-throated Caray made the song a part of ballpark culture but Norworth wrote it for the female voice. Witness that the famous chorus is Katie Casey's rebuke to her beau that she wants a day out at the ballpark rather than the theater.

Norworth had collaborated with the composer Albert von Tilzer since 1906 on such classics as "Good Evening Caroline," "I'm Glad I'm Married," and "Bessie and Her Little Brown Bear," so it was only natural that he should take his poem to his friend for the music. After all, von Tilzer had never seen a baseball game either. Von Tilzer came up with a waltz melody and Norworth turned it over to his wife who introduced the song in Florenz Ziegfeld's *Follies of 1908*. It was an instant sensation onstage, although it didn't seem to get much attention in the outside world. Edward Meeker's oom-pah-pah version of the tune for Thomas Edison's National Phonograph Company was a flop. The song began to catch on when nickelodeon movie theaters started using it for singalongs, flashing the words on the screen, and, by Opening Day 1910, it was a ball-park standard.

Almost a century later, "Take Me Out to the Ball Game" is the third most frequently sung musical composition in the United States, behind "Happy Birthday" and "The Star-Spangled Banner." Every major-league park except Baltimore and Toronto incorporates the song into the seventh-inning stretch. (Baltimore's seventh-inning song is "Thank God I'm a Country Boy" recorded by John Denver, and Toronto uses "O.K. Blue Jays.")

Von Tilzer finally made it to a game in 1928, but it would be 1940 before Norworth finally showed up at a ballpark. He was honored at a Brooklyn Dodgers game and, when asked how he liked this game of baseball, he replied, "Not bad. The peanuts were good, too."

Norworth was frequently criticized for having written the song without ever seeing a game. His response, according to Carl Sifakis in the book *Three Men on Third,* was measured: "Harry William wrote 'In the Shade of the Old Apple Tree,' and I am sure he never saw a blade of grass. If he ever got three blocks off 26th Street in Manhattan, it was a great occasion."

The beer men are hustling up and down the aisles this inning; it's last call for alcohol. The Reds, and other major-league teams, cut off sales of beer after the seventh inning. They don't want fans driving home drunk, and they don't want to be sued for getting them drunk.

Our beer man is a roundish, thirtyish fellow who has grown progressively more brash as the game has progressed. Now he stands at the fence, faces the crowd, and begins his pitch: "Ice coooooooooooooooooold beer!" He holds that "cold" note for a full thirty seconds, and the crowd applauds him for it.

Bill Douglas has been selling beer at the stadium since 1989. Of all the beer men I've heard over the years, and I've heard many of them, his signature call is the most striking, and the most appealing. It has an operatic quality to it, and the way he holds a beer bottle out emphasizes the connection. He's like a poster for "The Beer Man of Seville."

It's not an easy job, hustling a 30-pound tray of beer up and down stairs for two hours, but Douglas says he plans to do it as long as his back and knees hold up.

And he'll be a success as long as his singing voice holds out. How did he come up with his unique beer call? He says he can't pinpoint any one factor that shaped his style. "It just developed over the years."

Does it help sales, does it help tips? "Oh yeah."

Every stadium seems to have its famous beer man. In Baltimore it's Danny Hahn, the "whoo whoo" man the *Wall Street Journal* calls "king of the beer men." In Minneapolis it's Wally the Beerman, Wallace McNeil, with his "Coldbeerhere! Coldbeerhere!" And, in Cincinnati, it's Opera Bill, Bill Douglas, and his drawn out "Ice cooooooooooooooooooold beer."

Beer men agree on two things: to sell beer you need a loud voice and a little salesmanship. Combine those two qualities and you can turn an extra fifteen grand a year in, well, beer money.

According to a 1999 study in *The Journal of Political Economy*, beer vendors are overwhelmingly young and male, and the reason is simple. You have to be in good shape to spend three hours walking up and down stairs hauling a beer tray that can weigh upwards of fifty pounds when full.

While you and I are still at home, deciding on our stadium attire, the beer men are already at the park, picking product and section. This is done at most parks by seniority. If you have been around a decade, like Bill Douglas, you get beer in the box seats. If you're new, you might get hot coffee on a muggy afternoon in the upper deck. The senior vendors always want the beer concession. The junior vendors may sell coffee one game, popcorn the next, depending on who shows up.

Vendors are independent contractors, not employees of the Reds or their concessionaire, Sportservice. Vendor wages vary from game to game and from team to team, and all vendors have other jobs: Wally works for a pharmaceutical company, Danny is employed by Legal Aid.

They make their money on commissions, anywhere from 10 to 20 percent. So, that $4.75 beer I bought from Douglas nets him about 80 cents. Wally the Beerman has sold as many as 660 two-dollar beers at one game—that's the Twins record—earning him almost $250.

For beer guys, it's constant movement. The national anthem is the only opportunity they have to stop and they seldom get a chance to watch the game. Douglas says he catches the team on television when they're on the road.

Gerald S. Oettinger of the University of Texas at Austin has done the only research into Major League Baseball concession vendors. He studied all 127 vendors for the entire 1996 season at an unnamed stadium (which, we can assume, was one of the two Texas big-league stadiums), and his report in a 1999 edition of *The Journal of Political Economy* found the highest-earning vendors had average earnings of more than $100 per game, but the earnings fluctuated wildly. The average vendor earned only $43 per game, and a few averaged only $26 per game.

Earnings were lower, by about 30 percent at weekday night games and higher, by about 15 percent, on promotional dates. When he held attendance constant, Oettinger found earnings were 11 percent higher at Saturday night games. By way of explanation, he theorized that, "This might reflect that any given individual spends more on a Saturday night (or) that high spenders are a larger fraction of the crowd on Saturday nights."

I still find beer vendors fascinating. I grew up in the alcohol-free environs of the Bible Belt, so my first baseball game in 1959 was an eye-opener for more than just the game. I was struck by beer: Beer was everywhere, sloshing in cups, foaming in bottles, spilling out of cans. I knew about beer from television, but my parents didn't drink. In the South at that time, it was a behind-closed-doors event. Redneck was not yet a term of endearment.

So, here were guys walking up and down the stadium aisles, lugging wire baskets of brews and demanding your attention with their cries. My favorites were at Griffith Park in Washington, D.C.: "Get your beeeah heeeah!"

Those guys remained my picks for number one until I met Bill Douglas. Opera Bill is the best.

Baseball and beer seem like a natural combination, but it wasn't always so. In fact, the Reds are the reason that fans can buy a beer at the stadium today.

The club was virtually broke in 1880, so the team rented

out its park, Avenue Grounds on Spring Grove Avenue, to semipro teams on days the Reds weren't playing. Beer was sold at those nonleague games and the Reds profited handsomely. When word got around the fledgling National League that beer was being served in a league park, the fur started flying. In October of that year, at a special league meeting, the other seven clubs in a puritanical frenzy voted to prohibit the sale of alcoholic beverages at league parks at any time, even at nonleague games. When the Reds refused to abide by the rule, the team was expelled.

Oh, it wasn't as big a deal as contraction is today. The league had already lost five of its eight founding teams since the initial season of 1876. Philadelphia and New York had been booted for not completing their 1876 schedule and Hartford, Louisville, and the St. Louis Brown Stockings left after the 1877 season in the wake of a game-fixing scandal. The Cincinnati team expelled for its loose morals in 1880 wasn't even the original Reds National League club; that one had disbanded for financial reasons after the 1879 season.

The disenfranchised Reds helped form the new American Association in 1882, a league known around the country as the beer-and-whiskey league because it allowed, even encouraged, beer sales at games. By the time the American Association broke up in 1891, National League clubs were selling beer in their parks.

Beer is by far the most popular concession item at the ballpark. When the 2001 season opened, Sportservice tallied up the items it expected to sell on opening day at the seven stadiums it serviced. Number one, in number of items sold, was beer. The company said its vendors would sell more than a quarter of a million cups of brew.

Here's how Opening Day food items ranked in popularity:

272,415 cups of beer
105,000 hot dogs
101,450 cups of soft drink
37,477 grilled sausages
32,100 servings of nachos
21,165 one-pound bags of peanuts
17,390 orders of French fries
16,611 bags of popcorn
15,000 slices of pizza
12,347 hamburgers

Baseball and beer are so closely identified that it's easy to forget that vendors are marching up and down the aisles selling other products, too. Beer outsells soft drinks by more than two to one. Sportservice, sells about 38,916 cups of beer at a Cinergy Field sellout. At that same game, the vendors will sell only 14,492 cups of soda.

I bought a 24-ounce diet soda when we arrived, and it was gone by the National Anthem. That's a big drink, it's not that hot at the park, and I wasn't that dry, so I performed an experiment: I bought another one, poured the drink into a cup and measured it. A 24-ounce drink is really a 16-ounce drink and eight ounces of ice. I did the same experiment with a 16-ounce drink and found it has only 8 ounces of soda.

• • •

Concessions are big business for baseball. The Reds average $136,000 at the concession stands per game, about $11 million for the season. That will buy you a couple of second basemen. Cinergy Field, built in the days before scientific marketing, is actually underconcessioned.

Stadium designers recommend parks have one concession window for every 180 fans—Cincinnati's yard, with 18 concessions stands, has a 1-to-300 ratio. The new park, the Great American Ballpark, will have 28 concession stands, each serving 190 spectators.

Concession items are reasonable at Cinergy Field. Beer is slightly higher than the league average, according to the 2002 Team Marketing Report. Reds fans pay $5.25; the league average for a 20-ounce brewski is $4.82. Soft drinks are cheaper, $2.25 for a 16-ounce pop, versus the league average of $2.45. A hot dog is only $1.75. Fans around the league pay an average of $2.72 for a wiener.

Even nonfood items are cheaper: a program is $3.50; the league average is $4.13. A souvenir cap is $10, less than the league average of $12.67.

Even though Jack Norworth neglected to mention hot dogs in "Take Me Out to the Ball Game," the lowly frankfurter is the most popular food item at the ballpark, way ahead of peanuts and Cracker Jacks.

Here are ballpark food items in order of popularity at the seven ballparks served by Sportservice (including Cinergy Field):

1. Hot dogs
2. Sausages
3. Nachos
4. Peanuts
5. French fries
6. Popcorn
7. Pizza
8. Hamburgers

At an average major-league baseball game in a Sportservice park, fans buy:

22,000 hot dogs
6,500 sausages
4,500 servings of nachos
3,300 one-pound bags of peanuts
2,400 slices of pizza
1,700 orders of French fries
1,300 bags of popcorn
1,000 hamburgers

Major League Baseball fans scarf down 26 million hot dogs at the park over the course of a season. The top dog in 2002 when it came to hot-dog consumption was Dodger Stadium, where Dodger fans chowed down on 1.5 million dogs, topping Cleveland's Jacobs Field, where fans downed a mere 1.1 million. Cincinnati's Cinergy Field doesn't even rank in baseball's top ten of hot-dog eaters.

.   .   .

Some credit the original baseball concessionaire, Harry M. Stevens, with putting the lowly frankfurter on a bun and creating the hot dog, shortly after he moved to New York in 1895 and won the scorecard and food concessions at the Polo Grounds. Others credit St. Louis saloon keep Chris Von der Ahe, who owned the Browns and introduced sausages to Sportsman's Park as a sop for his beer.

Actually, sausage had been around since the time of Homer—that would be Homer the Greek poet, not Homer the Geek Simpson. Homer (900 B.C.) was an early fan of ground meat, writing in the *Odyssey*, "When a man beside a great fire has filled a sausage with fat and blood and turns it this way and that and is very eager to get it quickly roasted."

The sausage we call the hot dog traces its lineage to the Middle Ages, 1484 to be specific, according to the folks in Frankfurt, Germany, who claim to have invented the little fellow, and celebrated its 500th birthday in 1984. The people in Vienna, Austria say they invented it; witness the name, *wiener*, Austrian slang for someone or something Viennese. There's even a story that a butcher from Coburg named Johann Geurghehner created an elongated sausage that some thought resembled a dachshund in the 1600s. It came to be known as the dachshund sausage. He promoted it in Frankfurt, thus another name, frankfurter.

See where we're going here?

We don't know who invented the long sausage, but it was probably created in the Germanic states sometime before the Pilgrims arrived on these shores. During the Civil War, German immigrants to the United States began placing dachshund sausages in buns with mustard and sauerkraut, and selling them from carts on the streets of New York City. We are reasonably sure that the German butcher Charles Feltman first sold wieners, soon to be known as Coney Dogs, on Coney Island in 1871.

So, Harry M. Stevens didn't invent the hot dog, but one account has it that his red hots gave the hot dog its name. The story goes like this: In 1901, *New York Evening Journal* cartoonist and columnist Tad Dorgan, famous for his dog cartoons, sketched a dachshund stuck in a bun to spoof Stevens' Polo Grounds vendors, who roamed the crowd shouting, "Get your red hot dachshunds!" But spelling wasn't Dorgan's forte—he didn't know how to spell *dachshund*—so he captioned the drawing "Hot dogs!"

No one has ever found that cartoon, and the truth is the name *hot dog* had been in general usage for at least a half dozen years by 1901. The Yale student newspaper used the term *hot dog* to refer to sausage in a bun in 1895. Stevens *did* popularize the drinking straw, handing them out at the park with soda pop, enabling fans to sip their drink and never take their eyes off the game, and he did add peanuts to the ballpark menu. That was in 1895, when Cavagnaros Peanuts, a New York peanut vendor, couldn't pay for its ad in the Giants program and traded product for the ad. Stevens sold the peanuts at the park and, according to *Amusement Business* magazine, this was the origin of the phrase "working for peanuts."

. . .

What exactly is this hot dog we so love at the park? There's a legal definition from the U.S. Department of Agriculture and it's not pretty: "Hot dogs are comminuted, semisolid products made from one or more kinds of raw skeletal muscle from livestock [like beef or pork] and may contain poultry meat." Ugh. That doesn't sound appetizing. A comminuted—that means powdered or pulverized—semisolid of raw skeletal muscle. (Shiver.)

The definition continues: "Smoking and curing ingredients contribute to flavor, color, and preservation of the product. They are link-shaped and come in all sizes , . Water or ice, or both, may be used to facilitate chopping or mixing or to dissolve curing ingredients. The finished products may not contain more than 30 percent fat or no more than 10 percent water, or a combination of 40 percent fat and added water. Up to 3.5 percent non-meat binders and extenders (such as nonfat dry milk, cereal or dried whole milk) or 2 percent isolated soy protein may be used, but must be shown in the ingredients statement on the product's label by its common name."

So, that dog may only be 56.5 percent meat, the rest being fat, water, and cereal. Yum yum.

Harry M. Stevens' company is no longer around. It was sold in 1995 to Aramark, one of six concession companies serving major-league baseball stadiums. Aramark had contracts with thirteen teams in 2002, making it the largest baseball concessionaire. Sportservice and Volume Services tied for second with seven teams each. Prodine, Fine Host, and Olympia each serve one team.

Sportservice is my host today at Cinergy: I've already given them $21.75 ($8 for two soft drinks for me, $5 for Will's nachos, $3.50 for my peanuts—I have to have peanuts at a baseball game (more on that later), $3 for Will's bottled water and $2.25 for his hot dog). That would qualify me as a big spender. The average baseball fan spends about $7.46 on food and drink per game. I should be up in one of the luxury suites. Those fans spend an average of $30 per game on food and drink, according to the *Wall Street Journal*.

With the sale of Harry M. Stevens to Aramark, Sportservice becomes the oldest baseball concessionaire. The company was founded in 1915, in Buffalo, by the Jacobs brothers, Marvin, Charles and Louis, to sell peanuts and popcorn at a local movie theater. They got into the stadium game in 1927, when Louis landed the concessions franchise for Detroit's Navin Field. Legend credits the company's expansion to other parks to an episode of honesty by Louis Jacobs, who, after a particularly profitable first year, shared the wealth, presenting Tigers owner Frank Navin with a bonus check for $12,500, and telling him, according to Amusement Business, "You had a bad contract. We made a lot more money than we expected—a lot more than is fair to you. You're entitled to this share of our profits." Navin spread the word and, soon, Sportservice was the concessions contractor in other stadiums.

· · ·

Will says the Sportservice dog is a good one and he's a hot-dog connoisseur. However, it's missing something, and he heads to the concourse to add that special ingredient: mustard.

A hot dog is not a hot dog without a condiment, and the condiment of choice at the ballpark is mustard. In a 2002 poll by the National Hot Dog and Sausage Council, 30 percent of adults chose mustard as their favorite hot-dog topping. Ketchup finished second with 22 percent of the vote, followed by chili with 12 percent, and relish with 10 percent.

Mustard didn't begin as a sausage condiment. It was a curative, back in the days when leeches were on the, ahem, bleeding edge, of medical knowledge. Mustard was the aspirin of its day, its day running from 3000 B.C. to a couple of weeks ago. Actually, mustard plasters are still used medicinally in many cultures and, over the years, mustard paste has been used as an anti-inflammatory, a digestive aid, a laxative, a diuretic, a decongestant, an irritant, and an emetic. Its medicinal claims included preventing frostbite, stopping toothache, and curing the common cold. Pythagoras recommended it as a cure for scorpion bites. It was a long time before anyone figured out it's damned good on a hot dog. Of course, someone had to invent the hot dog and that didn't happen until well into mustard's career as a food.

The plant, a leafy bush that can grow up to four feet tall, was first cultivated in India around 3000 B.C., and was brought to Britain by the Romans, but none of those cultures used it as a condiment. That innovation was left to

French monks in the ninth century, who earned almost as much from selling mustard preparations as from passing the offering plate. By the thirteenth century mustard was a staple of Paris saucemakers, who peddled the product on the street every evening around dinnertime. We don't know who first combined mustard paste and long sausages in a bun, but we thank him (or her) for it.

Mustard is relatively easy to make, provided you have some mustard seeds. The tiny kernels—a quarter million weigh a pound—are crushed into a powder, then mixed with a liquid, either vinegar, wine, beer, or water, and combined with spices. Check the label to see what your favorite mustard is made from. French's, for instance, is made from vinegar, water, mustard seed, salt, turmeric, paprika, spice, garlic and the ever-popular "natural flavor." The pungency of the blend depends on the type of mustard seed used. White seeds are relatively mild; brown or Oriental seeds are strong.

I've been resisting all afternoon. After all, I've already dropped a twenty on food, none of which qualifies as dinner. That'll be another twenty on the way home, but I have to get a bag. Peanuts are my number one ballpark treat, though popcorn is a close second.

The hot dog comes from Germany; beer from Egypt; peanuts from Brazil, nachos from Mexico; French fries from, well, Belgium. Of all the ballpark favorites, only popcorn is truly all-American. The oldest known popped kernels, dating to 2000 B.C., were found at a site in Bat Cave, New Mexico in 1948. Aztecs called this corn *momo-*

chitl—thank God that name didn't stick—and demonstrated its popping quality to the Spaniards who thought it "a very white flower."

Popcorn was strictly a southwestern delicacy until the 1820s, when street vendors began selling it in northern cities. After the Civil War, popcorn became a popular treat at ballparks and fairs. Charles Cretors of Chicago invented a steam-powered popcorn roaster that he mounted on a wagon and took to the 1893 Colombian Exposition, where it became a sensation. He sold hundreds of them to street vendors and grocers, and popcorn became a staple of the American ballpark diet.

Popcorn, like television, is one of the mysteries of life. How does a hard little kernel burst into a soft flaky treat? Popcorn is known to scientists as *Zea mays everta:* On the outside it's hard and dry, but inside the kernel has just enough moisture to transform into steam once it's heated The steam expands, bursting the hard coat and, literally, turning itself inside out, into a white, starchy bloom.

It was a wonderful salty treat but there was still room for improvement. Enter another Chicagoan, Fred Rueckheim. The German immigrant, who arrived in the city in 1871 and opened a popcorn shop, didn't invent molasses-coated popcorn; popcorn balls using molasses or maple syrup had been a delicacy since the 1840s. Rueckheim's contribution was bagging this candy-coated popcorn in combination with candy-coated peanuts. He sold it out of his shop to no great acclaim. Then, came the Chicago Colombian Exposition in 1893. He set up a stand and sold his little treat under the breathtakingly original name "Candied Popcorn and Peanuts," and visitors gobbled it up. Just one problem, the customers said: It all glopped together. In 1896, Fred's brother Louis came up with a secret method of keeping the molasses-coated popcorn and peanuts from sticking together and the Rueckheims were on their way. The company would later replace the molasses with caramel, but preserved the method for preventing the glop. It still worked, it's still used today, and it's still a secret.

Something was still missing from this concoction—a catchy name. That came that same year that Louis offered some to a friend who took a bite and exclaimed, "That's a cracker jack!" Fred recognized a good thing and trademarked the words.

And thus was born Cracker Jack. Not Cracker Jacks; not plural. It's singular. Check the box if you don't believe me, or turn back a few pages and check the original lyrics to "Take Me Out to the Ball Game." Cracker *Jack*.

In 1912, Fred Rueckheim made another contribution to the brand, adding prizes to the box and, six years later, he supervised the creation of the sailor boy and his dog logo. That's Sailor Jack and Bingo, one of the most recognizable logos in America among adults. Kids just think Jack and the dog are weird.

Cracker Jack is a staple on ballpark menus but, the fact is, it's not a big seller. It doesn't rank in the top-ten food items at Cinergy or any of the other six Sportservice major-league ballparks. Aramark ranks it fifth in popularity among food items at its thirteen ballparks, just barely topping burgers.

The number one complaint about Cracker Jack? According to Frito-Lay, which now owns the brand, "Not enough peanuts." In fact it's almost a joke at the company, because the first thing Frito-Lay did after buying Cracker Jack from Borden was add 10 percent more peanuts.

The number two complaint: inferior prizes. This, too, is something of a Frito-Lay joke since the company reintroduced three-dimensional prizes in 1998.

The number three complaint: All the peanuts sink to the bottom. True. Unfortunately, Frito-Lay has no solution.

Even if caramel-coated popcorn were to suddenly come back in vogue, the outlook for Cracker Jack is not good. In a 2001 blind taste test of six commercial brands of caramel popcorn by the *Detroit News*, Cracker Jack finished tied for fourth, with the aptly named Poppycock.

Of the four panelists, two complained, "Not enough peanuts."

Chapter Eleven

Heckle the Ump

It's 5–4 in the top of the eighth, and though the Reds are still in it, the Marlins are threatening to blow the game open. After Mike Lowell reaches first on catcher's interference and Derek Lee doubles to deep, deep left, Bob Boone has seen enough, and replaces Gabe White with Carlos Almanzar.

As Almanzar warms up, second baseman Todd Walker and second-base umpire Kerwin Danley appear to be having a friendly conversation about the interference call, with Danley feigning what catcher Miller did to get the call—but you won't find them sharing drinks in the hotel lobby later. There may be a little on-field camaraderie but, when the game is over, they go their separate ways.

Like the policeman in *The Pirates of Penzance*, the umpire's lot is not a happy one, and never has been. Atlanta newspaper columnist Furman Bisher once described the umpire as "submerged in the history of baseball like idiot children in a family album."

Umpires didn't start out that way. The first recorded umpire was attorney William R. Wheaton, who officiated a

Knickerbockers club intramural game on October 6, 1845. The only record we have of that game is the scorebook Wheaton kept, but we can assume the umpire was treated with respect. It was a gentleman's game and, besides, he was vice president of the club. But things were soon to get testy as more ungentlemanly types took up the game. Club matches soon required three umpires, one chosen by each club and a third neutral party, presumably to cast the tie-breaking vote when the two partisans disagreed.

Early umpires were not yet the "men in blue." Prints from the time show umpires in top hats, with canes and formal coats, standing or sitting on a stool in foul territory near first base. They umpired for the honor of it.

It would be more than three decades before umpires became true professionals. It wasn't until 1878 that the National League of Professional Base Ball Clubs required the home club to pay the umpire. Remuneration was a handsome five dollars per game, about eighty in today's dollars. Not bad for an afternoon's work. Until you find out about the work. What started as a gentleman's game had devolved into a public scrum, particularly where the umpire was involved. Ernest Thayer didn't invent the epithet "Kill him! Kill the umpire!" for his 1888 poem "Casey at the Bat." Umpire-baiting was blood sport for fans, and team owners even encouraged it, thinking it boosted attendance.

Insults were the least of it. Umpires were targets of spitballs, spikes, even assorted missiles. Umpires were supposed to be the ultimate authority at the game—in 1879, they were given the right to fine players—but team owners seldom supported their decisions, and even paid player fines. No more the gentleman ump. It was a combative era and umpires were a part of the mix. They yelled back, threw things back into the stands, even got in fights with fans and players. "Rough and tumble" is the phrase you're thinking of.

But at least umpires were paid. And the following year, 1879, the fledgling American Association assembled an entire staff of professional umpires, paid and assigned by the league office. Pay was pretty good: $140 a month (about $2,500 today) with $3 a day for expenses. One of those expenses was a uniform. The league required its umps to wear blue flannel coats and caps. And thus was born umpires' permanent nickname, the men in blue.

But gentlemen were gone from the game. It was now a rough and rowdy sport and umpires were routinely spiked, kicked, and cursed by players—was Billy Martin active back then?—and baited, harassed, even mobbed by fans. Owners seldom supported the umpires. It was better for business to let the fans and players have their way.

Enter Ban Johnson. Appointed president of the upstart Western League in 1894, the former Cincinnati sportswriter set out to clean up the game, instructing his umpires to crack down on the rowdies. The result was an increase in respect for the umpire and a corresponding increase in attendance. Where once a player might defy an umpire's ejection, Johnson's umps had the full backing of the league and could enforce their discipline. When the Western League changed its name to the American League in 1899 and moved up to major-league status, Johnson's ways were copied by the National League. By the Babe Ruth era, umpires enjoyed respect, authority, and dignity. American League umpire Clarence "Pants" Rowland paid Johnson tribute, saying, "All umpires ought to tip their hats whenever Ban Johnson's name is mentioned."

Two umpiring styles had evolved to handle this rough-and-tumble nineteenth-century game. Robert Vavasour Ferguson, known during his days playing outfield for the Brooklyn Atlantics as "Death to Flying Things," typified the dictatorial style. He made the call, the call stood. It should be no surprise then that his other nickname was Fighting Bob. John Gaffney, one of the first to shift from behind the plate to the field when a runner reached base, typified the other style. He preferred using diplomacy to maintain order on the field.

When the National League and the new American League made their peace in 1903 it was Gaffney's style that eventually won out, at the insistence of American League president Ban Johnson, who wanted his umpires respected.

It was quite a bit to expect of one man, to run the game and keep everyone happy, and Johnson knew it. He pushed his owners to employ two umps per game—that option had been sanctioned by the rule book in 1898—and, by 1912, both leagues were using the system. During the twenties, the league office would assign one of its reserve umpires to a critical game or series and, by 1933, three umpires were the norm. The leagues went to the four-man umpiring crew in 1952.

Gradually, as pay increased, umpiring became a profession, not an avocation. In 1910, top major-league umps

were making $3,000 annually, which is about $57,000 in today's dollars, and good money in that period. By 1937, umps could make upward of $10,000, which translates to about $122,000 in current wages. No more fighting their way out of the park, they were pros treated with the respect professionals deserve. Their uniform at the time, the blue serge suit, reflected their standing. The blue suit remained the official garb until 1968, when the American League decided to update its image by putting its umpires in gray slacks and maroon blazers. Reflecting the casual Friday mood of the nineties, umpires began wearing short-sleeved shirts without jackets during the summer heat and satin warm-up jackets on cool September nights.

They are still the men in blue —usually wearing light blue shirts—but, some days, you have to look hard to find any blue. Maybe that jacket is navy blue, even though it looks black. There's some blue in the Major League Baseball logo. Or maybe they're like the bashful bride; the blue is hidden in the undergarments.

It was during the time of the two-man crew, shortly after the turn of the century, that umpires began using hand signals to signify balls and strikes. William "Dummy" Hoy, a deaf mute outfielder whose nickname predates political correctness by about a century, claimed he invented the signals as a way of communicating with his third-base coach. After each pitch, Hoy would look to his coach, who would raise a finger on his right hand if the ump had called strike, on his left hand if the call had been ball. In the 1944 Reds yearbook, Hoy claimed, "That gave the umpires an idea, and they began raising their rights with the violence of a pile-driver to emphasize an indisputable strike." Newspaper stories from the 1890s confirm that part of the story, but this is where historical fact and myth diverge. Most every baseball historian credits National League umpire Cy Rigler with starting the practice of raising the right hand for called strikes. Some accounts claim Rigler did it to aid Hoy, but Rigler was still umping in the minors when Hoy retired. For certain, Hoy devised hand signals for his coaches to communicate the count to him. But there are no contemporary newspaper accounts to verify Hoy's claim that the umpires adopted the practice on his behalf. Let's go with the most popular stories: Rigler invented the tradition of raising his right hand on called strikes when he was umping in the minors in 1905. It was a signal to his friends in the stands, who might not have heard his cry, the story goes. That same year, National League umpire Bill Klem began using expressive hand and arm signals to denote outs, balls, and strikes. So, who gets the credit? The 1909 edition of Spalding's *Official Base Ball Guide* is the closest we have to a contemporaneous account: It says umpires adopted signals so fans could follow the game. No mention of Hoy, or Rigler, or Klem.

Where do umpires come from? Umpires traditionally came from the playing ranks. Witness umpiring pioneers from the nineteenth century Ferguson and Gaffney. Ferguson was an outfielder for nine years in the majors, most of them with Troy, and Gaffney knocked around the minors as a third baseman for an assortment of New England teams including Lynn, Westboro, and Clinton.

After all, you don't become an umpire to get back at all the boys who said you threw like a girl. You umpire because you love the game and aren't quite good enough to play at the highest levels, or are too old to play the game anymore.

But as the game grew so did the demand for a more professional umpire. Playing credentials were no longer important. The road to respectability began in 1935 when George Barr, who'd been umping in the National League since 1931, opened the first umpire training school. It took eleven years but the school bore fruit when Bill McKinley became the first umpire-school grad to reach the big leagues in 1946. Within two decades virtually every professional baseball umpire was a training-school grad. In 1964 the leagues created the Umpire Development Program to oversee the training of future umpires. In 1995 the big leagues turned over umpire development to the minor leagues.

Despite the occasional missed call, today's umpires are better than their predecessors because of the extensive training, seasoning, and evaluation they receive. In fact, former umpire union head Richie Phillips believed that all sixty-four big-league umpires were, in his words, "marvelous." That's why baseball, unique among all professional sports, does not pick the best umpires—as determined by the league's secret ratings—to umpire in the postseason. Those choice assignments, by union contract, are spread around. According to the contract, an ump can work only one special event (All-Star Game, Division Series, League Championship Series, or World Series) per season. There is one exception: An ump can work both a Division Series and the World Series. And even the best umps are prohibited from working two World Series in a row. That ensures that three-fourths of the umps get a little postseason work, and some postseason money. It also ensures the best umps won't always get the most important games.

Glasses were once a sign of weakness. Look at early baseball cards and team pictures and no one is wearing glasses. Dom DiMaggio, who came up to the Red Sox in 1940, was one of the first players to wear his specs on the field and, for that, he earned the nickname The Little Professor, not a real manly sobriquet. For umpires, glasses were an even bigger no-no. Ah, the taunts that might come from both player and fan. For a full century, umpires left their spectacles back in the clubhouse. In 1956, Ed Rommel and Frank Umont took the field wearing their glasses and the world didn't end. Some players even saw it as a move in the direction of honesty. Today, most umpires with less than 20/20 vision wear contacts for comfort.

A high school sports official once told me, "No matter what call you make, you're wrong. If you go against the home team, that crowd screams for your scalp. And if you call it for them, the opposing coach comes after you." The umpire may be looking over the catcher's shoulder, but someone is always looking over his. There's even a league office charged with reviewing umpires' work.

It's a high-stress job, being the arbiter of a game where one call can mean dollars to teams and players. How do umpires handle this responsibility, this pressure? In other words, does umpiring shorten your life?

As it turns out, a study in the May 2000 issue of the *Physician and Sportsmedicine* addressed just that question. The authors, spurred by the on-field death of John McSherry at Cinergy Field in 1996, decided to examine the question statistically. They looked at the birth and death dates of 195 major-league umpires, the oldest born in 1836, the most recent in 1945. All had been full-time umpires. One began his major-league career at seventeen, another didn't make it to the big leagues until he was fifty. The results, in short: Umpires seem to lead normal lives, dying at about the same age as everyone else. Umpiring does not shorten your life expectancy the way, say, dentistry does.

The authors conclude that either "the factors suspected of placing Major League Baseball umpires at risk are simply not at work" or "perhaps their personality makeup, in ways not currently understood, insulates them from work stressors and, therefore, from a premature death."

Apparently thirty years of hearing "Kill the ump!" doesn't.

The taunt "Kill the ump!" first appeared in Ernest Thayer's "Casey at the Bat." After a called strike one, the poem notes, "'Kill him; kill the umpire!' shouted someone from the stand/And it's likely they'd have killed him had not Casey raised his hand."

Shouting "Kill the ump!" might now land you a lawsuit. Modern fans seldom use that jeer anymore. According to baseballtips.com, modern umpire taunts don't threaten physical violence but, instead, fall into one of two categories: accusing the umpire of being blind, or accusing the umpire of being partisan. Most umps don't hear the heck-les anyway, because they are positioned far from the fans.

What does stress out an ump? Researchers A.H. Taylor and J.V. Daniel developed a survey for the 1987 First World Congress of Science and Football to measure types of stress among soccer referees. The Soccer Officials Stress Survey (SOSS) was later adapted by D. Rainey for baseball umpires. While soccer officials had experienced the most stress from fear of failure, Rainey reported in *Sports Psychologist* that umpires felt pressure from four directions: fear of failure, fear of physical harm, time pressure, and interpersonal conflict.

Say what you will about them, but they're tidy fellows. So, why *do* umpires carry those little pocket brooms? To clean off the plate, yes. But they used full-sized brooms until 1904, when Cubs outfielder Jack McCarthy sprained his ankle by stepping on the umpire's broom at home plate. The order went out from the league office for umps to switch to the little whisk brooms. The American League followed suit the next season.

After Charles Johnson is intentionally walked, Pablo Ozuna pinch-hits for pitcher Hansel Izquierdo. After missing wide on ball one, Carlos Almanzar then fires a wild pitch into the dirt that allows Lee to score from third, making it 7–4 Marlins. Almanzar tries to sneak an inside fastball past Ozuna, but the pinch hitter catches it on his fists and sends a foul heading our direction. Will and I are on our feet, but the ball sails into the upper deck. We hear an anonymous cheer from above. Someone must have caught it.

I've been to hundreds of professional baseball games over the years. I've won door prizes and ballpark-quiz contests. Once, I won fifty gallons of Shell gasoline by picking the winners of all the major-league games on one day, but I have *never* caught a foul ball. In fact, I've never even been close to catching one.

I did get a practice ball once, but that was just because Clete Boyer was a rookie and didn't know any better. It was at old Griffith Park in Washington D.C., in 1959. I had moved down to the front row to watch batting practice. In Griffith Park it was no big deal moving down to the first row; there wasn't much competition for seats. When Boyer and Andy Carey got through passing the ball, Boyer turned to me, made eye contact and faked tossing me the ball. I put my glove up and he threw it to me. I still have that ball. It's dirty and scuffed but it does allow the imagination to run wild or, at least, my twelve-year-old imagination to run wild. I used to imagine that Mantle and Berra had passed that ball back and forth, that Whitey Ford had used it to practice his grip, that Bill Skowron had spit on it, that Bobby Richardson and Elston Howard and Tony Kubek and even Casey Stengel had all come in contact with that ball at one time or another. If balls could talk.

But I've never caught a foul ball.

I haven't been going about it right, according to author Zack Hample, who claims he averages six balls a game. In his book *How to Snag Major League Baseballs* he advises prospective foul ball chasers to heed the following bits of wisdom:

- Be ready. Don't be downing your drink.
- Don't sit next to a tall guy with a glove.
- When a batter hits a foul ball in your direction, don't run toward it. Try to find a spot three rows down from where it will land, because most balls aren't caught and most roll downhill.
- Ninety-nine percent of fouls are sliced, so be on the first base side for a righty and the third base side for a lefty.

Arrive early. You get most balls during batting practice.

What if I'm ignoring Zack's advice and I'm not ready? What if I'm looking the other way and I catch a foul in the back of the head? Can I sue? Not that I would, but what are the guidelines?

The precedent is set by an opinion rendered in the land-mark 1981 New York Court of Appeals case, *Akins* v. *Glens Falls City School District 17*. A woman was at a high-school baseball game, standing behind a three-foot fence on the third-base line when she was injured by a foul ball. She sued, claiming the school district should have put a screen up along third. A jury agreed, as did an intermediate appellate court. The high court reversed the decision and dismissed the complaint, defining "the duty of due care owed by the proprietor of a baseball field to its spectators." The court said the ballpark owner, like any landowner, had a responsibility "to prevent injury to those who come to watch the games played on its field," but that responsibility did not include screening the entire field, because the court also recognized that a field owner has a "legitimate interest" in serving spectators who prefer to view the game unobstructed by a screen. The decision said the field owner must screen "the most dangerous section of the field," defined as the area behind home plate, and to provide screened seating "sufficient for those spectators who may be reasonably anticipated to desire protected seats on an ordinary occasion."

So, if I get hit by a foul ball, I can't hold the Reds responsible; I knew what I was doing sitting here along third base.

It's the bottom of the eighth now, and Austin Kearns' blast into left barely slips outside the foul pole, making it nothing more than a long foul. The fans around me start talking about last night's game, when Aaron Boone hit what appeared to be a game-tying home run down the right-field line. Boone was well into his home-run trot and pumping his fist when first-base umpire Randy Marsh signaled foul. In most ballparks, a drive down the line is an easy call: Did it hit the foul pole, or did it curve past it on the inside or the outside? Not so at Cinergy Field, where construction of the new ballpark has altered a number of things, including the foul poles. Neither pole is flush against the fence; it's three feet or so back, a fluke of the ongoing construction. That means a ball can cross the fence in fair ground, then curve into foul territory.

No one is sure whether Boone's ball would have hit the pole—except his dad, manager Bob Boone, but this isn't

Little League, so there are no other dads to fight—but everyone is sure the pole is positioned wrong.

And, I think, named wrong.

Why is the foul pole fair? Why don't they call it the fair pole? And, for that matter, why is the foul line fair?

In football, the out-of-bounds line is out of bounds. Touch it, and you're out. Same for basketball. In baseball, however, the out-of-bounds line is *in-bounds*. The line separating fair from foul ground is called the foul line, and it's in fair territory. Huh?

Like so many things, it goes back to Alexander Cartwright and his New York Knickerbockers. The original 1845 rules made no provisions for base lines or foul lines—they aren't even mentioned. The fourth rule says, simply: "The bases shall be from 'home' to second base, forty-two paces; from first to third base, forty-two paces, equidistant."

Foul lines were introduced in the 1850s, but not to aid the umpire in determining whether a liner to left was fair or foul. The game was catching on with fans, and foul lines were introduced to create an area where spectators could stand without interfering with the action on the field. They really were foul lines. In 1886, a rules change moved first and third bases inside the foul line. They had been out of bounds, which defied logic. It meant the runner was in foul ground, which meant he should be out.

What made the foul line fair was a change to home plate.

The original home plate really was . . . a plate, or a close approximation. It was a plate-shaped station that served more as a base than as a pitcher's target. We're talking about an era when the batter gave the pitcher instructions on where he wanted the ball, so the plate was just a place to step when you scored.

The great leap forward in plate design came in 1887, when the rules committee decreed that home plate should be a twelve-inch square. It didn't have to be rubber; in the early days it could be marble or rubber, and it sat square atop the intersection of the first- and third-base lines. After a few players suffered nasty cuts from the marble plate corners, the rules were changed: Home plate could be made only of rubber.

With a new century, came a new home plate. The modern plate design was adopted for the 1900 season: It was no longer one-foot square, but an imperfect pentagon, a square with the back corners cut off and the angles darting in to meet at a point, the point where the third- and first-base lines met. This was to eliminate the back corners. Pitchers were kicking mad when curveballs nipped in across the back corner and the umps weren't giving them the strike. The rules committee, with all the logic of Bud Selig, decided that if it did away with the corners, it would do away with the complaints. Did any of those guys know a pitcher personally? Pitchers always complain about calls.

This pointed, pentagonal home plate was designed as the meeting place for the first- and third-base lines. Since the bases had to be in fair territory, according to the 1886 rule change, that meant the foul lines were now fair.

And that, friends, is why the foul line—and, in turn, the foul pole—is fair.

The field bases took a similar path to modernity as home plate. In the beginning, in a carryover from the kids' game of stake ball, four-foot-tall wooden stakes served as the bases. As you might imagine, this wouldn't exactly pass OSHA muster. Players were getting hurt, so the switch was made to flat objects—rocks, rags, whatever was handy. In 1850, teams went to sand-filled sacks, which evolved into cloth-filled canvas bags. The size was standardized at fifteen-inches square in 1877.

When I played baseball, there was a metal rod in the ground and the canvas bag was strapped to the rod. They still do that in many amateur leagues, but the big leagues have gotten fancy. Now, there is a recessed plate with a one-inch hole; the base is mounted on a support with a one-inch rod that fits neatly into the hole, anchoring the bag and keeping it firmly in place, unless Rickey Henderson should steal another landmark base, in which case he can just pull the bag straight up, take it to the dugout, and list it immediately on eBay.

Today, rules 1.05 and 1.06 specify field bases must be filled with a soft material and be 15 inches square and three to five inches thick. Most are closer to three; no one wants to stand on a mountain. The official base of Major League Baseball is the Jack Corbett Original Hollywood Base. It has a rubberized cover that is weatherproof and darned near spikeproof. A set of three bases may run a club upwards of three hundred fifty dollars, but they last three or four years.

That Jack Corbett was not the one who owned the El Paso minor-league team in the forties, and sued the majors to get the reserve rule abolished. This was a different Jack Corbett, a Californian who developed the rubber-coated base and started a company called Hollywood Bases to market his product. Hollywood Bases is now owned by Schutt Sports of Chicago.

When I was a kid—have I used that expression before in this book?—we lined the field with lime. The coach had a cylinder about the size of a fire extinguisher on two wheels that he rolled down the base path with a little stream of white lime pouring out. Sometimes, he even got the line straight. You never wanted to score the first run of the game, when the lime was still fresh, because when you slid into home, the last thing you wanted to do was get some of that stuff in your eyes. It burned like . . . well, it burned a lot.

Playing rule 1.04 specifies that "the foul lines and all other playing lines . . . shall be marked with wet, unslaked lime, chalk or other white material." In the professional leagues, it's done with the mandated chalk or other white material. At Louisville Slugger Park, groundskeeper Tom Nielsen and his crew hand draw the baselines with a mixture of water, gypsum, and latex paint. They use a plumb line to get it straight. Each line is three inches wide. The batter's box is drawn with chalk. Nielsen built a wooden frame that he sits on the plate. He dumps in chalk that filters through a screen to create the perfect batter's box, one that will be almost completely obliterated by the first batter.

Baseball started out with the pitcher 45 feet from the batter. In 1881, rule-makers moved the pitcher's mound back five feet to another round number, 50 feet. Then, in 1893, with pitchers now throwing overhanded, the rules committee made one last change, shoving the pitcher back ten-and-a-half feet to what today seems like a magical distance, 60 feet 6 inches. Why the sudden shift from round numbers to what is a really awkward number, 60-6? Did the rules committee members realize that this was the perfect distance, an expanse that would stand the test of time and still be in use a century later? Of course not—60 feet, 6 inches was a mistake. Baseball's rule-makers intended it to be another round number: 60 feet. However, the surveyor read 60 feet 0 inches, as 60 feet 6 inches, according to Hirsh M. Goldberg's *The Blunder Book: Colossal Errors, Minor Mistakes and Surprising Slipups That Have Changed the Course of History.* (How's that for an authoritative source?) The six inches stayed in the picture and it's been that magical, mystical number, ever since.

How important is that six inches? If you are facing Randy Johnson, who can throw a baseball 100 mph, you'd

probably say very important. Some would say it is of paramount importance. I contend that baseball evolved around that extra half foot. If the original surveyor had read the plans correctly, the game would have adjusted in some other way. The mound might have come down a couple of inches, bats might be lighter, batters quicker, fences shorter, the plate narrower. The game adjusts; the players adjust; and Babe Ruth would still have hit 60 home runs.

Chapter Twelve

You Can't Tell the Players

The man five seats down from me is keeping a scorecard. I've looked up and down my row and scanned the crowd in front of me all the way to the field, and he's the only person in sight tracking the game so intricately. Up in the press box, everyone keeps a scorecard, but it's their job to report on the game. Down here in the stands, keeping a scorecard is a forgotten, perhaps even lost, art.

The Reds don't even *sell* scorecards anymore. The man down the row is keeping his in his program. That's what the Reds and most teams offer now. Instead of a dollar scorecard, they prefer to sell a $3.50 program, with lots of pictures and stories and, oh yes, ads.

Scorekeeping isn't what it once was. There's a fascinating photo in Paul Dickson's book *The Joy of Keeping Score,* a black-and-white grandstand shot of the crowd at a 1938 New York Giants home game. I blocked off a section and counted: eleven of sixty-eight people are keeping a scorecard.

If I were to take a photo of my section today and count, it would be one of sixty-eight keeping a scorecard. Scorecards are now collectibles from the past, bought and sold on eBay.

What happened?

The scorecard was once more than a hobby for stat-heads; it was the only way you knew the score. In baseball's beginnings, ballparks didn't have scoreboards. In fact, many owners were reluctant to install the devices for fear of cutting into the scorecard concession.

The earliest known scorecard, lodged in the New York Public Library, dates from October 6, 1845. It was printed for the Knickerbocker Ball Club and had spaces for names, "hands out," runs, and remarks. So, fans were keeping a scorecard long before the first enclosed ball field and long before the scoreboard.

It wasn't until late in the nineteenth century that score-boards appeared. They were just crude boards where young men in newsboy caps hung out and hung up num-bers that showed the score. A funny thing happened after the arrival of the scoreboard: People kept buying score-cards. They liked keeping score and comparing their tallies to those on the big board.

At today's park, the scoreboard is more than just a tally board. It tells you what the batter did last time up, what he's hitting for the season, how he's fared in the past against this pitcher, lots more than your scorecard could. So, why do people still keep a scorecard? Obviously not for the stats. Who goes home and logs all the data into a computer? A kid maybe, but this is a grown man keeping this scorecard.

I can't find any sociology studies that address the ques-tion of whither the scorecard, so we are left to the opinions of experts.

Lisa Leigh Parney writes in the *Christian Science Monitor,* "Usually it's because it [keeping a scorecard] gets them more involved in the game and its strategies." Ah yes, a reasonable theory: keeping a scorecard keeps your head in the game.

Paul Dickson offers another hypothesis, a sort of us-versus-them explanation. Writing in *The Joy of Keeping Score,* he says, "The world is divided into two kinds of baseball fans. Those who keep score at the ballgame . . . and those who have never made the leap." We keep a scorecard because we are a more serious class of fan. We are not part of the teeming mass enticed to the park by offers of free car flags or free umbrellas. We come for, dare I say it, the game.

For the gang up in the press box, there's a third reason. If the big red PR machine were to falter, the sportswriter could create his or her own box score for the next day's paper.

The scorecard is indispensable because of what it yields, the box score, and the box score is what separates baseball from all other sports.

There, in tiny type, blocked off from the rest of the sports section, is a story without verbs, a series of fragments that can tell you more about a game than a thousand-word game story.

Football and basketball try, but no other sport can rival baseball when it comes to statistics. Football's quarterback ratings system is indecipherable; basketball continues to discover new categories to count. What exactly is a triple double? Double figures in what, whatever? Basketball didn't even count blocked shots until 1980, so you can't compare a Shaquille O'Neal to a George Mikan or even an in-his-prime Bill Russell.

But, four for four, everybody knows you had a great day. Throw in five RBIs and a couple of runs—the line would look like this: 4 2 4 5—and you have a hero.

From box scores you can re-create a game, and a season, and a career.

Henry Chadwick, one of the first writers to champion the game of baseball in the newspaper, is often called the father of the box score, but that is true only in the sense of father as nourisher; he didn't invent the form. Cricket matches already had box scores; the first baseball box score appeared in the October 22, 1845 edition of the *New York Morning News,* a decade or so before Chadwick included box scores in his baseball stories in the *New York Clipper.*

That first box score appears as a compliment to a story about the previous day's "friendly match of the time honored game of Baseball" between the New York Knickerbocker club and the Brooklyn club. The New Yorkers won 24–4.

It was a rudimentary box score, listing player names, positions, runs and outs. But, somehow, it made the game seem more serious, less like a boy's game, more like the cricket matches that men played.

Chadwick popularized the box-score form, adding his own flourishes, including fielding statistics. Because he wrote for many publications, including the *Sporting News, Sporting Life,* and the first weekly magazine devoted to baseball, *Ball Players Chronicle,* he spread the gospel of the box score.

It would be impossible to compute a batting average from a Chadwick box score, because that statistic hadn't been invented. In Chadwick's day, the batting champion was determined by who scored the most runs. Still, the box score remained in Chadwick's image for half a century. The opening-day box score of an 1895 game between the New York Giants and the Brooklyns, as the reporter called them again and again, listed players' last names, positions, then R, 1B, PO, A, E.

Foutz, Brooklyn's first baseman, recorded one run, two 1B's, ten PO's, one A and no E's. In the small type below, it noted that Foutz had a 2B. Also noted in the small type at the bottom: Earned Runs (each team had two), Stolen Bases, First Base on Balls, First Base on Errors, Struck Out (by pitcher), Left on Bases, and Double Play. The umpire was Mr. Lynch. Attendance was 20,000. The Giants made four errors, two by the new "red-faced" second baseman from Massachusetts, Stafford. Brooklyn won the affair 7–4. Ten years later, the box score was the same except for the addition of time of game.

Henry Chadwick also devised a scoring system for the scorecard. In the 1883 edition of Peck & Snyder's scorebook, published by the sporting goods company, he wrote, "Over twenty years ago we prepared a system of shorthand for the movements of the contestants in a baseball match, which system is now familiar to every scorer in the country."

That no longer holds true. Most of Chadwick's cryptology has fallen by the wayside, and is no longer familiar to every scorer in the country. He used what he thought was a mnemonic-friendly system for scoring: the letter D for a ball caught on first bounce, which was then an out; an L for a foul ball. The D came from the last letter of "bound" and L from the last letter of "foul." All that remains from his scoring system is the K for strikeout, K being the last letter of "struck."

He *did* give us the numbering system for scoring, with the pitcher as 1, the catcher 2; then around the infield, the first, second, and third basemen are 3, 4, and 5, respectively; back to shortstop for 6; then 7, 8, 9 around the outfield in reverse direction, from left to right.

When I was a kid, I always had trouble remembering the outfield numbers because it seemed backward. Why did the infield go one direction and the outfield the other? I finally developed my own mnemonic system for remembering the outfield numbers: Roger Maris was number 9 and he played right field. Then I remembered Ted Williams was number 9 and he played left field . . .

By the time I started devouring box scores, in the fifties, the four-column box score was the standard: at-bats, runs, hits, runs batted in. The box score had started to evolve in the teens with the addition of hits to the line. A 1914 line for Joe Tinker goes like this: 5 0 2 6 0, indicating 5 at-bats, 0 runs, 2 hits, 6 putouts, and 0 assists.

By 1927, errors had returned, making it a six-column box. A 1927 line for Ty Cobb goes like this: 5 2 4 4 0 0, with 5 at-bats, 2 runs, 4 hits, 4 putouts, 0 assists, and 0 errors.

That six-column style held throughout the forties and

up into the fifties; the four-column form wasn't adopted widely in newspapers until 1958. A line from the *New York Times* box score for a 1958 Dodgers game went like this: Hodges 5 0 2 1; the year before it would have read: Hodges 5 0 2 6 0 0.

Sports editors are still tinkering with box scores. In the early eighties, many newspapers across the country were dropping box scores in favor of the less-informative line scores. My own paper at the time, the *Louisville Times*, did just that, over the vocal protests of myself and our assistant managing editor Mike Kallay. *USA Today*, led by sports managing editor Henry Freeman, bucked the trend, adding information to the box score. "The Nation's Newspaper" tried to pick up fantasy-league players by adding a scoring summary and incidental stats, including caught stealing. Then, in 1990, the ill-fated national sports daily, the *National*, added updated batting averages.

Today, the five-column box score is the norm, including the old standby four: at-bats, runs, hits, runs batted in—plus updated average. *USA Today* uses an eight-column box: the big four, plus walks, strikeouts, runners left on base, and updated average.

USA Today, once praised only for its color weather map and its exhaustive sports section, continues to innovate when it comes to the box score. There's now a note at the end for weather and wind data. So, if some spindly infielder hits a home run, I don't automatically say, "Aha, steroids!" I check the weather data: "9 mph out to left." "Aha, wind blown!"

. . .

I didn't invent fantasy baseball; Lance Harris and I did. At least, in my neighborhood, we did. For the 1958 season we decided to divide up real players and create a league around them. We weren't clever enough to see the possibilities of using real box scores. No, we used the fifties game standard: dice. Roll a 2 and hit a home run; 12 and leg out a triple, and so on. We held our own draft with the other neighborhood kids, then kept elaborate records for each player and team. We soon discovered two things: keeping the records was a lot of work and, we really liked playing baseball more than playing this game. Our league disbanded after a couple of weeks, and Harris Kitchen Table League never entered the vocabulary.

Instead, the fantasy game is known as Rotisserie League, after the New York restaurant (*La Rotisserie Francaise*) where, in 1979 Daniel Okrent, convinced a trio of friends to join him in this pretend game. It was a few weeks later, at another restaurant, P. J. Moriarty's, that they drew up the original rules for fantasy baseball.

Baseball strategy games using real players have been around almost as long as the game itself. There's even a price guide, *Baseball Games: Home Versions of the National Pastime, 1860s–1960s,* detailing all the hundreds of baseball board games marketed over the years. In the fifties, you could order two popular versions, APBA or Strat-O-Matic, from ads in the back of the *Sporting News,* but all the various versions involved rolling dice or spinning a wheel.

It was Okrent who came up with the earthshaking idea

of basing the game on a player's actual performance. Holy moly, how simple, yet, how right.

The world learned about this creation when Okrent wrote an article titled "The Year George Foster Wasn't Worth $35" for a 1981 issue of the *Sports Illustrated* wannabe magazine, *Inside Sports*. The idea took off, breathing new life into baseball and attracting a new kind of fan, one with no interest in a team other than his own fantasy version.

Here's the kicker: Okrent, now an editor at *Time*, no longer plays. He lost interest and quit fantasy baseball in 1996. He had played the game he invented for almost two decades, yet never won his league.

My early fantasy-league experience wasn't a complete bust. As my parents would point out, it sharpened my math skills, figuring out all those averages. It also made me a cynic when watching baseball on television. The announcer might pontificate that the opposing pitcher, Johnny Podres, perhaps, had enjoyed much success this season against my favorite player, Orlando Cepeda. "He's held him to two for nine in two previous meetings." From my painstaking calculations, I knew the illusion of small numbers. I knew that, if Cepeda got a hit, he could magically transform that dreadful .222 average into a magical .300 (three for ten). I've never trusted sports announcers with numbers since.

There's no question, though, that fantasy leagues are driving the innovations in box scores. Who are these people, these fantasy folks?

In 2000, The Sports and Entertainment Academy at Indiana University's Kelley School of Business surveyed a group of students and young executives to find out. They discovered that rotisserie players are overwhelmingly male: fewer than 10 percent who participate in fantasy leagues are female. Building and maintaining friendships was the number one reason cited for playing; a close second was having fun. Other reasons were competition, bragging rights, and the challenge. Prize money was a nonfactor, with fewer than 40 percent even mentioning it.

Despite its statistical underpinnings, baseball was not the favored fantasy sport: Football, with 80 percent of those surveyed admitting to owning a fantasy football team, was vastly more popular. Baseball was a distant second, tied with golf at 40 percent participation.

Who doesn't play? Those who said they don't participate said they lack the time or the interest.

In the nineties, when I was the video columnist for the *New York Daily News*, the paper was trying to attract more of the city's immigrant population. Focus-group research conducted at the time revealed that for immigrants the most mystifying feature in the newspaper is the box score.

The box score can be mystifying even for the hard-core fans. I've read box scores for fifty years; I own every Bill James *Statistical Abstract* except the first mimeographed one, and I don't know some of these newly invented statistics. I know how to decipher GIDP (grounded into double plays). But what's an RMU? (a runner moved up). An RLISP? (a runner left in scoring position). And, my least favorite:

IRS? No, it's not what you think, or dread. It's "inherited runners scoring."

Are all these stats necessary, or, as a recent study by the *Newspaper Research Journal* asked: Are baseball box scores helpful statistics or sports hieroglyphics?

C. A. Tuggle of the University of North Carolina in Chapel Hill surveyed fans at two Florida Marlins games to see how many understood all the abbreviations and notations in a box score. His conclusion: few.

One-third of those surveyed claimed to read nearly all the box scores every day. Yet, not one of the 307 participants could correctly identify all thirty abbreviations in a box score, and only one could identify twenty-nine. Six percent identified twenty-eight of the notations and another 6 percent were correct on twenty-seven.

Nearly everyone surveyed knew that AB stood for "at-bat"; 92 percent got that right. Eighty-five percent knew E meant "error"; 80 percent correctly identified ERA as "earned run average"; and 65 percent recognized HBP as "hit by pitch." Only 30 percent knew BF stood for "batters faced," and only 1 percent knew that the pitching abbreviation H meant "hold" by a middle reliever. Men did significantly better than women. Those who played high-school sports scored significantly better than those who didn't.

Not that the sports section isn't hard enough to decipher anyway. Tuggle cites a 1992 study that pegs the readability of sports articles at 18.7, meaning you need to be a second-year doctoral student to understand them. He compares box scores to the financial tables of the business section, "a never-never land filled with arcane codes and hidden formulas that are not designed for mere mortals to comprehend or act upon."

According to Tuggle's study, 40 percent of people teach themselves to read a box score; dad is responsible for teaching another 30 percent; the remainder learn from a coach, another family member, or a friend.

About one-quarter of the participants in Tuggle's study said they never read box scores, claiming they could get all the statistical information they needed from television or the Internet. Other non-box–score readers said they were "confusing, too complex, and boring."

In my boyhood, I read every line of every box score; Will is a sophomore in college, and he still reads them all.

However, my box-score reading has declined over the years. I now check the Giants box, then the Reds, and our minor-league team, the Louisville Bats. Even in my fantasy league years, I only checked the Giants and my players.

Still, today if I see four numbers in sequence, I read them as a box score. On our drive in Will and I passed a bus with yesterday's Pick Four lottery numbers on the side. We both burst out laughing: 1-8-1-3. That makes no sense. One at-bat. One hit. Eight runs! Three runs batted in! "Must have walked seven times," Will said.

After Larkin grounds out to lead off the eighth, and Encarnacion strikes out, Austin Kearns strides to the plate. The rookie from nearby Lexington, Kentucky has had a tough day: a pop out to third, a line out to third and a painful plunk in the shoulder. After swinging and missing on two curves, he pulls a 2-2 fastball over the left-field wall and all eyes turn to right center field. It's a fireworks show, a celebration of Kearns' blow. It's the old exploding scoreboard.

As ballparks have become fancier, so, too, have the scoreboards.

Originally, they were just tote boards. They evolved into inning tallies. There's a famous story about Dizzy Dean's beef with his manager and the scoreboard when Diz was in the minor leagues. It was 1930 and Ol' Diz was playing for the Houston Buffaloes of the Texas League when he hit a home run. But his pitching didn't equal his hitting that day, and manager Joe Schultz later pulled him for a reliever. Incensed at being removed, Dean raced out to the scoreboard and took down the run from his home-run inning, telling manager Schultz that if he didn't want him to pitch, he couldn't have his run either.

The watershed event in scoreboard history was the 1908 invention by George A. Baird of the first electronic scoreboard. Ballparks didn't jump on the invention immediately. In fact, it was newspapers that bought into the idea: They would erect these electronic scoreboards outside their offices and crowds would gather to follow the home team's fortunes. This was especially prevalent during late-season pennant races and during the World Series. The first to attract attention with this gadget was the *Chicago Tribune,* which put up an electronic scoreboard at the intersection of Madison and Dearborn during the pennant race of 1908 when thousands would gather to follow the Cubs-Giants race

These electronic scoreboards began gaining a foothold in the thirties, when America's passion for baseball was fueled by the Depression. George H. Leland's 1930 patent for a Circuit Controlling Device for Electric Signs and the Like meant electronic scoreboards could be visible during night games.

Eventually, scoreboards included places for game scores from other parks. Still, that was only three other games. By tradition, scoreboards would only show other games in the same league and at that time each league had only eight teams. It wasn't until 1946 that Bill Veeck, maverick owner of the Cleveland Indians, added scores from the National League to his scoreboard.

Scoreboards looked pretty much the same around the league for the next three decades. Enter Mitsubishi.

At the 1980 All-Star Game at Dodger Stadium, the Japanese electronics giant unveiled Diamond Vision, which turned the old-fashioned scoreboard into a giant television. Virtually every stadium now has Diamond Vision or one of its competitors, like Sony's JumboTRON.

These boards are huge: Stadium designers recommend that the height of the screen be 3 to 5 percent of the maximum viewing distance from the screen. If spectators on the far side of the stadium are 500 feet away, the screen needs to be at least 15 feet high. A Diamond Vision scoreboard can be 15 feet by 20 feet in size, weigh more than 5 tons and cost $4,000 per square foot or more, but maintenance is low. Most parks use their screen only about 250 hours per year; a screen has a life span of around 20,000 hours, so a Diamond Vision scoreboard can last forty years.

They provide more information during the game than a fifty-page program, keeping fans posted on today's stats, scores from other games, even offering mug shots of the players and highlights. Between innings you can win a drink if your choice of an animated ball wins an animated race. At Cinergy Field, there are sometimes as many as fourteen people working to program the scoreboard. Scoreboards have become so elaborate that kids often pay more attention to the flash on the scoreboard and ignore the game on the field.

There are still a few manual scoreboards around the league, the most famous being the hand-operated tote in the wall of Fenway Park's Green Monster, the left-field wall. It takes two guys to keep the scoreboard current, to lift the 16-inch by 16-inch numbers and hang them under the appropriate inning designation.

A number of the new, fun ballparks have manual scoreboards, just to keep the spirit alive, even though it's an addition to the payroll.

Fenway's scoreboard is famous, but the most notorious stadium scoreboard was at old Comiskey Park in Chicago. When he bought the team in 1959, maverick owner Bill Veeck (you are not allowed to identify Veeck without using the words "maverick owner") got a bright idea. He would celebrate the home team's accomplishments with fireworks. Stealing the flashing-lights idea from a pinball machine, he installed ten mortars on top of the scoreboard to shoot off Roman candles, then placed a fireworks crew behind the scoreboard to fire off cherry bombs, rockets, and firecrackers. The fireworks were set off by an employee with a Mafia-sounding nickname, The Torch (hey, this was in Chicago), who would physically light the fuses. Today, that task is done remotely.

The exploding scoreboard went into action after a White Sox home run or victory in the 1960 season, infuriating opponents (Jimmy Piersall, who had his own issues to deal with, once threw a ball at the board) and helping the Pale Hose set a club attendance record of 1,644,460. Of course it didn't hurt that the Sox were coming off their first pennant in forty years. (Also their last—they've won only a handful of division titles since then.)

Bill Veeck, meanwhile, is a book unto himself. In fact he wrote that book, *Veeck as in Wreck*, in 1962. With only eleven dollars, he turned the Milwaukee Millers into a minor-league sensation in 1941, staging beer nights, live pig nights, fireworks night. After only four years, he sold his stake for a quarter-million-dollar profit, then turned around and bought the Cleveland Indians, where he was also a promotional genius. His crowning stunt came in 1951 when he owned the miserable St. Louis Browns. He sent 3' 7", 65-pound Eddie Gaedel to the plate, with number 1/8 on his back, to face Detroit Tigers lefty Bob Cain. Gaedel walked on four pitches, making major-league history, and earning Veeck the undying enmity of every other major-league owner, all of whom considered his stunt detrimental to the game. (Canceling the World Series isn't detrimental, I guess.) The Tigers went on to win the game

6–2, making any protest moot. Gaedel was paid one hundred dollars for his performance. Eight years later Veeck used him again in a stunt at Comiskey Park. He dressed him up like a Martian and had him jump out of a helicopter to present ray guns to the Chisox keystone combination, Nellie Fox and Luis Aparicio. Fox was two feet taller than Gaedel, Aparicio two feet and an inch taller. Gaedel reportedly told the two, "I don't want to be taken to your leader; I already know him."

The first time I visited Riverfront Stadium, in 1976, I remember being impressed by the scoreboard. It was the biggest I'd ever seen but, what most amazed me, was how it could display a drawing of each player—they looked like low-grade baseball cards—as he came to bat. There was his name and his number in letters that had to be six feet high. In retrospect, that scoreboard was pretty tame; there were no colored lights, just yellow against a black background, so the player portraits were stylized, but it was so modern looking, in stark contrast to the dated Crosley scoreboard with its Longine clock (with hands, not a digital readout!) on top.

In 1987, the Riverfront scoreboard that I marveled at was replaced by a modern JumboTRON with TV replay capabilities. It's still there in right center field, but scoreboard technology has passed it by. The image is dim in the bright sun and it's not razor sharp.

When the Reds' new stadium, the Great American Ballpark, opens in 2003, the scoreboard will once again be state of the art. The $3 million Trans-Lux–brand scoreboard will be 24 feet high and 164 feet wide, with a display that offers more than 273,500 pixels in an 8.6-billion-color LED matrix. I don't know what that means either, but I suspect it means a really sharp picture. It's being billed as the "largest incandescent scoreboard, ever constructed for a professional sports facility," which means it's probably the largest incandescent scoreboard, period. What other kind of facility would need a giant scoreboard? What other activity keeps "score"?

I'm not crazy about the new stadium name: Great American Ballpark. Sounds like an incredibly hokey name, until you learn it's named for the Great American Insurance Group. I'm not saying that isn't a hokey name for an insurance company either.

The Reds have joined the march to stadium commercialization. All they are doing for the new park is switching sponsors from Cinergy PSI to Great American Insurance Group. Cinergy signed up in 1996, paying $6 million to slap its name on the stadium for five years, a move it called a "strategic marketing decision." Great American is paying $75 million over thirty years for the naming rights.

It's the trend these days: Pacific Bell Park in San Francisco, PNC Park in Pittsburgh, Safeco Field in Seattle, Comerica Park in Detroit, Edison International Field in Anaheim, Tropicana Field in Tampa, Network Associates Coliseum in Oakland, Bank One Ballpark in Phoenix, Coors Field in Denver, Miller Park in Milwaukee, Enron Field—er, Minute Maid Park in Houston (shouldn't Minute Maid Park be in Florida somewhere?), Pro Player

Stadium in Miami, and Qualcomm Stadium in San Diego. You literally can't tell the playing field without a program. ("Now, which team plays in Comerica and which in Qualcomm?")

Fourteen of thirty big-league parks have sold naming rights to giant impersonal corporations, and a fifteenth is in murky waters: Busch Stadium is ostensibly named for the family that owned the St. Louis Cardinals, at least that's what August Busch told the newspapers back in 1953 when he bought Sportsman's Park. He tried to change the name to Budweiser Park, but there was such a kick from fans and the press that he switched to Busch Stadium. And then the following year his brewing company introduced a new brewski, Busch Bavarian Beer.

Austin Kearns' homer down the left-field line certainly brought the crowd to its feet. We were all leaning, trying to body-English the ball into fair territory. It worked. The ball just slipped to the right of the foul pole, giving the rookie his fourth home run of the season, and finally giving the crowd something to cheer about.

While everyone else is watching Kearns' home-run trot, my attention is still in left. On the cement wall, behind the foul pole, are paintings of the five retired Reds jerseys, numbers 1, 5, 8, 18, 20, plus a generic number 42, a tribute to Jackie Robinson.

(In a rare moment of clarity, the players and owners agreed during the winter of 1997 that they would commemorate the fiftieth anniversary of Jackie Robinson breaking the color barrier by officially retiring his number from the league. No player would ever again wear number 42, except the twelve players who were already wearing the number. Half a decade later, only three of the exempt dozen—Mo Vaughn, Mike Jackson, and Jose Lima—have insisted on sticking with the number. Two of the original twelve guys are out of baseball; the other seven have switched numbers. Vaughn and Jackson are both in their late thirties (in Vaughn's case, that's chronological age, not maturity) and Lima's arm appears to be at least that old, so the number 42 should be gone from the game—fully retired—in a couple of years.)

The Reds were late to the retired-numbers game. They retired their first numbers on September 1, 1996: number 1 for manager Fred Hutchinson and number 5 for catcher Johnny Bench. They've since retired three more numbers: number 8 for second baseman Joe Morgan, number 20 for outfielder Frank Robinson, and number 24 for first baseman Tony Perez.

Notable by its absence from the retired-numbers roster is number 14, the number Pete Rose wore from his rookie days

in 1963, until he was fired as manager and banned from baseball 125 games into the 1989 season. They can't retire it officially, since Rose is banned from baseball but no one has worn the number except for eleven games in 1997 when his son Petey Jr. wore it during a brief stint with the club.

Still, the number is unofficially retired. The club's general manager Jim Bowden told the *Cincinnati Enquirer* in 2000, "You have to respect tradition and history. . . . I wouldn't give (Pete Rose's) 14 to anybody. The only way you can wear [that number] is if the person who wore it gives his permission."

Pete's number 14 is retired in Philadelphia, where he led the Phillies to their only world championship in 1980, but it's not retired to honor him: Hall of Fame pitcher Jim Bunning wore 14 when he was a Phillie.

Retiring numbers is a relatively modern phenomenon. Tiger Mapes, George Selkirk, Allie Clark, and Bud Metheny all wore Babe Ruth's number 3 before the Yankees officially retired it in 1948.

The Yankees hold the distinction of having retired more numbers than any other team. In fact, they are the only team in danger of running out of uniform numbers; they've retired fourteen numbers: 1, 3, 4, 5, 7, 8, 9, 10, 15, 16, 23, 32, 37, and 44. They retired number 8 twice, for Bill Dickey and for Yogi Berra. The Dodgers are next in number retirements with ten, and they could have enshrined more. They've never retired Gil Hodges' 14 or Steve Garvey's 6. Both players have been honored with a number retirement, but Hodges' 14 was retired by the Mets, and Garvey's 6 by the Padres.

The most frequently retired number, as you might guess, is number 1, with seven teams taking that number off the shelf, but it's actually in a tie for tops: Numbers 4, 5, and 20 have each been retired seven times.

. . . .

The first time I saw film of Ty Cobb, a scratched-up print of the Great Man sliding into third, spikes high, I was struck by his uniform. There was no number. The old "can't tell the players without a program" line was still a few years away.

The first players didn't have uniform numbers. The Reds were actually pioneers in numbers, as they have been in many areas, sewing little digits on the players' uniform sleeves as an experiment for the 1888 season. The players hated it, complaining it made them numbers to the fans, not people, so the numbers came off.

The Cleveland Indians tried the numbers game in 1916, but fans complained it made the players look like convicts. Then, in 1924, the St. Louis Cardinals tried the experiment again. Again, it failed.

Fans were just about ready and, for Opening Day 1929, the Yankees added numbers to the backs of their fabled pinstripes; because the Yankees were the Yankees, the practice finally caught on. By 1930, every team except the Philadelphia A's sported numbers. Obstinate Connie Mack held out until '31.

With no history for assigning numbers, the Yankees decided they would give out numbers according to position in the batting order. That's how Ruth got his famous number 3 and Gehrig his famous number 4.

Left fielder Earle Combs batted first, and wore 1; third baseman Mark Koenig batted second, and wore 2; then came Ruth; Gehrig; center fielder Bob Meusel with number 5; second baseman Tony Lazzeri with number 6; shortstop Leo Durocher sporting number 7; and catcher Johnny Grabowski wearing number 8. So, who got number 9? The opening day pitcher? No, the pitchers got 11 through 21 (but no 13 for superstitious reasons). Benny Bengough, the third-string catcher, got number 9. Bill Dickey, a rookie, who would quickly win the starting catching job, wore 10. Backup infielders and outfielders got the last four numbers. Who was number 25, ostensibly the worst player on the opening day roster? Outfielder Ben Paschal, who lived up to expectations, hitting only .208 that year.

Unlike football, which has a number-by-position formula, so the referees can tell when an ineligible receiver is downfield, baseball numbers are assigned willy-nilly. The National League tried a position numbering system in the early fifties (managers, coaches and catchers were to wear 1 to 9; infielders 10 to 19; outfielders 20 to 29), but it met with resistance from players who didn't want to switch numbers. Who's going to tell Stan Musial he can't wear number 6 anymore?

Uniform numbers have infested our national conscience. If I see the number 27, I think Juan Marichal. Eight is, of course, Yogi Berra. I find when I park in a downtown pay lot I try to get in a numbered spot of a favorite player. Easier to remember where my car is: I'm in Roger Maris's spot, number 9.

And, yes, I even use those numbers when playing the numbers. I'm not going to tell you my lottery numbers—you might steal them and win. (Because they're still due to win.)

Chapter Thirteen

The Tools of Ignorance by Any Other Name Would Still Weigh Eight Pounds on a Muggy August Afternoon

It just hasn't been Reds catcher Corky Miller's day. In the top of the eighth, he was called for interfering with Mike Lowell's swing, giving Lowell a free pass to first. Lowell made it to third on Derek Lee's double, then scored on a Carlos Almanzar wild pitch. And don't we all think that, unless the pitcher fires it into the upper deck, the catcher should stop it?

Now, it's the top of the ninth and Miller has just overthrown second on a stolen base attempt by Andy Fox. As the ball skips on into center, Fox rounds third and scores easily.

Chalk up two runs next to Miller's name. He's just as responsible as the pitcher, but he doesn't have an ERA.

I'm being too hard on Miller. Catching has to be the most difficult position to play. When I was a sophomore in high school, my classmate Tim Thayer led the Big Seven conference in hitting. At the end of the season I overheard the baseball coach telling him that he was switching him to catcher for his junior year, and that he could expect his batting average to drop about sixty points. That was forty years ago, and it hasn't gotten any easier.

I never played catcher in my baseball career. I played hind-catcher in backyard games, but hind-catcher is a far cry from catcher. Hind-catcher stands about ten feet behind the batter and tries to knock down anything that gets past the batter, whether a bad pitch, a foul tip, or a swinging strike. In our games, that meant keeping the ball from getting in Mr. Price's garden so he wouldn't yell at us.

In our neighborhood we had no mask, no chest protector, no shin guards, so whoever was hind-catcher, usually the on-deck batter, was on his own. Even standing back ten feet and fielding the ball on the hop was a dangerous position.

The greatest hazard of the hind-catcher position was also the funniest one. You know what I'm talking about: the most dreaded injury in baseball, the one that elicits snickers from everyone else but has the affected player doubled up on the ground in pain. It's getting hit in the nuts.

I don't have any statistics from my childhood backyard games but, reflecting on it, it seems to have afflicted everyone in the neighborhood at least once. I can recall at least twice it took me out, once at shortstop and, of course, once at hind-catcher.

Mike Wampler was batting and I was standing the usual ten feet back with my glove in the protective position right in front of my crotch. The pitch came in, a low grazer that suddenly hit a clump of dirt and jumped straight up into the family jewels. Mike Wampler could have circled the bases five times for all I cared. First was intense pain, then nausea and dizziness. When I opened my eyes, I was surrounded by all the neighborhood kids, every one of them biting his tongue to keep from laughing. I must have laid there ten minutes anyway. Mike kept talking to me; he was feeling the guilt, thinking it was his fault.

This was a monthly occurrence in our games, and not once did anyone ever summon a mother. We called in the mother brigade for cuts and bloody noses, for getting the wind knocked out of you and for shin bruises. But, never once, was a mother called in for the ball-in-the-nuts injury. We knew their limits. Sympathy only extends to things you understand. Women don't understand this particular injury.

Medical science has a name for it; they call it *testicular trauma*. Ask any man, and he will tell you it is the most painful injury he can suffer. According to *Men's Health* magazine, about 250,000 American men suffer sports-related groin injuries of some kind each year, and 31 percent of those are blunt testicular trauma. (You don't want to know what the second most common, at 20 percent, is; let's just say the medical term is *penetrating testicular trauma*. Ouch, ouch, ouch!) Blunt testicular trauma means you got nailed by something, usually a ball or a foot.

The pain and nausea usually subsides within an hour but, for those sixty minutes, you see your entire sexual future pass in front of you, waving bye-bye. It's almost never that serious, but it feels that grave every time.

Why? Why is this the man's burden to bear? Perhaps it's payback: women bear babies, men suffer bad hops to the crotch.

The testicles are extremely sensitive to the touch, porn

movies to the contrary. All other reproductive organs are protected by muscle and bone, but not the testicles. They have a unique design, a natural thermostat that raises and lowers them according to body temperature to keep those budding spermatozoa just the right temperature. Apparently, God didn't plan for the bad hop.

Fortunately for the male of the species there is a way to protect against this painful, and embarrassing injury: It's called the *cup*.

We are, however, putting the cup before the strap.

Before there was, or could be, the cup, there was the jock or the jock strap. No one knows where the name came from, at least not the *jock* part; the strap part is pretty easy to figure out. James Villas searched for the origin for *Esquire* magazine, and finally went with *Webster's Third New International Dictionary*, which says *jock* is British slang for penis. Villas says he is British and that he has never heard the term used that way, but it'll do till something else comes along.

So, it's really a *penis strap*.

The device was created in 1874, by the Bike Web Manufacturing Company for the Boston Athletic Club, whose members needed support while riding their bicycles on the city's bumpy cobblestone streets. Union suits, the traditional male undergarment of the day, were uncomfortable, and rubberized girdles, created originally as modesty undergarments for male swimmers, caused chafing and blistering.

It was originally called the Suspensory, and was just a belt with a silk or cotton pouch. There were no straps under the cheeks. Bike patented the design in 1897, and began its first marketing campaign in the 1902 edition of the Sears, Roebuck and Co. Catalog, which touted the device as "medically indicated" for men engaging in sports or strenuous activity.

A century later, Bike Athletic remains the world's largest supplier of athletic supporters, selling one million per year. The company has sold more than 300 million jock straps worldwide over the years. However, jock-strap sales are not what they once were. Jock-strap sales are off 40 percent from their high in the 1960s.

Today's athletes prefer what are called *compression* or *bicycle shorts,* tight-fitting nylon-and-spandex shorts that give support to the genitals, while stretching and breathing better than regular cotton underwear. These compression shorts don't do much to protect the testicles from bad hops; for that, baseball players still need a cup.

Exercise physiologist Dr. Bryant Stamford says the only reason jock straps are still around is to serve as a holder for the plastic cup that protects the testicles.

Cups work, take it from one who knows. A hard grounder to the cup may feel like having your bell rung, but it beats sterility by a couple of steps.

Cups have been around almost as long as the jock straps they were created to fit in. The first use in professional athletics apparently dates to 1904, when White Sox rookie catcher Claude Berry took the field as a defensive replacement wearing one, determined not to let happen to him what happened to his predecessor.

You just have to wonder how many catchers were

turned into sopranos between 1880, when a new rule required them to catch a third strike on a fly for a strikeout, and 1904, when Berry waddled to his spot behind the plate. That may be the reason there are only two pre-1904 catchers—Buck Ewing, who made his big-league debut in 1880 and Roger Bresnahan, who came up in 1897—in the Baseball Hall of Fame.

Berry didn't have much of a career—245 games over five seasons—but his introduction of the cup would seem to rank up there with Candy Cummings' curveball and merit a little Hall of Fame attention. Ask any catcher about the importance of a good cup.

Those early cups were made of aluminum and rang with every bad hop. Over the years, manufacturers shifted to magnesium, then plastic, and, finally, today's favored material, Kevlar. Shapes too have changed, from the triangle shape of a pool rack to today's banana shape that follows closely the contours of the, er, banana-shaped thing being protected.

Today, cups come in all shapes, materials and sizes. (That's right, you can brag to your girl that you need an extra large cup). Foam and soft plastic cups are favored in soccer and basketball, while baseball and football need the added protection of hard plastic or metal. Soft cups have more give, but that's not exactly what you want when trying to block a Randy Johnson fastball in the dirt. You want something like the International Jock brand Kevlar Banana Cup ($18.95), in white or clear (clear? Ugh!). Kevlar is what they use to make bulletproof vests and, if it can stop a bullet, it ought to be able to slow down a fastball.

The banana shape protects the family jewels and the sensitive area under them.

If catchers had never moved into a crouch directly behind the batter, they might not need cups but, in 1880, the rule-makers said the catcher had to catch a third strike on the fly for a strikeout. No more parking back at the fence, now the catcher had to move up and into the line of fire. Eleven years later, the transformation was complete when the catcher was permitted an oversized mitt, the pitching distance was increased from 50 feet to 60 feet 6 inches and the pitching box was replaced by a foot-long rubber slab. Now the catcher would need all manner of protective equipment.

The first catchers had none. They were as naked as the rest of their teammates when it came to protection from the hard ball. The first bit of protective equipment for the catcher was introduced in 1869 when Cincinnati Red Stockings' manager Harry Wright bought a fifty-cent boxer's mouthpiece for his catcher Doug Allison. A few games later Allison donned a gentleman's mitten to protect his hand. That was pretty much the height of catcher's protective gear for a decade, a buckskin glove on the hand and a stub of rubber in the mouth.

Still, catchers resisted protective equipment, because they considered themselves the tough guys of the team. In the early 1870s, almost a decade before the rule change, Nat Hicks of the Brooklyn Eckfords had moved up behind the batter. According to Hicks's *New York Times* obituary in 1907, he and Bill Craver of the Troy Haymakers were the first and forced others to follow suit. Their close proximity to the batter immediately bore results, and game scores started coming down. I should note that pitchers threw underhanded at that time, so Hicks and Craver weren't snagging 90 mph fastballs without a mask. It also bore results in increased injuries and, even with slow pitching, squatting immediately behind the batter was not without its hazards. A *New York Times* story about an 1876 match between the New York Mutuals and their bitter rivals the Brooklyn Atlantics reported, "It was considered doubtful whether [Nat] Hicks could play so frightfully had he been injured by catching behind the bat. . . . He went into the game with his right eye almost knocked out of his head and his nose and the whole right side of his face swollen to three times their normal size." Pretty. Hicks toughed it out that day: He was struck four times in the game, once in the mouth by the ball, once in the chest, and twice by bats. The paper paid tribute: "No man ever exhibited more nerve and pluck."

Help for Hicks and his backstop brethren was on the way, however. Frederick Thayer, president of the Harvard University Baseball Club, had observed the catcher's lot up close, and crafted a primitive catcher's mask from a fencing mask and installed it on his Harvard Nine catcher Jim Tyng for an April 12, 1877 game against the semipro Live Oaks. When Tyng went out and committed only two errors in a single game (!) other catchers took notice. Thayer's mask, "the rat trap," opposing players mockingly called it, looked very much like a fencer's, with wire mesh replaced by a few strategic coat hangers. It resembled a grocers' egg basket more than anything but, over the next few years, manufacturers made adjustments according to catcher's recommendations.

Still, change came slowly. The *New York Clipper*, Henry Chadwick's paper, wondered aloud in August 1877 why more catchers weren't adopting this newfangled bit of equipment. "It is really surprising, in view of the serious injuries catchers, facing swift pitching close behind the bat, are subjected to, that the wire-mask—a perfect protection against such injuries—is not in more general use among professional catchers. The idea seems to prevail among a prejudiced few of the fraternity that it is not plucky or manly to wear the mask. It is nonsensical to run the risk of such severe injuries simply because a pack of foolish boys may ridicule you. Look at [John] Clapp of the St. Louis nine, who now lies ill and disabled with a broken cheek-bone, due entirely to the fact of his not wearing a protective mask. We regard the Harvard collegian's invention as one of the best things out for saving a catcher from dangerous injuries."

Clapp had been felled in an August 8, 1877 game and his replacement, Mike Dorgan, took a mask with him to the plate, apparently becoming the first major-league catcher to don the mask.

Thayer patented his invention in February 1878, Patent Number 200,358, and it was listed for sale in that year's Spalding catalog. Slowly, it began to pick up adherents.

By the twenties, the mask had been widened and a vertical bar eliminated to give the catcher better visibility. In 1921, umpire James E. Johnstone patented the platform mask, a one-piece mask with solid horizontal crossbars, which enjoyed a brief vogue in the sixties, but catchers soon went back to the wire-mesh models because they allowed more air movement, important for an August day game in St. Louis. The wire mesh also had more spring, allowing the mask to absorb more of a foul tip's impact, instead of the chin. Most catchers today wear the carbon-steel wire-mesh mask, but another innovation is on the horizon.

The new vogue among catchers could be the Darth Vader look.

Jeff Sipos, equipment acquisitions manager for the Cleveland Indians since 1996, says All-Star Sports Equipment, which supplies catcher's gear to the major leagues, has adapted the hockey goalie's mask for use by catchers. The mask incorporates a fiberglass helmet, now required for all catchers, with wire mesh. "It's very light. In some ways visibility is even better. It's much more protective." He also says that you don't lose as much vision peripherally. Even though the contraption looks like it might have catchers breathing like Vader, it doesn't. "The new masks are lighter and lighter and lighter; even in the '80s it was like wearing cast iron."

Developed by former Blue Jays catcher Charlie O'Brien, a journeyman who caught for nine clubs in a fifteen-year career, this combination helmet and mask was inspired by the ice hockey games O'Brien had seen while playing in Toronto. He wondered how a goalie could get clobbered with a hard, dense puck, and shake the hit off. He got in touch with the Canadian hockey helmet manufacturer Van Velden Mask to create a helmet for himself. He had no intention of marketing it. Together, they developed the All-Star MVP Adult Mask, an extreme-games–looking catcher's mask that is light years—and light sabers—ahead of the standard-issue mask. The shell construction, seven layers of fiberglass, Kevlar, plastic, and polycarbons, is the only thing taken straight from the hockey mask. The rest is a rethinking of the old mask. The cage sits closer to the face, providing less obstruction. The surface is angular, deflecting balls, instead of sending the impact straight into the catcher's head. The wire is solid core so it doesn't bend; it doesn't even need to bend because the helmet acts as the shock absorber and, because it's form-fitting, it doesn't slide to the side like conventional masks when making a hard toss to second. The back of the helmet is hinged, making flipping easier for a pop foul. Because the visibility through the cage is so much better—40 percent more vertical visibility and 50 percent more peripheral visibility—flipping, and, too often, stepping on the mask may soon be as old fashioned as wool uniforms.

Despite the cool look—Zorro meets Jason—the mask has a serious purpose: protecting the catcher's head, face, and eyes from injury. Not just any good old boy with a blowtorch and some carbon steel wire can whip up a mask. Catcher's masks and helmets must measure up to standards set by the National Operating Committee of Standards for Athletic Equipment, a group formed in 1969 to, set standards for athletic equipment.

NOCSAE also sets test standards for football helmets, baseball and softball batting helmets, baseballs, softballs, lacrosse helmets and face masks, and football face masks.

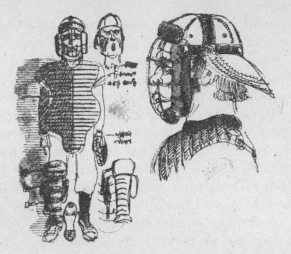

To pass the NOCSAE test, a catcher's mask and helmet must withstand the force of a baseball fired at 70 mph from an air cannon two feet away. Since Astros closer Billy Wagner has been clocked in triple figures and Randy Johnson regularly hits 98 on the radar gun, and the mask standard is only 70 mph, you have to wonder if catching is the position for your child.

The throat protector, that dangly thing on a catcher's mask that resembles a turkey's wattle, was invented in 1903, but didn't become popular until Dodger catcher Steve Yeager wore it in the seventies. That was a result of the change in catching style, from two-handed to one-handed. Sneaking the throwing hand behind the back helped cut down on the gnarly-fingers syndrome that catchers had suffered since time immemorial, but exposed the throat to foul tips.

You don't see the throat protector any more; modern masks have it built into the wire cage.

Early ballplayers could accept the catcher wearing a glove and a mouth protector; even the mask was grudgingly accepted. But a chest protector? That was just unmanly. A real man should be able to block a wild pitch with his own chest, at least that's what the *real* men out in the field thought. Catchers might have disagreed.

Naturally, it took a woman to bring the chest protector to the game.

In the October 15, 1914 issue of *Leslie's Illustrated Weekly*, old-time catcher Charles Bennett boasted it was his wife who created the first catcher's breast protector. "It was a constant source of worry to Mrs. Bennett to watch her husband acting as a target for the speedy twirlers of thirty years ago and she determined to invent some sort of an armor to prevent the hot shots from the pitcher playing a tattoo on the ribs of her better half. After much planning, assisted by practical suggestions from her husband, she shaped a pad which answered the purpose and which bore some resemblance to the protector of the present day. In a private tryout it worked well and Charles, after permitting the ball to strike him repeatedly without feeling a jar, decided to use it in public. . . . It made a hit with the catchers and they were quite ready to follow Bennett's lead."

Other catchers had experimented with stuffing inside their uniform jersey but, when Bennett took the field in 1886 wearing his breastplate, he was the first professional catcher to display one as proudly as a peacock.

Other sources credit left-handed catcher Jack Clements, of the Philadelphia Keystones in the short-lived Union Association as the first pro to don the armor. In an 1890 story tracing the gradual acceptance of the chestplate, the *Cincinnati Enquirer* noted, "This most useful piece of base ball paraphernalia had a hard time getting a foothold. The catchers were slow in adopting it, and the spectators at first guyed [mocked] it as baby-play. Clements, the great catcher of the Philadelphia League team was the first to wear a catcher's protector in a game before a Cincinnati crowd. He was then back-stopping Jersey Bakely with the Keystones Unions, of Philadelphia, in 1884. Considerable fun was made of the protector, and the writer distinctly remembers that it was made the subject of adverse newspaper comment by one of the best baseball authorities in America. Now it is different. A catcher's protector is of as much importance to a back stop as are his mask and gloves. In other days a visitor to the dressing room of a ball team when the players were getting ready for a game did not need to ask who were the catchers. He could tell them by the black and blue spots that appeared on various parts of their anatomy, the result of hard thumps from unruly foul tips. The protector, mask and padded glove have made the life of a catcher a bed of roses to what it used to be."

For a time, a short time, in the nineteenth century, catchers preferred inflatable chest protectors, but they made chasing wild pitches and fielding bunts cumbersome and so they reverted to canvas and leather protectors stuffed with everything from fur to kapok. (The same material used for many years in life jackets, making catcher the only position that would float.) Umpires stayed with the inflated bladders for much longer. National League umps, at the urging of their colleague Bill Klem, began switching to catcher-style chest protectors in the late twenties. American League umps stayed with the balloons, gradually switching with the rise of the Umpire Development Program, staffed mostly by retired National League arbiters, in 1964. The last American Leaguer to wear the balloon protector was Jerry Neudecker, who retired in 1985.

The modern catcher's chest protector is a miracle of science, with Kevlar and shock-absorbing polyfoam stuffing and plastic inserts to protect the heart, lungs, and rib cage.

After Bennett and Clements made their first appearances wearing the chest protector, the catcher's armor was almost complete. The final addition came on April 11, 1907, opening day, when Giants catcher—and future Hall of Famer—Roger Bresnahan took his position wearing mask, mitt, chest protector, and something new: shin guards. "Bresnahan created somewhat of a sensation when he appeared behind the bat for the start of play, by donning cricket leg guards," wrote the *New York Times*. The cricket leg protectors made his shins look like an upholstered couch but the *Times* approved. "As he displayed himself, togged in mask, protector, and guards, he presented no vulnerable surface for a wild ball to strike. The white shields were rather picturesque, in spite of their clumsiness, and the spectators rather fancied the innovation." The paper also noted, "The crowd howled with delight when a foul tip in the fifth inning rapped the protectors sharply."

The shin guards were made of cane rods covered by padded fabric with more padding at the knees. There had been some experimentation with shin guards earlier, and football players were already wearing them. Best & Co. advertised athletic shin guards for boys in an 1893 issue of the *New York Times,* and Red Dooin of the Phillies had worn homemade papier-mâché protectors under his socks in 1906. But Bresnahan was apparently the first baseball catcher to go public with them.

Once catchers showed a willingness to pad their shins, sporting-goods manufacturers were quick to market the innovation. Fiberboard shin guards first appeared in the Rawlings catalog in 1916, and fiber soon replaced cane as the preferred material. Later manufacturers tried leather, eventually settling on plastic.

Bresnahan's shin guards were the final pieces of the "tools of ignorance," that great descriptive phrase for the catcher's equipment. There are conflicting stories about who came up with that wonderful moniker: Some sources credit Herold "Muddy" Ruel, a Senators catcher who caught for Walter Johnson and later became a lawyer. The more likely—and earlier—story, from the "Diamond Jargon" column in the August 1939 issue of *Baseball Magazine* accepts Yankee catcher Bill Dickey as the true author. Dickey supposedly coined the term while donning his gear and brooding over why anyone would want to be a catcher in July heat.

I like the Dickey story because it was published sixteen years before the Ruel claim, but wouldn't it be sweeter if "tools of ignorance" had been first muttered by a Washington lawyer whose nickname was Muddy?

. . .

Each team starts the season with six complete sets of catcher's gear, compliments of All-Star, and the sporting-goods manufacturer replaces equipment as needed. Not every catcher wears All-Star, though; for instance, Cleveland catcher Eddie Perez is under contract to Mizuno, so he wears their equipment.

The tools of ignorance, even with modern lightweight materials, are not light. The All-Star FM25LMX mask weighs 29.1 ounces, then add on the All-Star CP25 PRO chest protector (19.3 ounces), the All-Star LG21WPRO shin guards (64 ounces) and the All-Star CH910 helmet (12 ounces) for a total of seven and three-quarter pounds. That doesn't even include the mitt, which can be as much as eight ounces heavier than a regular glove. It's like playing with four-pound ankle weights on each leg.

As the Reds race off the field in the middle of the ninth, happy to escape with the Marlins tacking on only one run, thanks to catcher Miller's overthrow, second baseman Todd Walker leaps over the baseline, landing on both feet on the other side and smiling as he looks back at Adam Dunn, who has just touched the second base bag on his way in from left field. Two players, two superstitions. Don't step on the baseline or you'll have bad luck; be sure and touch the bag coming in, so you'll have good luck.

Superstitions and baseball go hand in hand.

I could fill a book with all the baseball superstitions: don't change socks during a winning streak, don't change underwear during a hitting streak, whirl the bat over your head three times for good luck.

I could go on. Cross yourself before every at-bat, keep a buckeye in your pocket, don't shave on game day.

A 1997 study of college students, published in *Sport Psychologist,* found college baseball players were more superstitious than non-baseball–playing students and more baseball players had a lucky charm or object (like a lucky dirty sock) than their non-baseball–playing fellow students. I'm sure that study would translate to the big leagues in spades. When I was briefly in the Reds locker room after a game I spotted troll dolls, religious artifacts, all manner of lucky objects.

The study also found that the average college baseball player makes 82.6 unrelated movements—or tics—each at-bat. These range from arm flapping to bat tapping to head swirling, all intended to bring good fortune, while getting the player focused on hitting. My favorite batting ritual belonged to Indians slugger Rocky Colavito, who stood in the box and ended his warm-up swing with the end of the bat pointing straight at the pitcher. I think all the pitchers understood that nonverbal bit of communication.

The Reds try to make a game of it in the bottom of the ninth. Todd Walker skies one to deep right that has the few remaining faithful on their feet—clearly, half the fans have gone home already.

After an Encarnacion pop out to third, Casey and Dunn walk, setting the stage for pinch hitter Barry Larkin. The local favorite is getting up in years—he was thirty-eight in the 2002 season—and can't handle the everyday wear and tear any longer. But he's a local boy and still a crowd favorite after fifteen years. He gives the fans a thrill when he rips one into the air toward center, but it is not to be. Preston Wilson reins it in and we head for the exits.

Final score: Florida 8, Reds 4.

I can understand fans abandoning the home team late in the game in football and basketball. A football team down by four touchdowns with five minutes to play is done. So, too, is a basketball team trailing by twenty in the final quarter. But one of the charms of baseball is its timeless frame of reference. Three outs can take three minutes or it can take half an hour. The Red Sox in a 1953 game scored 17 runs in one inning (that's the record). Down four in the bottom of the ninth is not an insurmountable lead; after all, the Reds got the tying run to the on-deck circle.

Fans of the Dodgers are credited (blamed would be a better verb) with starting this beat-the-traffic trend, scurrying to hit the notorious L.A. freeways ahead of the Dodger Stadium throng. But why spend all that money—Will and I went through fifty bucks, not including gas—and not even see the end of the game? One of the great experiences in sports is walking out of the stadium, surrounded by like-minded fans, after a big win by the home team, particularly a come-from-behind victory. There are no strangers in that crowd.

I just don't understand leaving early.

Why do fans leave early? There are no studies addressing that question, but a 2000 survey commissioned by *Sports Illustrated* hinted at the answer. The survey asked 894 fans what would make them less likely to attend a pro game. Two factors seem relevant: the number four answer, "traffic and parking," which bothered 38 percent of respondents, and the number six answer, "lateness of games," which irked 26 percent. Fans leave early to beat the traffic and to get home before dawn.

I've never forgotten an experience my childhood pal Lance Harris had. His first big-league game was in Boston between the Red Sox and the Tigers. Frank Lary had held the Sox down all day and it was 4–1 Tigers, going into the bottom of the ninth. Lance's family insisted on leaving to beat the traffic in this unfamiliar city. The Bosox came back to win 5–4.

I was hoping the Reds would come back today, so I could yell at the people sitting in traffic outside the stadium: You missed a great game!

Chapter Fourteen

The Fan Heads Home

As we stand to leave, the public address announcer intones, "Tickets sold for today's game: 25,006."

Will looks at me. I look at him. "What's that about?" he asks.

It's an unusual phrasing, one I don't think I've heard before at a baseball game. Usually the announcer just says, "Today's attendance: 25,006." And we are left to wonder what that means.

We know exactly what *tickets sold* means. It doesn't mean 25,006 fannies in the seats; it means that since the Reds started selling tickets back in the winter and up through game time today, the team sold 25,006 tickets to this game. It also means there weren't 25,006 fannies in the seats.

That's because every game has its share of *no-shows*, people who buy tickets but don't use them. The number of no-shows has been climbing steadily in all professional sports over the past few years. On the one hand, yeah, the Reds got their ticket money. But, on the other, there is money that they didn't get: parking revenue, concessions revenue, souvenir revenue.

The percentage of no-shows at Major League Baseball games is now 18 percent. For comparison's sake, the NBA averages 16 percent no-shows, while the NFL average is 20 percent. That means that there were probably only 20,504 fans in the stands today. That seems more accurate than the tickets-sold number. The red seats in the upper deck were deserted.

So, 4,502 fans with tickets didn't show. The average fan spends $15.40 at a baseball game. Multiply that by the number of no-shows and you get $69,330.80. That's how much the Reds didn't get from those absent fans. Now multiply that by 81 games: $5,615,794.80. Five-and-a-half million dollars they might have earned had those fans used their tickets. Five-and-a-half million dollars will buy you a pretty good second baseman, maybe a serviceable relief pitcher. It might even help on the Griffey Jr. mortgage.

Five-and-a-half million is actually a little high, that's because I used a weekend game to calculate missing revenue. Attendance at weekend baseball games is 20 to 25 percent higher than weekday games.

The league average is $3.2 million lost per team for the season from no-shows. (The NBA loses $800,000 per team; the NFL $1.7 million per.)

I wish I could say that Will and I are despondent over the Reds' loss. We aren't. We are happy to have been to a game, but the Reds aren't our team. The Giants, that's our team, and the Giants lost last night, 6–3, to a pathetic team, the Expos, who finished last in the NL East last year.

So Will and I aren't happy. We live and die with our team.

. . .

Baseball is a cruel mistress.

If your favorite football team is playing miserably, you have, at most, sixteen bad Sundays. If your favorite pro basketball team is a joke, they may lose sixty games in a season. If your favorite baseball team loses a mere 60 games, it's in the playoffs. A baseball team having a bad season can lose 100 games, or more. Ask the 1962 Mets: They lost 120 games and might have lost more but two games were rained out. What am I saying, "might have." They definitely would have.

Baseball is relentless. Day games, night games, road trips, home stands, box score after box score to be pored over, studied, analyzed. Why?

Because you are a fan. Because in the ancient mists of your history you fell in love with a team—God knows why—and now your moods depend upon that team's success. You fall asleep to *Baseball Tonight,* you rise to *Sportscenter,* you surf the Internet, and fine-tune your radio dial, trying to find out what happened on the West Coast.

Maybe you picked your team because of proximity. It would have been difficult to grow up in Cincinnati in the seventies and not be a fan of the Big Red Machine.

Root, root, root for the home team is one of the most common connections between a team and its fans. Robert J. Fisher, in a study published in a 1998 edition of *Advances in Consumer Research* reports that, "Sports fans tend to cheer with the home team, i.e., the team that represents their country, state, community, university or other group. The team is connected to the individual because they have a shared group affiliation." Makes perfect sense, right?

There is another kind of affiliation besides physical location—call it location of the psyche. Fisher says some fans identify with a team's personality, using as an example the Reds of the mid-1990s, a blue-collar bunch that found a bond with Cincinnati's blue-collar population. "Similarity is a more important predictor of group-derived self-definition than attractiveness." (And everyone knows about the thuggish reputation of the NFL's Oakland Raiders and their rowdy fans.)

Maybe you picked your team because of success. If they had tracked such things as souvenir sales in the fifties, you can bet the New York Yankees would have been atop the best-seller list every year, with fans spread out all over the country. They were America's Team. (There was, and is, an opposing force, the Yankee haters, also a large group.)

A 1976 study reported in the *Journal of Personality and Social Psychology* concluded that fans want to associate themselves with a successful group in order to bolster their self-esteem, a process that researcher R. B. Cialdini called "basking-in-reflected-glory." We all want to be a part of a winner.

Maybe you picked your team because of one player. My best friend as a kid, Lance Harris, was a Yankee fan because his favorite player was Mickey Mantle. I think Lance felt a connection. He was blond; Mickey was blond. His name was Charles Lance Harris; Mick's was Mickey

Charles Mantle. It didn't hurt that Mickey Mantle was just about the best player on the planet at the time.

Or maybe you picked your team for reasons that no longer make sense. I fall into the latter category. I grew up in East Tennessee in the fifties, far from the sphere of influence of any major-league club. There was no home team effect; you didn't automatically become a Reds fan or a Cardinals fan or, today in the South, a Braves fan. They were all a day's drive away. There was no local rooting interest. You could pick your team.

I picked the Giants.

They had just left the Polo Grounds for San Francisco. It was a fresh start in a new ballpark and a new town, but that wasn't why I picked them. In fact, forty-five years later I can't say exactly why I picked them. Maybe I liked their uniforms, all black and orange with the interlaced S and F on the hat. Maybe their baseball cards were more exciting: Valmy Thomas couldn't hit his way out of a minor-league training camp but he looked sharp cocking his bat in front of a yellow background on his 1958 Topps card. Mike McCormick looked unstoppable at the top of his windup in front of a blue background in that same year's cards. And there was no way Jim Davenport was going to let a ground ball get past him in that fielder's crouch with a blazing red background on his card. Maybe that was it. Maybe

But the nearest I can figure out it was one player—and it wasn't Willie Mays.

I remember reading the *Sporting News* in the spring of

1958—I devoured every copy as soon as it came out. There was a note at the end of the Giants' write-up; "Giant Jottings," they called it. The writer asked incumbent first baseman Whitey Lockman about the big rookie who was pushing him for playing time. What about this kid, the writer asked. Is he ready? Lockman responded— and I've never forgotten this quote—"He's about a year away . . . from the Hall of Fame." Suddenly, I had a favorite player, Orlando Cepeda, and a favorite team. Half a century later, the thrill fueled by that seemingly insignificant quote affects my daily existence.

Because I am a fan.

If my team loses, I expect a bad day. If my team wins, I look forward to a day of good fortune. There are days when I dread opening the morning paper for fear of finding out my team lost, plunging them another game back of the league leaders. If my team is on a losing streak, even though I don't believe there's such a thing as momentum, my dread is palpable. Did they lose again? A loss sinks me deeper. A win brightens me even more than normal.

If you're shaking your head, thinking, "boy, that guy is weird, letting his team's fortunes influence his life," you don't know very many sports fans. I am not atypical. Arnold Beisser in his 1967 book, *The Madness in Sports,* found that fans can experience pregame symptoms such as nervousness and an increased heart rate. E. R. Hirt and his colleagues in a 1992 study reported in the *Journal of Personality and Social Psychology* found that, after his team loses, a fan will feel worse about himself and about his own abilities.

The gloom that I feel because my team lost has been

documented throughout psychological literature. In a 1998 study, reported in *Advances in Consumer Research,* Robert J. Fisher concluded, "Highly identified sports fans feel ecstasy when the team wins and despair when they lose because the team is an extension of themselves."

That's why I don't understand fantasy baseball. How can you separate yourself from your favorite team? I tried fantasy league for three years; I enjoyed studying the stats, preparing for the draft, and making the week-to-week personnel decisions, like picking starters, that can affect your success, but I hated the game. Hated it. It diluted my interest as a fan. Sure, I had a renewed interest in reading box scores, every box score, but I only wanted to know: Did Kenny Lofton score big last night? Was Curt Schilling on his game? They were on my fantasy team. I soon discovered that to be a good fantasy owner, I often had to pull against my favorite team. I had to hope that Barry Bonds went zero for five, because he wasn't on my squad. I had to hope that the Giants' starter, and with him, the team, lost, if I didn't have him either?

It was the most miserable three years of my baseball life.

I want to cheer for my team, whether I am watching them at the park, as today, watching them on television, listening to them on the radio, or just reading about them in the newspaper. J. H. Krause could have been describing me when he wrote, "With what an indescribable enthusiasm those present dedicated themselves to the spectacle! With what lively sense of participation did they share the athletes' fates and enact the outcome of the contests! How their spirits were excited by what they saw; they were impelled unconsciously to move their hands, to raise their voices, to jump from their seats now with the greatest joy, now with the deepest pain."

(Krause was actually writing in 1838 about the sports fans in ancient Greece.)

Compare those polite but excited Greek fans to these guys: "When they enter the stadium, it is as though they had found a cache of drugs. They forget themselves completely, and shamelessly say and do the first thing that occurs to them . . . at the games you are under the influence of some maniacal drug. It is as if you could not watch the proceedings in a civilized fashion . . . when you enter the stadium, who could describe the yells and uproar, the frenzy, the swatches of color and expression in your faces and all the curses you give vent to?"

The guy who was sitting next to me today? No. Philadelphia fans giving the business to Mike Piazza? No.

That was Greek orator Dio Chrysostom describing the fans at a chariot race in Alexandria some time in the first century A.D.

Things really haven't changed in the grandstand in, what, a couple or three millennia. I'm not the only one who takes these games seriously.

Why, why, why do we love our teams and our games so much? Philosopher Thorstein Veblen called sports a "manifestation of man's predatory instinct." In his classic 1934 study, *Theory of the Leisure Class,* he called sporting contests a "biological inheritance from man's predatory past, which is expressed in 'civilized' life through competition and aggressiveness."

Fans are neanderthals, in other words. And, more than that, we're delusional neanderthals. G. J. Smith, in a 1988 edition of *Journal of Sport and Social Issues*, identifies the one great unifying belief in the grandstands: "Fans have all accepted the illusion that the results of the contest matter."

It is the great denominator at the game. Everyone accepts that what is happening in front of us matters, although once we leave the confines of the stadium, none of it matters. If Ken Griffey Jr. or the Mighty Casey strikes out, the world will not stop spinning. As fans, we are united by this Grand Illusion.

And, yes, I do have what the aptly named psychology researcher Van S. Butt called a "dark side" to my fanaticism. In a 1987 volume of the *Psychology of Sport*, he pointed out that "annihilation has long been documented as part of a fan's desire and since the beginning of time fans have found delight in the physical destruction of others."

I love it when the Giants win. I love it when the Dodgers lose. I love it most of all when the Giants beat the Dodgers; 14–0, that would be a nice score, 15–0 would be better.

I've never taken the Sports Involvement Inventory Assessment, which determines the involvement level of a fan, but I have no doubt I would score as a high-involvement fan. (The other end of the scale is, naturally, low involvement.) According to a study in a 1998 edition of the *Journal of Sport Behavior*, by Matthew D. Shank and Fred M. Beasley, the average person watches 5.3 hours of sports programming a week on television. The low-involvement person watches only 3.2 hours. The high-involvement fan, on the other hand, averages 7.5 hours. Heck, that's not even a good week for me.

And, where the average person spends an hour and eighteen minutes a week reading sports periodicals, the low-involvement person spends only 36 minutes a week. The high-involvement fan spends two hours.

For me, that's next to nothing.

At a baseball game, there are fans, and then there are the rest of them. In a 1998 study in *College Student Journal*, Franklin Krohn divided the people in attendance at a sporting event into two categories, spectators and fans. He defines the spectator as one who fulfills "enjoyment by simply viewing a sporting event and not getting caught up in the logistics of the event." The fan, on the other hand, is a fanatic, "an enthusiastic devotee of a given diversion."

I am a baseball fan. Maybe I should phrase that in twelve-step recovery program terms: My name is Vince and I am a baseball fan.

And, I'm not alone: A 2000 study in the *Journal of Sport Behavior* found that 73 percent of women and 83 percent of men consider themselves sports fans. Those results mirror pretty closely a 1986 *New York Times* national opinion survey in which 71 percent of people said they consider themselves sports fans.

But, after proclaiming themselves fans, the two sexes diverge. The study found that men have a significantly stronger identification with being a fan than women.

While the two sexes spend equal amounts of time attending sporting events, men spend significantly more time talking sports, watching sports on television, and reading about sports. For women being a fan "is not an identity that is especially important to them."

The study concludes that women "tend to think of themselves as sports fans for primarily social reasons. These reasons include watching a sporting event with friends and family, cheering at a sporting event, and watching and attending sporting events . . . Males, on the other hand, report being a sports fan because they play sports, like sports in general, and seem to enjoy acquiring information about sports through such means as reading the sports page."

Why aren't women as gung-ho about sports as men? My wife Judy says she can tell you in one word: testosterone. "Men are just more competitive. They like that physical stuff. Plus women don't like to sweat."

If Judy were along on this trip, the conversation on the drive home would be different. We'd be planning where to eat, and when we can make the trip to visit Grandma. She's not here, though, so Will and I talk baseball. We rehash the game, reflect on the strategy, even ponder when we'll head back up for another game. The Giants don't come back to town this season, but the Dodgers do. Maybe we'll go then and jeer those Hollywood pretty boys.

Why are we plotting our return when we are barely out of the parking lot from today's game? What makes us want to come back?

A study by Wann and Wilson and published in 1999 in *Perceptual and Motor Skills* tried to identify variables influential in attracting people to sporting events. Although they studied college basketball, their conclusions seem transferable. The number one reason for spectator enjoyment, cited by 49 percent of respondents, was the competition. Second was the social nature, followed by exciting plays. Other reasons cited: entertainment, the players, talent of the team, atmosphere, supporting the team, filling time, and being a fan.

We liked the competition; we liked being together; we liked those moments of thrilling play. But the last reason says it all for us: We are fans, baseball fans. We love the game.

The topic of conversation between Will and I inevitably turns to Ken Griffey Jr. His is an amazing presence considering that he has missed two-thirds of the season. Every conversation about the Reds seems to turn eventually to Griffey's return. When? Where will they play him? Can he return to form? His presence in the lineup will force someone to the bench. Will thinks it will be the current center fielder Juan Encarnacion, who has been playing well. I think they will move Adam Dunn to first and trade Sean Casey while he still has value. Whatever happens there will be turnover.

In baseball, the only constant is change.

The Reds' situation reminds me of my team back in the early sixties. The Giants had Willie Mays in center, Felipe Alou in right, and a first baseman in left. One game it would be Cepeda, the next Willie McCovey. This abundance of talent let them trade away a procession of slugging outfielders because there was no place to play them: Willie Kirkland, Leon Wagner, Matty Alou. But, eventually, they came to the inevitable conclusion that neither Cepeda nor McCovey could play left.

The worst day of my baseball life occurred in the winter of 1966. I was a freshman in college, long before email and instant messaging, and I got the word on the radio. I was stunned: The Giants had traded Orlando Cepeda to the St. Louis Cardinals for Ray Sadecki and a broken bat. I knew my favorite player had a reputation as a clubhouse lawyer, but he also had a reputation for smashing curveballs over distant fences. Who was Ray Sadecki?

I have to admit my devotion to the Giants has never been the same since. I understand how Reds fans must have felt in the late seventies and early eighties when a tightfisted management allowed the Big Red Machine to be dismantled, first Perez, then Rose and Foster, departed by trades and free-agent signings.

Fan loyalty is a dicey thing. In a 1997 report in *Applied Economics*, economists Leo Kahane and Stephen Shmanske did the math to see what all the trades and free-agent losses mean to a team. As it turns out, quite a bit.

Using a lot of numbers and formulas that I don't understand—and I was a math major in college—they concluded: The loss of an important player who constitutes 10 percent of the total team payroll can cost the team half a million to three quarters of a million in ticket revenue. Attendance falls by 12,058 for every percentage point increase in turnover. The loss of one player means a 48,000 drop in attendance (that's using the slope estimate, whatever that is) or a 62,000 drop (using the elasticity estimate and the mean attendance, whatever that is). In the seventies, team turnover was about 21 percent from year to year. Now, it is about 27 percent.

In the end, being a fan comes down to one thing: loyalty to your team. None of the players I grew up with are on the field for San Francisco anymore. I'm no longer pulling for Mays, McCovey, or Marichal. The next generation, Gaylord Perry, Chris Spier, Bobby Bonds, is gone too. I'm fifty-four, and I've seen my team's lineup turn over fifteen times. First base alone has gone from Cepeda to McCovey to Will Clark and, now, to J. T. Snow. And yet I'm still a Giants fan.

Maybe Jerry Seinfeld is right. "Loyalty to any one sports team is pretty hard to justify. Because the players are always changing. The team can move to another city. You're actually just rooting for the clothes when you get right down to it. You are standing and cheering and yelling for your clothes to beat the clothes from another city."

An hour later, Will and I are forty miles down the road to home. The windows are down, the breeze is blowing, the radio is blaring the Reds postgame show. It's a great evening, perfect for a night game. No humidity, just a pleasant crispness to the air.

But the Reds chose to play in the sunlight and I have an idea why. Traffic is starting to back up the ramp at exit 55, the exit to the new Kentucky Speedway. In a couple of hours they'll be racing trucks around the oval track. Thousands of fans will be standing, chanting, cheering. There will be applause and sighs, nail biting and deep exhaling. And no little white ball will be involved.

And, when the fans swarm out at midnight their announcer can say, "Tickets sold for tonight's race, 66,089." Truck racing outdrew major-league baseball.

A sports fan in my town, Louisville, Kentucky, has a world of choices today: horse racing at Churchill Downs, minor-league baseball at Slugger Park, big-league baseball ninety minutes up the road in Cincinnati, the NBA playoffs a mere hundred miles away in Indianapolis, ice hockey three hours down the interstate in Nashville or, you can stay home and watch any or all of it on television.

Once, baseball had summer to itself. Now basketball lasts till June, hockey almost as long. Football starts in September just as the pennant races are getting hot, and then there's this new competitor, NASCAR, less than an hour from the Reds ballpark.

It's a new sports world and baseball isn't as important as it once was. Except to me.

About the Author

VINCE STATEN was born and raised in
Kingsport, Tennessee. A graduate of Duke
University and the University of Tennessee,
his articles have appeared in *Food & Wine,
Bon Appetit,* and the *New York Times.* He is the
author of nine previous books including *Do
Bald Men Get Half Price Haircuts?* and *Did
Monkeys Invent the Monkey Wrench?* Staten lives
in Prospect, Kentucky, and loses sleep over
the San Francisco Giants.